The Last
Civilization

Is this the last civilization so far or the last one forever?
An objectively severe look at our long past, <u>and future</u>, made possible by the whole new science of social evolution

Charles Brough

Printed in the United States of America.

ISBN: 978-1-4269-4057-6 (sc)
ISBN: 978-1-4269-4058-3 (hc)
ISBN: 978-1-4269-4059-0 (e)

Library of Congress Control Number: 2010912716

Trafford rev. 11/14/2010

 www.trafford.com

North America & international
toll-free: 1 888 232 4444 (USA & Canada)
phone: 250 383 6864 ♦ fax: 812 355 4082

To

Christa

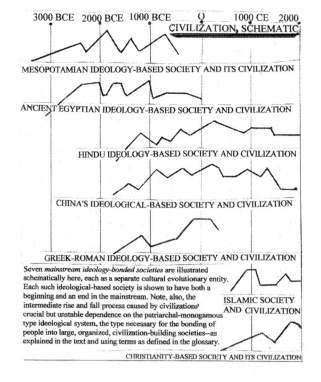

3000 BCE   2000 BCE   1000 BCE   0   1000 CE   2000

CIVILIZATION, SCHEMATIC

MESOPOTAMIAN IDEOLOGY-BASED SOCIETY AND ITS CIVILIZATION

ANCIENT EGYPTIAN IDEOLOGY-BASED SOCIETY AND CIVILIZATION

HINDU IDEOLOGY-BASED SOCIETY AND CIVILIZATION

CHINA'S IDEOLOGICAL-BASED SOCIETY AND CIVILIZATION

GREEK-ROMAN IDEOLOGY-BASED SOCIETY AND CIVILIZATION

Seven *mainstream ideology-bonded societies* are illustrated
schematically here, each as a separate cultural evolutionary entity.
Each such ideological-based society is shown to have both a
beginning and an end in the mainstream. Note, also, the
intermediate rise and fall process caused by civilizations'
crucial but unstable dependence on the patriarchal-monogamous
type ideological system, the type necessary for the bonding of
people into large, organized, civilization-building societies—as
explained in the text and using terms as defined in the glossary.

ISLAMIC SOCIETY
AND CIVILIZATION

CHRISTIANITY-BASED SOCIETY AND ITS CIVILIZATION

TABLE OF CONTENTS

INTRODUCTION/ABSTRACT ix

PART 1 ---- PREHISTORY

one   --- NATURAL SELECTION................................ 1

two   --- OUR BASIC BEHAVIOR 8

three   --- THE PRECURSOR SYSTEM..................... 17

four   --- THE FIRST WORLD-VIEW SYSTEM..... 22

five   --- THE MATRILINEAL WV SYSTEMS 27
         the fishing-based society and the end of the hunting
         society

six   --- DEVELOPING THE FIRST PATRILINEAL
             SYSTEM 40
         fem-fertility & fishing/megalithic WV systems in
         decline

seven   --- THE REVOLUTIONARY WV SYSTEM IN
             MESOPOTAMIA & EGYPT............................ 49
         the evolution of the Kurgan feudal system....
         the end of the Fem-Fertility WV system in the
         mainstream.....monotheism and the state

PART 2 ---- HISTORY

eight   --- THE MECHANISM OF CIVILIZATION 65

nine   --- THE HINDU CIVILIZATION 75

ten   --- SHANG CHINESE SOCIETY 89

eleven   --- THE GREEK-ROMAN SYSTEM 100

twelve   --- CHRISTENDOM 110
         the scientific age.....the artistic age.....the empire

thirteen --- ISLAM 130

PART 3 ---- THE PRESENT ERA

fourteen --- BARBARISM AND MODERN TIMES..................... 145

> the empire.....problems with the world order.....the
> end of history?.....the affluent class and its economic
> empire.....where the US ruling class comes from.....
> the wave of regression.....present trends in the US.....
> the walls between us.....the corpulent crowd.....terror

fifteen --- SOCIAL EVOLUTION 179

sixteen --- THE SOCIAL BIOLOGY OF OVER
POPULATION... 186

seventeen --- PROBLEMS AND SOLUTIONS 192

eighteen --- A LIKENESS OF THE NEXT WV SYSTEM 200

PART 4 ---- "PROPHESY"

nineteen --- HOW EVENTS MAY UNWIND 207

twenty --- THE ALTERNATIVE... 226

> the First Period.....the Second Period.....the Third
> Period.....the global economy.....the drift to a
> subsequent system

GLOSSARY: 241

> --- Single meaning and functional definitions used
> for important terms.

APPENDIX 249

> --- to-be-avoided word-use stratagems
> subconsciously or intuitively used in consensus
> social theory

BIBLIOGRAPHY..257

INTRODUCTION/ABSTRACT

Is Western civilization just the last civilization so far? In light of present world problems, it is perhaps time to at least consider the possibility that civilization itself might not be able to recover. World population keeps growing, with a leveling off expected only after 2050. Meanwhile, the thirty-year-old "green revolution" is falling behind, climate is heating, and in large areas we are running low on available fresh water. World wide, energy supplies lag as we have to use even more energy to extract energy. Species loss is accelerating, and top soil thickness has been declining. The threat of terrorism continues, we are unable to stop the expansion of piracy, and (in the US) the infrastructure is crumbling.

Worst of all, for decades, the number of nuclear armed nations has been increasing.

With all that in mind, we may have some cause to believe our civilization is in decline, possibly even approaching its end.

If so, could we reverse its course or, possibly, build a new one? In our universities, social science theorists have been unable to explain what needs to happen to cause a civilization to change from its decline course or for a new society and civilization to arise. If conditions grow worse, we need to know what would have to be done in order to avoid an approaching collapse. If we are to replace the declining civilization with a new and more advanced one, we need to know what *are* civilizations and what causes them to "rise and fall." Are our problems really caused by the world, or such things as cultures, urbanization, memes, bad leadership, climate change, or mankind's "troubling (or Divine) nature?" Perhaps the above so-called causes are only convenient excuses used to avoid admitting the real cause, that is, the inability of the world's present ideological systems to unit us. We are, after all, just one race, the human race, and what divides us into tribes, nations, ethnic groups and skin color always has to be caused or abetted by religious and/or secular ideology and its dividing.

Clearly and without doubt, the ideological systems people use to think with determine how well or poorly they deal with their problems. But why is what we believe failing us?

The only logical way to find out is to treat divisive religious faiths with unaccustomed and brutally frank objectivity. It also means subjecting our *secular belief system* to the same treatment. It has, after all, failed to replace the old religious systems. The old ideologies still survive even though grossly unscientific. They also still cut and divide our now crowded world. Since they still do survive, even flourish, we have to depend on the secular system to at least replace the old faith's leadership in the world. The growing list of world problems indicates the secular system is losing its ability to do even that.

Human ideologies function by shaping the way people think and hence, the way they cause their society and civilization to function. The ideologies, in turn, are shaped by human nature and need. The complex inter-relationship is dealt with in this text by isolating the natural selection processes involved. It becomes possible to explain how ideology-based societies evolve through natural selection and, thus to explain history and even present world affairs. Doing all that should even afford us a glance at what lies ahead. All this is social theory, the process of interpreting the data of the social and natural sciences in order to build the most accurate possible picture of the whole human story.

The many world problems and lack of answers indicate that the most accurate possible social theory picture is not what we have been getting. The reason may be that consensus social theory has not been able to be *objective*. Most social theorists consider objectivity to be even impossible. It is as though the whole science had been turned into only a philosophy.

Actually, however, social theory is everyone's secular view of the world, including that of scientists in the other fields. The secular theory consensus is simplified, fitted to the various age groups, and taught from grammar school through the universities to become the secular ideals that supplement the way the whole world thinks. It is called "a liberal education."

For centuries, social theorists have been adapting the West's eighteenth-century-Age-of Enlightenment and Age of Reason-based secular world-view and fitting it to coexist with liberalized Christianity to provide necessary stability to Western society and civilization. In the last century, it was even adapted to similarly co-exist with other faiths in order to spread abroad so is able to recognize and know at most only a couple hundred people, and that we tend to feel more compassion for the suffering of a single individual we can visualize before us than for thousands of other people outside of our "group." Our common world-view (WV) and way-of-thinking systems are the only means we have to expand the ultimate size of our concern and hence of our groups.

There have to be such world-view ideological systems to make "nations" possible. The Christian, Islamic, Hindu and East Asian Marxist world-view (WV) systems have all managed to bind their nations, their smaller groups and their individual citizens into their own particular, massive-sized groups, ones which are referred to here, and defined in the Glossary, as "*societies.*"

The concept of society as being the bond of ideological systems has far-ranging implications which are, here, for the first time, fully exploited and applied to the whole human story. Because of that, it becomes possible for us to see the natural selection process causing human social evolution, to explain human history, modern world affairs, and even to give us some insight into where human civilization is going from here.

it could achieve the cooperation needed to build and sustain "the
community of nations." To do that, the social theory consensus has
be reconciled with the rest of the world-civilization's stubbornly enc
old "spirit"-based religious systems. It had to avoid being in conflic
their ancient doctrines.

In order to serve that task, the basic beliefs of our secular systen
not been questioned because they have been vital to the whole v
unifying and stabilizing process. The social theorist consensus has a
interpreted social science data in ways that allow both secular and reli
doctrines to still be regarded as "inherent Truths." So, social theor
had a different function than the sciences have, but if society is in de
and heading for eventual collapse, at least *some* social theory nee
be scientific. We need a clear and objective understanding of wh
happening so we know what to do about it. Social science data nee
be re-examined and re-interpreted wherever necessary. It needs to fi
data, be logical, be objective, involve natural selection and be able to
some insight into the future.

Is all that really possible? It would be impossible to re-interpret
whole mountain of data now available in the some twenty to thirty s(
and natural sciences.

Fortunately, that is not necessary. In most cases, we only nee(
more accurately, more objectively, *re-interpret* the social theory conse1
interpretation of the data. To do that, however, we need an effective p
The plan followed consists of these three steps:

First, we must work only from a glossary of important social the
terms. Each important social science term used here has only one mean
or definition, the one in the Glossary. Other and inconsistent meanii
or usages are consistently avoided. In other words, we have to oper
as scientists do in all the physical sciences. Also, every word that can
defined functionally is defined functionally.

Second, all subjective word-use stratagems intuitively but necessar
used in consensus social theory must be avoided. Twenty-one of them a
listed and described in the Appendix.

Third, we need to start with a vitally important, but consistent
avoided, explanation of why we humans have always and must aways ha\
massive ideological systems. We cannot live in just the hunting-gatherin
sized groups which we were instinctively shaped to live in by millions (
years of evolution. We evolved genetically as *small-group primates* an(
remain so to this day. Researchers have found that the average individua

PART 1

one --- NATURAL SELECTION

Millions of years of evolution shaped us into a distinct social animal, one so capable at tool technology as to be able to rapidly populate the Earth. We did not descend from a monkey-like creature. We *ascended* instead and ended up dominant on this planet. We are the ones who organized our ability to speak in an ideological way, one that has enabled us to swiftly build technology and, hence, grow in number at a far faster rate than would be possible with biological evolution alone. If we look back at our rise, it is with barely concealed pride, and if we look forward, unlike with the other creatures, we can shape it to our needs.

But who _are_ we? We are not just a "HOMINID" nor are we a fellow Neanderthal or Homo Erectus, nor are we just an evolutionary blur. The present anthropological/bio-geneticist consensus currently points to our immediate ancestor evolving from one of the later African HOMO Erectus species about 195,000 years ago. It had attained the same gross anatomy and gross genetic structure we have today, but for the next 155,000 years, most of those archaic Sapiens continued to have the same primitive Mousterian, upper Paleolithic tool-weapon technology as the Neanderthals. Those Sapiens were archaic; we are not. They were not "us."

We are the ones who organized our ability to speak in a way enabling us to swiftly build technology and, hence, grow in number, an ability that has been carried on in our genes.

1

Speech began to develop in our ancestral line millions of years ago, but its development was genetic. It evolved through the brutal and ponderously slow process of biological natural selection. The snail's-pace biological evolution became largely irrelevant when the vocal speech apparatus and the brain's speech capability reached the level we now have. That capacity appears to have developed in isolated places in South Africa, in Kenya's Rift Valley Tugen Hills and other places such as in the Drakensberg, all over 100,000 ago. It spread north and reached its peak in Europe beginning more than 35,000 years ago. It is during this long era that Ancient Sapiens became "us" by acquiring the ability to adopt and use ideology. We are the ones who organized our ability to speak in a way we could build technology fast and, hence, grow in number at the gradual expense of the others. That ability was carried on in our genes. Since then, we have had little need for the slow, million-year-long process of biological evolution. Since then, some small genetic changes have occurred, such as a slightly smaller brain case, thinner leg bones, adult lactose tolerance, beards in Asia, and a better immunity to influenza, but those minor changes do not account for or explain our cultural-technological success and hence our growth in numbers. Instinctively we have not changed and our success as a species is still dependent on our primitive, but basic human nature. When it began is what marks the point of transition from biological to social evolution. That point begins the explosive growth of our cultural heritage that still continues to distance us from our Ancient Sapiens ancestors.

The quick spread of the Upper Paleolithic stone tool and weapon culture world-wide means that "we" had arrived with the same biological/brain/lingual capacity everywhere by 35,000 years ago. No matter how anthropologists classify us within the various hominid species, what *we* are, what is *human*, the human race, began at the transition point from biological evolution to social evolution more than 35,000 years ago.

What is proposed here is that a special form of ideology evolved in Africa and Europe that alone enabled small Homo Sapiens hunting-gathering groups to merge and/or expand in size. The increase in group size has been essential to the growth of the human cultural heritage, essential to what we call "progress." Moreover, as we shall see later, the social evolution of our ideology-bonded groupings (societies) explains human history, even how and why civilizations rise and fall.

Back in 1896 Benjamin Kidd explained in his work, "Social Evolution," that natural selection occurred between societies, and that "religions" were the major component of "societies." The thesis had important implications which appeared to be highly offensive to the religious faithful, even to secular-based non-theists as well. To the faithful, it inferred that "religions," instead of being "the sacred Truth," were merely transitory ideological systems playing a natural selection, evolutionary role. To secularists, it defied the doctrine of "free will" and implied the secular beliefs were also "ideology" instead of inherent and self-evident "truths." For these reasons, Professor Kidd's concept has never been effectively developed. He understood the importance of ideology ("religion") to the success of a society, but our long primate history of hunting-gathering groups was not known then. He was unable to conclude that ideology is what makes a society, that it was what bound people into large, "ultimate-sized" groups. The largest ones, the ones uniting people, kingdoms or nations together, are bonded by a common ideological World View (WV) and determine what is a "society." He was unable to think of Christianity, for example, as being the means used to shape Europeans into an immense and far more technologically advanced "hunting-gathering group."

Millions of years of evolution as small-group primates have fitted human nature, human emotions, or instincts, only to small group living. As mentioned in the Introduction/Abstract, research has shown we can identify and know only a couple hundred other people and feel much more compassion for any one of them than for scores to thousands of people in another society. Among other mammals, their groups break up into smaller groups when the size widely exceeds the norm for that species. They break up because being in too-large a group is innately disturbing to the individual. Mankind has no means, other than language-developed ideologies, to minimize that distress. We are able to create much larger and more successful societies only because of the social bonding ability of ideology.

A "mainstream society" is accurately, usefully, and exclusively defined here as "a mass of people who have their own territory and are bound together by an ideology that gives them a common world view (WV) and way of thinking." Conversely, a "WV system" is what binds people into such a society. Defined as such, the term "society" has specific meaning, not just a vague, catch-all social theory word merely meaning "more than one person."

So the social theorist consensus has never been able to move on from Professor Kidd's beginning and develop a coherent theory of social evolution. As to what causes civilizations to rise and fall, no one could give a credible explanation, one that involved natural selection. In order to avoid offending the public with a "society=religion" line of reasoning, the social theory consensus position has been that a society and its civilization could not be based upon a religion because civilizations change religions. As we will see in Part 2, that is a miss-conception.

Some of the most respected social theorists have tried to explain the rise and fall of civilizations in other ways, yet all have failed. This includes E. O. Wilson's genetic social evolution, Karl Marx's "Economic Imperative," Arnold J. Toynbee's "Challenge and Response," Ellsworth Huntington's climate change explanation, Pitirum Sorokin's "divine will," Lewis Mumford's urbanization, and Richard Dawkins' "memes." Other proposed "causes" have been depleting the environment, great men, "free-will," warfare, and plagues. Taken separately or together, they all still fail to explain the social evolution, natural selection mechanism responsible for the rise and fall of civilizations and the accumulation of the human cultural heritage.

Could it be because they had not been objective enough? Perhaps referring to a civilization as "declining" was being subjective, and that civilizations simply "changed." Social theorists decided to carry that idea forward and concluded that as entities, "civilizations" do not exist, they were just "changing cultures." In that way, the term, "culture" was substituted for "society" and "civilization." That enabled social theorists to free themselves from the problem and focus on more productive research. How could they explain the rise and fall of something that did not exist? They had turned the term, "culture," into an *omnibus word*, one of the rationalizing stratagem listed as item #4 in the Appendix.

Millions of years of biological evolution shaped Ancient Sapiens to live in hunting-gathering troops. What heralded our arrival less than 40,000 years ago was the first application of our supreme lingual-speech skills to the creating not of "cultures" but "societies." A society is "the maximum-size group which we subconsciously use a common world-view (WV) system to bind ourselves into." Social evolution has, ever since, occurred in the competition between mainstream societies, that is, those that occupy the most territory.

Is it really necessary for people to be ideologically bonded together by anything, that is, to be "bound" into societies? Characteristic of ideological systems is that they shape the very way people think, so the ideology itself is naturally regarded as made up of "eternal truths" and even being "above question." It is almost impossible for them to think without it and, hence, even to question it. When things keep going wrong, their ideological system has to be what keeps them from dealing effectively with their problems, but they never blame it. Instead, they find something else to blame, something usually coming from a society bonded by a different ideology

People are unable to understand what their society is now because they are bound by a combined old-religion and secularized world-view, both of which are shattered into such a multitude of conflicting sects, cults and theories that it is difficult to see the whole for the parts. Even so, each of the world's ideological systems, that is, Christianity, Islam, Hinduism and East Asian Marxism, all still comprise their respective societies. The one the Westerner at least subconsciously favors is generally the one he or she was brought up in, feels most apart of, and most at ease in, the one that is "home." Most people feel an affinity for their own particular ideological heritage, its history, languages, holidays, art, accomplishments, and traditions, including what they eat and how they eat it. Even Western non-theists still subconsciously consider the geographic limits of Christendom to be their society. They identify with it, and feel more at home when in it. Westerners may love to travel and, because of the humanistic secular beliefs they also hold, they may convince themselves they "love all human beings equally." Nevertheless, they are normally less upset over people being killed in another society than in their own. When any part of their secularized Christian World View-bonded system seems to be threatened, they tend to drop their differences and come together in a way that makes them feel more secure and strengthens their will to respond, such as the aggressive way the US and the rest of the West reacted and responded to the 9/11 attack.

The growth of human numbers here on Earth forced our ancestors to organize into social groups or communes over 35,000 years ago, groups that were much larger than the hunting-gathering troops we were evolved to live in. The tens of thousands of years preceding that brought verbal speech skills to modern levels and enabled them, *us,* to develop the first whole world-view (WV) and way-of-thinking system. We were then able to step ahead in the mainstream from living in little hunting-gathering groups to being bonded into larger, many-people-sized stationary settlements. People then came to live longer, learn more, developed art and music, and increased drastically in numbers.

We had learned to create a whole world-view (WV) and way-of-thinking system that was intimately fitted to our social instinctive nature, that is to our evolutionary-based psychology. This first such WV was shaped

5

around the lore of hunting, fishing, netting and/or trapping. It bonded us into the first of our long run of mainstream societies, each of which in prehistory was based upon a different WV system and technology---such as (first) hunting, then agriculture and herding. The historic societies followed after that. Each went though its own life cycle, each benefited from the previous ones, and each proportionately decreased the scientific inaccuracy of mainstream mankind's general world-view (WV) and way of thinking. None of our WV systems have ever achieved "the Truth," but each, in succession, achieved a less inaccurate understanding of ourselves and the world about us.

It is in our nature to identify with the hunting/gathering size group such as the platoon, the school class, sports team, orchestra, congregation, etc., but we must also have WV systems to create ultimate-size groups (societies) into which the smaller groups are combined. The societies we form are the largest of our groupings, the ones that bind together our nations, cities, provinces, etc. In order to be bound into these societies, we have to have a common, complete and closed world-view (WV) and way-of-thinking. Such WV systems are popularly called "religions."

If they are called "religions," why not consistently refer to them as that? The reason is that we are bound into societies by something that is not necessarily the same as what dictionaries define as "religion." World view systems serve a function, one that provides people with the most practical and hence rational cause and effect explanation for things. Ideologies function to bind us into larger "groups," or societies. Early "religions" served that role by building practical, "spirit"-based, belief systems that were, then, the best way available to explain things. The dictionary definition of "religion" only describes its ancient form, not its function. When something serves a function for us, it needs to be defined as such. It would be inadequate to define a "chair," for example, as just "a frame supporting an elevated platform with legs and a back." Most important is explaining its function: "it is to sit on."

As mentioned earlier, all this applies to mainstream WV-based societies, that is, the main ones, those which occupy significant territory.

In order to bind us into a society, a WV has be able to "condition" or modify the way we express or respond to our social instinctive nature. The generation by generation conditioning process comes partially through the parents and they, in turn, are shaped by the belief system. Also, the WV system itself has to have been shaped by those very same social instincts.

WV systems guide how all people interpret what goes on about them but in a way shaped by human nature.

What is it, however, that limits our WV systems? What is "human nature?"

Human nature is often described by anthropologists and social psychologists as being "hard wired." Biologists see it more specifically as "genetic," but their ability to explain human nature from genes is severely limited. That is partially because of the endless mire of our epigenetic system. Trying to deal with genes and "hard wires" to explain human nature is an intuitive stratagem that enables social and biological theory to avoid using the ideology-offensive word, "instinct." We have many social instincts, all of which are adapted or *conditioned* by our WV ideological systems, as they are in other mammals.

As small group social primates, we have always instinctively adapted our world-view (WV) and way-of-thinking belief systems to condition our social instincts, as uniformly as possible, in how they are to be best expressed for the survival of the society.

The next task below will be to examine the social instinctive repertoire behind our group nature, the instinct repertoire which we condition with ideologies in order to create our societies.

two --- OUR BASIC BEHAVIOR

Throughout the some forty thousand years we have been here, we have operated ever more successfully because our social instinct motivational structure is common to most mammals, especially other primates. It even forms the basis for our moral systems. It evolved millions of years ago and has been indispensable to our success as a species even though remaining much the same for more than a hundred thousand years.

As far as we know, our instinctive social nature has not changed even as society has changed drastically in the last forty thousand years. What has significantly changed and evolved is our WV systems, and it is their changes that explain the accumulating of the human cultural heritage. They evolve in ways that condition our social nature to bond more efficient and successful societies. A WV system that conditions its society to deviate from our instinctive nature tends to have more limits to its efficiency and become less successful. It has taken both our ideological systems and our instinctive social nature to cause our success as a species.

An important clue to our instinctive nature is found, strangely enough, in the body mass disparity existing between men and women, something which is included within the term "gender dimorphism." A specie in which one gender is larger than the other lives a different way than one in which they are the same. In those species in which the males are larger than the females the dominant male normally cohabits with more than one female. The chimpanzee and the orangutan, for example, may exhibit slightly more gender-dimorphism than we do but much less than that of the polygynous gorilla even though all three of the species are polygamous. In us now, females, at the age of fifteen, are more mature than the male juvenile, but then the male continues to mature physically and mentally faster than the female until growth in both stops at the age of twenty one. By then, the average male is about thirteen per cent larger. This amount of size dimorphism between men and women is confused by the genetic-caused ease with which women add on fat. Men may be five to ten percent taller but weigh perhaps twenty per cent more because young men are known to have about fifty percent more muscle mass than women in the upper body. It is also confused by the fact that sexual maturity in human females changes, as it has being coming on earlier in modern times. All that adds up to us having approximately the same gender dimorphism as the Chimpanzee.

Of course, men do not go into rut, women do not "present," and the human brain has many more cognitive skills, but there is nothing that even suggests we are instinctively monogamous. Human nature is consistent with our modest degree of dimorphism in that we are instinctively, like the chimp, mildly polygynous. Indeed, many an unhappy wife would claim men are more than just mildly so. That is the way it is with us primates, none are monogamous, even the gibbon is sometimes unfaithful. If we were monogamous, we would never have needed to adopt, as we have, monogamy-based WV systems ("religions"). We would not have needed them to make us do what was already natural to us. Later, we will see why it was, and still is, essential for the WV systems of mainstream society to be monogamy-based.

The best way to detail our social instinct repertoire is to deal directly with the data and examine the less conditioned, instinctive repertoire of the great apes. With the gorilla, the males are about twice the size of the females. Their Alpha dominant males are the only male breeding member of their small groups. A dominant male orangutan will protect a large territory containing several small groups of his females and sexually active juveniles, but it is the chimpanzee, our genetically nearest living relative, whose motivation most resembles our own. Sub-dominant males among them exist within the group and mate with females of the dominant male's polygynous "household." Generally, however, the mating takes place only before the females ovulate. The shifting bonds of intimacy help to bind the larger wild chimp groups together, but the main binding force, is the dominant males' leadership. His extensive patrolling of his territory and aggressive response to any challenge to the safety of his "entourage" (the troop) provides security that attracts the females, juveniles and sub-dominant males and binds them together into a group. In the wild, it turns a gathering or crowd into a unit, an instinctively cohesive social entity.

The amount of information available on chimp behavior is extensive, but it is all reported in a separate, animal behavioral terminology in order to avoid "anthropomorphism," that is, the crediting of human emotions to other animals. Unfortunately, that keeps us from noting that many instincts which are common to the higher apes, especially the chimpanzee, are essentially the same as our own. Below, many of these traits will be examined and all have a direct bearing on the human instinctive motivation that goes with group living.

In the minimally polygamous chimpanzee group, those who leave a group, go to another one because all chimps favor living in groups. Membership is voluntary, not imposed by force. Important to the group is that the dominant males are *respected* (admiration + feared=respect) and, because of that, are constantly being monitored for cues. Alpha dominance exists in us also, but in the chimp, "dominant" does not mean "ordering individuals around." It refers to the one who's will is most respected and, because of that, the one who leads the others. With us, nations/societies tend to be led now by individuals who are not respected. When the leaders are not respected, the people are poorly led. Their members fees insecure and stressed. If a dominant male does not handle his troop so he is both admired and even in some sense feared, the members lack confidence that he is shrewd and tough enough to protect them and will seek a troop with an alpha they *can* respect. It is actually common for females to migrate to other groups for that reason. This means a natural selection process goes on between the different troop dominant male cabals to be both the toughest, shrewdest, and most responsible.

The females of the minimally polygamous wild chimpanzee troop prefer to mate with the dominant male because his very dominance makes him attractive to them. He is "successful." He has "power" and "prestige," but the most compelling of the instinctive ties the females and sub-dominant males have to the wild troops are protection and security.

It is much the same with us. The only exceptions with us are occasional hermits, autistic individuals, and rare cases of feral children.

Not only are women attracted to successful men, but all people feel more secure when protected by one or a few powerful, dominant males. Even tall and bulky politicians have an edge over short, skinny ones. That is also why people "huddle around" the more aggressive leader in times of crisis and why the public supported US President George Bush during the years after the 9/11 terrorist attack. Many even accepted his bold assertion that "he had not made any mistakes" and trustingly allowed him to compromise their "rights" and be led into wars against "evil" which they later regretted.

To polygynous primates, the extended troop is their family in much the same way we have made the monogamous nuclear family be for us. The Chimpanzee family-troop generally varies between twenty to a hundred individuals, but the preponderance of pregnancies coming from the dominant males mean it is not a group of families but a minimally polygynous *family-troop* (see Glossary). Our once monogamy-based family is not the only type of family. Human hunting-gathering groups are also "families," or family-troops.

With the chimp, the bonds created by kinship, sexual intimacy, parenting and the fear of outside threat all cause members to rally around the dominant male cabal. The different ape-human terminology should not obscure the instinctive, family-type-basis to the human social bond.

Briefly then, the chimp troop is a single-family entity even though a different type of family than that of the lone breeding alpha male gorilla and his harem. Being a minimally polygynous family, the dominant male chimp successfully mates with many of the females without being the only one who procreates. His offspring comprise the bulk of his loosely polygynous family, but subordinate males in the troop do access his females and do reproduce.

Pre-human evolution occurred over millions of years in which it appears that our more primitive ancestors lived as hunting-gathering family-troops more or less of the same size as that of the chimp. Human hunting-gathering family-troops that still survive are also approximately forty-members in size. Many of the groups congregate together for short periods for ceremonial purposes, but because most of us are unable to know and maintain a relationship with more than a about hundred and fifty people, we are are instinctively used to living in small groups. The more extreme is the group-size deviation from the forty or so individual size, the more each individual primate in it become stressed. Even the most successful troops divide when the membership number approached the hundred-and-fifty-people approximate maximum.

Much of our social instinct nature involves how and why members of the family-troop inter-react with the dominant male. The dominant male's most prominent role in the social instinct complex is not just to aggressively maintain his dominance but, as well, to bravely protect his family-troop from internal disorder and outside threats. These are *responsibility* traits and the basis for most male be behavior that is labeled "altruism." Most heterosexual men are instinctively programed to want the role and to be able to exhibit their innate sense of responsibility and thus achieve high

11

status. That responsible trait is generally maximal when the Alpha male senses he is dominant to the group and feels he *owns* it. We all tend to take good care of what we regard as our own. The advent of language and speech made it possible for the family-troops to have the type of common WV and way of thinking that could enable the dominant male to subconsciously regard a virtually infinite number of people all bonded by the WV system as his group. He can feel he "owns" it in the same way he originally felt he owned the smaller hunting-gathering family-troop.

What we humans constantly do is balance brain-stem basic individual need (including the male ego demand for more status) against our common group's ideological expectations. Most more Alpha heterosexual men are driven by an intensely emotional need for group status, even control. This is a drive that is normally expressed as a desire to be of benefit to the group Most more Alpha heterosexual men are driven by an intensely emotional need for group status, even control. This is a drive that is normally expressed as a desire to be of benefit to the group in order to be appreciated. In direct proportion to how divided the ideological system is and continues to become, the male leader looses the feeling the group tribe, kingdom, nation or society is his, comes to feel it is less his responsibility, and becomes less sincere in his dedication to it. The ideological disunity causes those who seek leadership of it to *feel* less responsible for its welfare. However, the individual consciously perceives himself still as being responsible because he knows he is supposed to be and needs to be seen as such to keep status. Slowly over many generations, the dividing WV system causes the leadership to deteriorate or, as we say now, for government to become corrupt.

Not only does the group, the society, lose good leadership but the group also looses the ability to take the emotional place of the small family-troop in the people. It becomes just a huge mass of "other people."

In order for people to feel they belong, the larger group's members all need to believe they all have the same common origin and that they all have the same general goal or "purpose," one that everyone benefits by working together to achieve. That needs to be apart of their WV system. In addition, common rules or taboos are needed that all can agree to observe so they can work better together in hopes of achieving the common goal.

In contrast, if the group is united by the goal of "pursuing happiness, of "scientific Truth," going to "heaven," "spreading democracy," and achieving "The Second Coming," then, not surprisingly, the group that has such divers goals is not easily recognized as a group at all. Its members live in little more a shadow than a society, one that has only the trappings of the type of group in which they evolved to function. In such a group, the individual young man feels intense frustration. Instead of wanting to work for its benefit, he fills with inexplicable emotions that he finds difficult to manage. The WV is too divided to bind him into the society. He feels isolated, left out, and even tends to become hostile. He may want to avoid people, become depressed, or suicidal. If he is rich, he may become corrupt and arrogant. If he is poor, he may become so hostile that he can no longer repress his feelings, and looses control. He may take his frustration and hostility out on others, such as his mate and children. He may even come to think everyone is trying to take advantage of him and that he has to strike first in his own defense. He may end up in prison.

Like all human beings, the alpha male tends to rationalize. When his society is pathologically divided, he can promote himself as a responsible public servant" even when he uses the weakened society as a tool to provide bounty for his more real-to-him family-troop entourage of parents, wife, and children. It is the logical way for him to satisfy his sense of responsibility. He feels justified in doing that regardless of the rules and regulations imposed by the weakened society.

We can next gain insight into our instinctively normal male-female relationship. With the chimpanzee groups, the dominant male tends to initiate more pregnancies than do all the other males. It is in that sense that all the females in his family-troop are his entourage. Even as the dominant male initiates the liaisons, the females also mate with non-dominant males, but such liaisons occur only at the tolerance of the dominant male. The females who are not currently his favorites feel neglected at times and flirt with subordinate males. In us, we could say that the females feel the need to flirt (to "present") because the lower status of the males causes them to be sexually inhibited. Repressed sexual assertiveness in the less-dominant males is a natural phenomenon and helps limit how much low-status male chimps actually reproduce. In humans, sexual inhibition is called, "shyness." It also helps explain the prevalence of impotency in sub-dominant men.

Instead of "presenting," human females initiate most sexual liaisons by means of willingness-cues or flirting. Involved is a whole repertoire of characteristics that include a passive show of interest and respect through subtle, non-aggressive and subservient body language and verbal cues collectively classified as "being feminine." Women do not "present," but they do have estrus. Researchers have discovered that when ovulating, they tend to be instinctively more open to mating, more inclined to shop for sexier clothes, and choose the closest thing they can to an alpha, that is, to a "successful," hence high-status, male.

Sub-dominant male apes generally do not take sexual initiative with a female without her presenting, that is, in us, without getting flirting cues from her. Even then, it would be early in estrus and hence less likely to result in pregnancy. The higher-ranking males would mate only later on and then, mostly with the higher-ranking females. It is this late-in-estrus-mating which results in most pregnancies. It all resembles the human class structure. Male juveniles tend to be excluded and kept at the periphery of the troop by the dominant males.

Of course, both human and chimp behavior has changed during the over four million years since they evolved away from our line of descent. Women do not "present"and men do not have "rut." Also, we gained more division of labor. In the hunting/gathering-group, men hunt, war, or play sports, and women gather or go shopping.

Female chimps are innovative and give us no cause to underestimate their role even outside of child bearing and rearing, but it is the dominant or alpha male who holds the family-troop together and protects it. It is the group, however, not the individual, that he "owns" and protects. This means that there is a instinctive difference between the sexes in that the dominant male is primarily focused on the welfare of his family-troop while the female's main focus is on the welfare of her offspring. When tension builds in the group because the males are struggling over dominance or they are lax in their protective role, it is the nature of the females to respond by being assertive or by placating them and thus easing tension. Male competition for dominance is a problem especially acute in crowded zoo conditions. In the Kansas City zoo, the females have been known to even mob and injure an unnecessarily aggressive male. Zoos may deliberately manipulate the gender rate in favor of females and keep groups small just to minimize male aggressiveness.

The dominant male's brain stem attitude seems to be that it is he who "services" the females and provides them with children genetically best fit for survival. He feels it is he who risks his life to protect them, recovers fallen infants, and beats up misbehaving juveniles. He even looks the other way when those "fawning male underlings" he allows to "hang around in his entourage" (but who help him in the hunt) take liberties with his "more restless wives." With all his responsibility, he instinctively feels that they had all better be responsive to his cues or leave his group.

Chimpanzees also have what we can call a *reciprocity* instinct. That is, they resent those who accept a favor but do not reciprocate. This is where our sense of "fairness" originates, our sense of justice. Chimps and even monkeys, such as the capuchins, share food with each other. When a favor that is extended, such as giving food, is not reciprocated, both the chimp and we humans feel the perpetrator deserves to be punished. Since we humans are social animals, we are then moral animals. We are not moral because some "being" tells us to be moral. We are moral beings but because we evolved that way.

Yet, another social-instinct we share with other apes is the way all group members continually monitor the dominant male(s) for cues as to when, whether, how, or where to eat, play, sleep, travel, and groom (socialize). In earlier times, people took their cue from the king. Now, our media and advertisers provide us with our society-shaping political-commercial dominance cues, and people are instinctively led by them. This able-to-be-led behavioral trait appears early with the human infant's intense, instinctive suggestibility to the mood of its mother. It shows later on in the way children learn more rapidly from teachers who are dominant (e.g., who are respected). It exists in what we see as "in," "trendy," or "hot," or even what is "cool." It is why placebos work. The cues come from whatever we have been conditioned to respond to as the dominant male.

All over the world, large, multinational corporations use their advertising, marketing, and public relations media to control all our sources of information and emit the cues that shape public opinion. These firms are masters at manipulating people because they have a deep and practical understanding of human instinct. Even though the income of immature teenagers is low, these firms focus on and exploit them because their more exaggerated response to cues makes them the most gullible buyers of their styled clothes and electronic products. Smaller "kids," who can buy even less, are indoctrinated through television on what is "fun" until they are programmed to successfully badger their grocery-shopping mothers into buying highly processed, addictive junk food.

Briefly then, cue influence is a primate group-cohesive behavioral trait that is instinctive. We, as well as all the other primates, instinctively think and behave as a family-troop in response to cues, cues which we perceive as representing the intent of the dominant males. In the wild, the survival of every member of the troop and, hence every individual's sense of security and self-worth, depends upon the dominant male. Failure of the individual to monitor his cues arouses fear of losing favor, being rejected and without protection in a dangerous world. In both apes and humans, the mere threat of being rejected causes feelings of fear, embarrassment, loneliness or depression, depending upon both conditions and social system conditioning.

Finally, primate troop members feel a sense of unity and togetherness which tends to pit them against other groups. Howler monkeys, for example, gather daily at the edge of their territory and howl at those in the next one. They are effectively "hurling insults" at the neighbor group, and in that way reinforce solidarity within their own group. The territory of the howler and other primates is an invisible border between the groups which covers their food supply and which is demarcated through a curious process. It is where intruding neighboring group members, when confronted, feel less and less secure the further they are in their neighbor's territory, and the further they advance away from what they feel is the core of their own territory. The resistance of the defenders, on the other hand, grows more intense the further they are backed up into their own territory. Ultimately, they may drive the intruders back and the reverse process occurs. The final result is a sort of equilibrium, and is ca phenomenon common to life, even fish, such as the stickleback. How territorial borders are established is an instinctive, swarm-theory process that, in modification, is similar to the balance of power and the territorial limits of and between nations. In most primates, the territory of each group is flexible and not just from "wars" but, as well, from moving seasonally which alters and reshapes the "territory" they move with them.

The human social nature therefore involves a whole complex of dominance and related instincts which, together, bind all the members into the family-troop. Our ideological WV and way-of-thinking systems affect how we express our instinctive nature. Our basic nature, in turn, modifies and shapes our WV systems. How "instinct" works, neurologically and physiologically, is not well understood, but explaining it is not in the least essential to understanding how it functions in human social evolution. Even "thinking" is shaped by the way our social-cultural environment conditions our genetic-based instincts. It is not possible to tell what one person will do in many situations, but what people do in general depends upon what they believe, and once that is ascertained, we can know what they will do in general, what they are in general thinking, even in general what they will say. When they need to adapt their beliefs, even switch to a new set of WV beliefs, they will do it when they need to. They always have.

three   --- THE PRECURSOR SYSTEM

We evolved from Archaic Sapiens. They and the Neanderthals evolved from a broad list of Homo Erectus types who, in turn, perhaps, evolved from a smaller Homo Habilis ape-li,ke hominid; but there is as yet no consensus. The anthropological theory consensus is flexible and changes, but it is fair to say that neither Homo Erectus nor the Neanderthals were especially eloquent conversationalists. The Archaic Sapiens that evolved from them did manage to develop a primitive "spirit"-based WV system which seemed to them to explain "cause and effect." Such a belief system would have been necessary as soon as speech developed to where a whole world-view and way-of-thinking could be communicated. What is proposed here is that it developed in the form of answers to questions people would have had. When people became able to ask questions, there developed a need for a common, ideology-based closed system of thinking, one that made it possible to provide practical answers. Early Sapiens came into the world not as "divinely created spirits" but as finite beings who were contending with a world that was as much a mystery to them as it has always been to all living things. Even newborn infants have to interpret what goes on about them according to the best theory they can manage. Everyone needs to have and, hence, manages to get, a core of belief. Ancient Sapiens, as well, needed a common WV in order to be in general agreement with the other members of their small groups about those matters which were important to all. They needed to agree on why some animals hide in burrows and others in trees. They needed to agree on why some animals sleep in the daytime and others at night---and why seasons change and animals migrate. Being gatherers as well, they needed to agree on why some tubers were edible and others not. They needed a world-view that formed a framework for coming up with answers to such issues which would become the common lore of the group and that helped them work together to obtain food.

Once Archaic Sapiens' speech ability became skilled enough, it was inevitable that a family-troop dominant male would subconsciously absorb from the group and from other groups what cultural/technological beliefs which were the most practical, that is, they were the most "advanced" by being less *in*accurate. He would have coalesce them all into a lore consisting of a primitive whole World View (WV) and closed way-of-thinking. It was also inevitable that the others in the group learned it from him because, as explained earlier, they instinctively responded to Alpha cues. The instinctive makeup of the group made it so that the whole WV (world view) and way-of-thinking held by the alpha and his cabal was subconsciously accepted by all.

The ideology in turn would have strengthened the Alpha male's concept of the family-troop as being *his*, and thus intensified his sense of responsibility for, and control over it. His WV ideology would strengthen the group's social bond, promote cooperation and cohesion, and thus improve the efficiency with which he and his cohorts led the rest.

It is of note but seldom noted, that animal groups are essentially *communes*. This is the case with primates, including human hunting-gathering groups. Communism has been the only economic system in the world until the development of our far more sophisticated economic system beginning with the rise of civilization.

Let us propose that one of the hunting-gathering groups that arose had ideological improvements that better adapted its members to the environment, brought them the most unity, and proved to be the more satisfying because of being the most consistent with their emotional nature. All that would have increased the success of the family-troop and improved its ability to compete with the other groups. This more successful group may have grown in size and broken into several other such groups with the same ideology. Also, because they were small-group-size social primates with an ability to speak and communicate, their more successful hunting-technology lore would have spread and been adopted by still other groups. The competition between hunting-gathering family-troops would have ensured that the WV and way-of-thinking that built the most successful family-troop was the one that spread the fastest and furthest to the other family-troops. Ultimately, the groups that adopted that WV would have crowded out all the other ones in the stiff competition that has always existed. Such a development did not happen because of one dominant male or all at once but that did happen over a period of tens of thousands of years. This was an early part of the natural selection process responsible for social evolution. The best ideological system appeared and spread by means of a natural selection process. It's beliefs would have even become a part of their very language. As both Ludwig Wittgenstein (1889-1951) and Karl Wilhelm Von Humboldt (1767-1835) observed, languages are separate world perspectives. The first language and the first whole WV system automatically became integrated.

Let us also propose that a sort-of federation of common WV believing family-troops developed, all of whom spoke the same WV-based language. The individual within these hunting-gathering family-troop communes felt no special awareness or loyalty to the larger, ideological federation of similar-believing groups, but the common WV tended to limit hostility between them. The communes even traded with each other as hunting-gathering groups tend to do, but the individual's own family-troop was still his or her real world. The groups did compete for space so that some hostility and infighting must have occurred, but because they all tended to have the same common WV, such wars were either rare or ritualized. Real and savage warfare is not known to be common among the human hunting-gathering groups that had survived into recent times. They even tended to come together for social occasions.

Thus, by adopting speech and ideology, the early Sapiens turned hunting-gathering technological lore into a group-bonding belief system, one which enabled the hunting-gathering groups to quickly adopt new methods from each other in the story form which are now referred to as "myths." In that way they were able to obtain more food and lower the death rate. The individual family-troops probably remained about the same estimated thirty-five to forty-five member size because the basic hunting band, as with the military squad and sports teams, is instinctively centered around about eight to ten adult males. Add females and children and the total comes close to some forty people, that is, the same size grouping common to human hunting-gathering commune groups that still survived in the last century.

The world-view systems that did not adopt the same language and similar beliefs but still survived the competition would have been "non-mainstream" and pushed to the more marginal areas of the continent. In the mainstream, only the most advanced belief system survived. Instead of a million-year-long biological process, a natural selection, social evolutionary one had developed, one that produced a growing body of cooperating hunting-gathering family-troops in only tens of thousands of years, a growing family of groups all speaking the same general language.

Certainly, linguists who trace back world languages conclude that the modern tongues trace back not to more, but to fewer languages.

The groups are believed to have migrated out of Africa some seventy to ninety thousand years ago. By some seventy to eighty thousand years ago, it would appear that the number of groups outside of Africa had dwindled sharply. By sixty thousand years ago, however, their number seemed to have recovered, and they spread North and East in small hunting-gathering family-troop communes, all with the same general WV-language system.

The migration was slow. Each group camped near water and hunted and gathered within an approximate five-mile radius. Each group's "territory" was only its current hunting/gathering range. Perhaps every five to six months a troop would exhaust its range and move some ten miles or so to another site. Population movement into new territory would have been at roughly that speed.

The dominant male in each group was the ideologically sanctioned headman or "chief." He maintained his authority with the help of several other dominant males. Dominance is an instinctive and essential feature of all society---even when people live in what appear to be egalitarian communes. In them, "consensus" decisions are actually still determined by subtle physical and verbal cues and from the body language of the dominant males. Otherwise, no consensus could be readily achieved; the groups would be rent by enough political controversy to be uncompetitive if not dysfunctional.

Within human hunting gathering communes, the death rate from murder has been much higher than in modern society. Most killing has been of "adulterers." It is the dominant male protecting his "wives" against "seducers" and, hence, "illicit" sex. His latent brutality attracts rather than repels the women. Even today, people are repelled by "too-soft" leaders. No Ancient Sapiens felt safe in a group without a few dominant males who were tough, ingenious and aggressive enough to protect their commune group.

Being common, murder even tended to help limit too-rapid population growth. To this day, murder has been a common cause of death within hunting-gathering communes. Of the Ache of Paraguay, for example, eighty one per cent died of violence, from accidents, war and murder. Such violence was characteristic, also, of most of the New Guinea tribes. Within the Yanomamo of the Amazon, murderers had, on average, twice as many women and children as non-murderers. Also, hunting gathering family-troops tend to murder or abandon one or both twins, also the impaired, the aged, and the infirm. Such WV doctrine-decreed-slaying or abandoning tended to protect the genetic, epigenetic and/or micro RNA heritage and preserve the mobility so essential to the survival of the group.

There was no system or code of justice we would now recognize in the hunting-gathering family-troops, but surely the males did take their "wives" (liaisons) discreetly so it could be more easily overlooked by the others to minimize friction. The females knew, however, and surely gossiped as they gathered while the males sought to minimize resentment that would weaken the bond so vital to the hunt. This meant the males were more oblivious of the "seductions" and, hence, to retribution. Instead, they surely talked only of past kills and other such more important subjects. The need to work as a team in the hunt stood above all other considerations

four --- THE FIRST WORLD-VIEW SYSTEM

The hunting-gathering WV belief system was still primitive, possubly because of being, in part, self-contradictory and incomplete, thus limiting its functional utility to the groups. What ultimately developed in order to bind the family-troops into larger groups was what can be described as a WV system master formula, one consisting of answers to a template of four questions, each one dealing with the so-called "eternal mystery of life." The formula ensured that the answers would be consistent with each other, create a coherent way of thinking, and provide a plan for how the people were to live. The four questions were and still are: (1) who are we or where did we come from? (2) what is our goal, our reason for existing? (3) what means (morals) do we use to achieve them, and (4) what stands in our way? In some primal way, our ancestors asked those "us" and "we" questions and came up with community-forming answers. The four answers shaped the group's core or theology, one forming their whole WV and way-of-thinking. Answers to them have formed the core/theology of every mainstream WV ever since.

It should be noted that since groups are never regarded as dying by their members, the question of one's personal fate and death is not included here among the four questions.

With the first question, "where did we come from?," the unity of the group would require that members believe they had a common origin, such as, for example, the Christian belief in our being created. Whatever answer was provided, if believed in common, would serve to reinforce solidarity. Even such answers as "our origin is shrouded in mystery" or "we have always existed," when believed in common, serve the same society-bonding function---as would the theory of evolution and social evolution in a more accurate/advanced WV system. Where we came from helps to shape what we think we are.

22

The second question is "what is our goal?" If the modern secular age "pursuit of happiness" were not our goal, and if the means to attain it was not set by our corporate marketing media as shopping, we would have a much different society. The ultimate core ideal and goal of the East Asian Marxist WV is still "an egalitarian, communal society with the withering away of the state" even though, in the mean time, in order to progress economically, it has adopted a capitalist economic agenda with the government tightly controlled by the Party. The goal of Christian fundamentalists is "individual salvation," and the "Second Coming of Christ and God's Kingdom." Hindus seek "enlightenment" and "Nirvana." Muslims seek "complete obedience to Allah" and await "the Mahdi"--- believed to be followed by *yawm al-Qlyamah* (the day of the rising) and the ideal "kingdom of Allah." In the past, the old spirit-based WV systems worded the goal question as "what is our *purpose?*"—that is what fate do the spirits have in mind for us?" To this day, the people still think their "spirit"-based purpose is "true. Their faith in that still, though weakly, bonds their societies even in this secular age of science.

The third question is "how do we achieve our goals?"---or "the means to the ends." People have to agree on how to behave so they can cooperate to achieve the common goal(s), and how they are to work together to achieve them is their moral system. The mainstream belief systems' moral codes or formulas have always been based on such social instincts as reciprocity, maternal care and placating, and the alpha male sense of protecting responsibility. Moral codes do not make us moral but merely condition our moral-social nature to enforcible standards. That improves harmony and enables the society to operate more efficiently.

The fourth and last question is, "what stands in our way?" When difficulties arise, people want something or someone to blame in order to agree on what to avoid. In the East Asian Marxist WV system, the Party claims to be establishing socialism while regarding the capitalist world as still being their enemy. It has been "the barbarians" in the ancient Chinese WV system. Christians made an evil god (Satan), as their scapegoat. Muslims are supposed to hate both infidels and demons. The short-lived racist Nazi regime aimed at "the Jewish Conspiracy."

Once the answers to the Four Questions Template are formed into a self-consistent core of belief or theology, the next thing the believers do is follow a subconscious but logical step-by-step process of tying into their new core of belief all that they subsequently observe. From then on, all questions and concerns are thought out only in those ways that are consistent with their Four Question Template core of answers. All that finally coalesces into a complete, near self-consistent, rigidly held closed system of thinking in which each part supports the rest. The result is a WV system which may become mainstream and survive for thousands of years.

We have no way now of knowing the precise myths and doctrines that formed the WV core of belief of the first mainstream society, but if we indulge our imaginations a little, we can visualize the logical path that was followed in setting it up. Imagine someone becoming aware of himself and recognizing that this consciousness or "self" was directing wn body. From that, he would then logically conclude that everything else was also run by his body what to do. He would logically see his body as having a "spirit" that controlled it, and that such "spirits" logically existed in other people as well. This early thinker would then logically reason that the "spirits" in them controlled their bodies in the same way his own consciousness controlled his own body.

The next logical step for him was to conclude that all cause and effect was the result of "spirit-power." Edward Taylor (1832-1917) is credited with drawing the first picture of this "spirit"-based way-of-thinking and which he called "animism." His picture of early religion has not been popular in social theory because it leads to recognizing the slow evolution of WV systems from belief in total "spirit" causation to polytheism and then to monotheism. That brought attention to the obvious trend down in the number of "spirits," leading to the valid but dangerous conclusion that newer mainstream WV systems always depend less on "spirit" causation and more on natural causation, meaning of course, that the still surviving animistic and polytheistic mainstream faiths of Asia were *inferior*. Social theorists avoid such a conclusion because the secular system had to keep being bonded with the old "spirit" based WV systems in Asia in order to continue bringing some order to the world. Much of non-Marxist, "spirit"-based WV systems (those of India, Nepal, Singapore etc.) in Asia would never have adopted the secular system. If the secular system taught that their WV systems were inferior, they would not want to be a part of the modern secular system's "Global Community of Nations."

The social science consensus justifies its position by mentioning that there are tribes on Earth which still have animistic WV systems. That response overlooks the obvious process in which such primitive WV systems have been weeded out from the mainstream by natural-selection and manage to survive only in ever diminishing numbers in the world's least desirable places. Also, an anthropologist would hardly be well received by animistic WV-believing tribes if he was known to regard their treasured beliefs as being the most backward on the planet.

The individual(s) who originated the "spirit"-concept would have created a practical system. A rock shaped to a spearhead could kill an animal and provide food, but if they threw rocks straight up, they could come right back down and seriously injure someone. Logically, therefore, rocks had "spirit power" to do "good" or "bad." That meant they had developed a system of thinking which established logical, cause and effect rules on how to deal with things. To them, rocks hated being thrown straight up but wanted to be chipped into spearheads and be of service to them. So, in order to efficiently utilize "spirit power," there developed guidelines for the use of rocks. The dangerous ways became taboo.

Mainstream WV belief systems are verbalized mostly only in terms of the welfare of those in the group, not the interests of the self, because all the members of the group want to be a part of the group, not separate from it. So, all lent a social instead of selfish bias to the growing communal WV and way-of-thinking. Because language and the WV are intertwined, the hunter-gatherers' language itself ensured that the very words of the WV system were always assembled and combined in a "for-the-group" way. Words are the evolutionary tool of the group, and all language is shaped by people's WV systems.

By being society-oriented, language is poorly adapted to selfish thinking. People's more selfish brain-stem-wants tend to be non-verbalized and, hence subconscious. They tend to be couched in rationalized social-welfare terminology. People prefer to believe they always care for and always serve others because they feel they are supposed to. Doing so builds their status in the group they need and want.

Language-speech made possible the full development of the "spirit" concept. All the first society-bonding WV systems were based on "spirits" because they were the only means we had then to make sense of things. They were our earliest way of explaining what we now interpret as "natural cause and effect."

So, the first "spirit" way-of-thinking shaped the Four Question Template answers into the first closed "complete understanding" of the world. The people had turned to a new way of thinking that was able to be held in common and became the first world-view (WV) system able to bond people into a "society" larger than the single family-troop.

The development of the "spirit theory" can be regarded as the dawning of the human intellect, probably the greatest step ever taken in human social evolution. It was so successful that the same old "spirit" theory has survived in an increasingly attenuated form, unfortunately, to this very day. The need of society to have a whole WV and way-of-thinking system of belief is no less vital to the forming and functioning of human society now than it was then, but time and the improving accuracy of human understanding has made obsolete the old "spirit"-based WV form of bonding.

five --- THE MATRILINEAL WV SYSTEMS

As the number of the Ancient Sapiens hunting-gathering groups increased, the territory and number of the Neanderthals decreased. Our Ancient ancestors' swelling numbers meant more need for a higher level of organization. That was achieved by adapting the "spirit" concept to answer the questions of the Four Question Template. The answers were able to form the central core of a common and coherent world-view, one that accommodated them to a myth-based and closed way of thinking that was successful in binding the smaller hunting-gathering groups into communal conglomerates, ones that were much larger than the less than one hundred fifty-people size hunting gathering groups.

The larger groups were so successful that their WV systems, and the technology bound up in their myths, managed to spread to other hunting-gathering groups and bind them into similar but even larger groups. All groups bonded by that same WV system came to comprise the first mainstream *society*.

The WV system of the first society was based on a tool-weapon technology that included a hunting, trapping, netting and gathering lore. This Hunting WV system's much larger groups were able to (1) dispatch large hunting parties to trap and net small herds of game and hunt and kill larger game, (2) send out separate tuber and berry gathering parties, and (3) trade with other such groups. Instead of dying before our thirtieth birthday, many of us then managed to live to be grandparents and teach skills to the young while our parents made and used the weapons they made. Finally, (4) we later developed such sophistications as cave art, weaving of cloth, formal burials, and even music.

By about 35,000 years ago, our social evolution had begun with this new type hunting-technology WV-based system. Its visible African and European *mainstream* (see Glossary) existence began with cave paintings.

The new system continued to spread and ultimately replaced the old hunting-gathering WV systems in much of the rest of the world. Relatively fast-paced social evolution had ended our need for further, slow-paced, biological evolution. *We* had finally arrived, that is, Homo Sapiens Sapiens, true humans, "*us.*" We had begun our unique social evolutionary progress.

Even though the more sophisticated new WV system did involve their early technology, it was still "spirit"-based and regarded then as "the Truth." Its doctrines were only what worked for them and only as long as they did. It was only the beginning of a long procession of WV systems, each succeeding one being based on a less inaccurate WV, one with a belief in fewer "spirits." A gradual natural selection process of weeding out older and less advanced WV systems was underway, one in which we humans gradually *decreased* the over-all *in*-accuracy of our understanding of ourselves and our universe.

As is always the case, now as well as then, nothing they then believed could logically be separated from their WV belief system. The new belief system provided the justification for everything they did, even how a certain stone blade was to be chipped to sharpness. Magic also played a part. No matter what question a member might ask, only the WV belief system provided the framework for answering it. The technology and lore it was based on has always been how we explained cause and effect.

The specific doctrines of this first mainstream WV system and its society may never be known, but they must have (1) attributed a common origin to the members of the group. Having a common origin would have helped to bind them together with a sense of unity and brotherhood, something especially important in the hunt. Also, (2) what would have worked would have been a mythology to explain why they existed, that is, what plan or goal the "spirits" had for them. What would have worked would have also been (3) a mythology that established the rules, taboos, customs, rituals, magic and spells to guide them towards achieving their "purpose" (goals). Finally, (4) they would have placed blame for the hardships, suffering and privations they endured. When they placed it on themselves for breaking taboos, they helped to reinforce their taboo (their moral) system. When blaming the "spirits," they generally decided they had to do better in order to placate them. What had developed was a new hunting-technology-based class of ideological systems, ones built around the same or similar core of Four Question Template answers.

We are able to note other clues by closely examining their cave paintings. Their art expressed the reverential idealism and awe with which they viewed the animals. They understood and respected them as massively muscular, horned and imposing animals, not just those they hunted but also those they tried to avoid because of being so fierce. Most were depicted in the narrow and more confining areas of the cave where acoustics were the best. Young males led by the older men must have crouched there, crowded in the dark with only a periodic flicker of a small, sacred-to-them, smoldering fire source they brought with them. There, they sang or chanted their hunting and net using lore. The ceremony was a fearful, "men-only" ordeal which downplayed the important gathering role of the women by emphasizing the hunter's ability to kill animals for food despite the animal's massive muscle weight, their horns, sharp teeth and belligerence. Their art showed the legs of the animals as being inadequate to bear all their muscular weight, an indication that they were depicting them as trophies. It seems to be the way they initiated their male juveniles into adulthood and shape their character, courage and group pride. It also served to educate them with the WV system's "spirit" explanation of what season each animal-type was to be found in, and where, as well as what they needed to do to trap, net and spear them. It would have all been memorized and handed down generation after generation as their "sacred truths."

Since the main technology of the new ideological system was based on hunting-weapon technology, it is appropriate to designate it as the Hunting WV-bonded society.

It is of further note that the cave paintings and drawings seem unusually sophisticated to us now when compared to the stiff and stylized art common to later societies during their decline. As we will see later on in the historical societies, idealistic, sophisticated art appears during the early crest of the society and portrays a feeling of idealism, even ebullience. That ebullience was later lost and eventually sank into almost melancholia during the subsequent decline. Characteristically, art portrays the attitude of people toward their society at that particular stage of their society's development.

Our new Hunting, "spirit"-based WV System and its society had enabled the hunting-gathering groups to coalesce into group-conglomerated communes that underwent a technological revolution in stone weapon and tool-making. From small portable stone cores properly heated, they chipped off small but sharp blades, ones which were fashioned into scrapers, spear points, awls, and horn-carving tools for making needles. With needles, they learned to bound hides, weaved and later sewed to make nets and crude fabrics for clothing. Their spears enabled them to kill animals from a range of up to fifty feet. With their better technology, they could set out on large hunting and gathering excursions. Their WV myth-based technology included the "spirit" rationale for setting up elaborate traps for catching big game *in mass*. They then dragged the carcasses to their encampments for the communal butchering of the meat. As hunting-age man, we had become the most effective and efficient hunter on earth, even killing mastodons and mammoths. We had begun the more than forty-thousand year long process of pushing the Archaic Sapiens' WV belief-bound hunting-gathering way of life into the peripheral and less bountiful, non-mainstream, areas of the globe.

The new Hunting WV system spread east from Africa through India to Malaysia, Indonesia and Australia. It spread north into Europe and Central Asia, then across Russia and northern China where it moved into Manchuria and then Japan. Some twenty to thirty thousand or more years ago, the Hunting WV System people began spreading into the New World. Clues are leading to possibly a much earlier, older migration. They may have come in boats, skirting across the southern fringes of the great Arctic ice mass, possibly first from Europe and probably Siberia. Once they had developed mainstream, society-binding WV belief systems, cultural-technological improvements followed and they were able to grow in numbers and populate more of the globe.

Once a better technology had arisen, it naturally spread. As we will later see, every new and better way of obtaining more food involved new and better "technology." In prehistory, each such mainstream technology was the main part of the WV ideological system.

Much of the focus in prehistorical research has been on the location and migration of racial-lingual groups. The accumulating evidence is that once the ancient Sapiens migrated into a region or continent and then developed society, we tended to stay there. Afterwards, mass conquests and migrations were rare. The early Sapiens that poured out of Africa some 60,000 years ago, ended up almost fifty-five thousand years later divided from the proto-Afro-Asian lingual/racial group into Afro-Asian, Indo-European, Semitic, Dravidian and other generally smaller lingual groups. In explaining all this, linguists, archaeologists, anthropologists, geneticists and others propose cultural, lingual and even DNA-based explanations. Social-evolutionary, natural selection, cause-and-effect explains the process.

In figuring out in detail which people settled where, race-type studies have played an important part. Even though genetic differences do not determine the culture, language or religion of a people, and even though the race-type differences are essentially only cosmetic, until now at least and human nature being what it is, "racial type" has tended to confine the limits of each lingual-religious system. This race-ethnic chauvinism served then to boost the common ideology-built sense of brotherhood among believers that is so useful in promoting unity and limiting strife inside a society, a tendency dealt with earlier. It also explains why the new Hunting WV System must have differed from one region to another.

Like all things, societies and their WV ideological systems are expendable. Success is ephemeral, and change is inevitable. As with biological organisms, no ideological WV system lasts indefinitely. The Hunting WV-based society was killing too much game in order to feed its then most certainly burgeoning numbers. As the population increased, the sizes of the game herds declined. Large animals were becoming extinct in every continent.

The dwindling supply of meat was especially hard on the less adaptive Neanderthals. Not only was the new Hunting society building up commune-communities of several hundred people in size, our technology had also improved. We were making warm clothing and could deal with the snow and cold even better than the more robust Neanderthal. With its poorer weaponry, smaller groups, and lack of resistance to human-contact-caused infectious diseases, the Neanderthal numbers dwindled. By about 28,000 years ago, they had become extinct. Surviving longer was a smaller hominid ape which inhabited the tiny Indonesian island of Flores, and perhaps much of the rest of Polynesia. It also died out less than perhaps seventeen thousand years ago, and there may have been other homids as well. Even the saber-tooth carnivore could no longer compete and became extinct.

Some 28,000 years ago, stress began to build up in our Hunting WV System and signs of decline were appearing. We can begin to draw a picture of what was happening from (1) basic human motivation described earlier, (2) anthropological, lingual and archaeological clues, (3) examining their art, and (4) extrapolating from the social evolutionary processes which can be accurately discerned from the more profuse data in the historical societies and described in Part 2.

It is logical to surmise that, as a result of less food causing a higher death rate and an increase in stress, the people's exuberant idealogical self-confidence waned. More paintings of predators appeared. The number of animal paintings declined. The religious center of their large hunting and trapping communes shifted from the caves to the Gobekli Tepe temple complex built about 11,000 years ago on the then lush "Garden of Eden" hill top "nexus to the heavens" just north of the Fertile Crescent. In it are sculpted headless humans, crawling, biting insects and vulture designs. After its construction, their society continued in rapid decline.

Female idols had begun to appear as far back as 25,000 years ago, ones that then seem to have served as fem-fertility fetishes to promote better gathering. The WV was shifting away from hunting. By about 9,000 years ago and the full development of agriculture, the shift to the female fertility symbols had been completed, and the drawing of hunted animals ceased. A drastic increase in female influence and decline in the male-role in society had occurred.

As explained earlier, when chimps feel crowded in captivity, stress builds up and the assertiveness of the females increases. Just as the Alpha prime males look for threats outside the group, the females are sensitively and subconsciously attuned to discerning trouble *inside* it. They will either gang up on a troublesome male or take to placating and thus minimizing dissension among the males. Female chimps will also leave a group they feel has become poorly led. Among us, women are also primed to protect their offspring by judging the security they find in their society. If the women sense group-weakness because the men are squabbling among themselves and allowing authority to break down, the women are programmed to become more assertive. As will be described later, the historical data on all of the mainstream civilizations shows that women have always become assertive and increased their role during the early decline of each mainstream society.

The proliferating fem-fertility idols depict a definitely corpulent and decidedly female human being. Was the intent to emphasize pregnancy or obesity, or both? What we can be most sure of is that it was only the female principle they were worshiping. Woman-ness alone represented fertility because people were not yet aware that the male played any role in reproduction. The tendency, therefore, was to regard all things as either feminine or non-feminine—e.g., "sacred" or "profane."

Obesity may have become representative of pregnancy by showing that woman-ness represented abundance, especially an abundance of food. In our modern society, we have long depicted obesity as a lack of will power or just a sickness, but in prehistory, in the bare survival of a growing mass of hungry people, corpulence would have represented high status. Women were transforming gathering into agriculture and may have used the small hand held pregnant female idols as fetishes that mocked their "great male hunters," the ones who went out to kill a mammoth and came back with a rabbit or a gopher. Gradually, the goddess figurines grew to become sacred symbols of "the great Fem-Fertility" principal. The old Hunting WV system had been transformed into a new Fem-Fertility agricultural WV belief system.

We have no written record of the age, just the era's mass of tool and pottery found by archaeologists and which they use to name separate cultures. Here, we add the mass of clues and evidence found in the ideological heritage that was passed on verbally from generation to generation but written down only later in historic times. We put it all together with the help of the primate instinctive group ways described earlier, and we have a picture of what finally became the Fem-Fertility WV System and the society it bonded.

The social theory consensus, for example, is that there has never been a matriarchal society, that is, that women have never ruled a society. Yes, they have never ruled but only because *no one* ruled the egalitarian commune democracies of the fem-fertility WV society. Even so, the women had total control of public opinion. They did not "rule," but since the men had no real status, in that sense, the women did rule. Human society did not develop the patriarchal-monogamous WV systems and, hence, government, until after 3,500 BCE.

By more than 10,000 years ago, women in the Near East, India and North Africa had taken to sewing seeds and watering plants. Their new WV system was being shaped by the need for an ideological lore that explained agriculture and carried the technology with which to manage it. Let us propose that its WV way-of-thinking was that the planting of seeds was an offering to the female fertility spirits, and that the people believed they were entitled to harvest what they had planted only at their "spirits'" indulgence. Considering how primitive and inaccurate was what people then knew, their fertility goddess belief system was both rational and practical. The very process of planting would have been loaded with taboos which required that the planting be done in an exact way, such as the seeds being sewed at a specific depth. Deviating from planting doctrine would have violated taboo and, logically, caused the Fem-Fertility spirits or goddesses to become angry and hold back the harvest. The WV system was unscientific and based on the supposed existence of spirits, but it was logical for them to believe that it was not what the plant needed but what their imagined Fem-Fertility force wanted that explained things and enabled them to know what to do.

So, control by the women came to be sensed as essential to everyone's survival. As it is with every such closed and successful new belief system, their new Fem-Fertility WV was fanatically believed. Any deviation from it was resisted. Its agricultural technology, being practical, enhanced its efficiency and contributed to its spread from language to language, people to people.

The Fem-Fertility society formed large communes. That is, their social-economic system was *communism* as defined in the Glossary, not Marxism. It was not capitalist, nor was any other ancient prehistorical mainstream society. The ancient communist societies operated under a barter system. As we will see later on, some later prehistoric communist societies were not egalitarian or democratic. Some exhibited clear class divisions, while others very little. No communist economy has ever been quite the same because none have been totally communal at any stage. Typically, people had their own personal property. If someone planted a tree, in many cases it was his or her tree, even though on communal land. In other communes, everyone might know who owns a tree but need no permission to take fruit from it. All or nearly all land might be "owned" by "the person in charge," whatever his or her title might be, such as the Feudal lord. It might, instead, be "owned by the gods" or "owned by the community," but all were just different forms of common ownership or communism.

For thousands of years, let us propose, the Fem-Fertility WV spread and evolved in the Semitic language system in the then lush region that is now the Eastern Sahara and Arabia where it spread into Mesopotamia. From there it spread into Jordan, Palestine and Turkey as well as east into the Indus and the then Sarasvati River systems of Pakistan and Northwestern India. Its Fem-Fertility WV agricultural-technology was often adopted into other languages. In Pakistan, frequent flooding forced the communes to rebuild often enough that they became expert in town planning. In east-central Anatolia, villages were built without streets, and the homes were communally built condominiums attached to each other. In both, organization was minimal, and community decisions were made mostly through the efforts made by the high-status shamanesses or wizardesses to obtain a consensus. They developed the solstice so they would know when to plant, as such early WV ideologically-bonded societies have long known to do. Later, the new "spirit"-based WV belief system's most high-status wizardesses became priestesses.

We can even reconstruct how the Fem-Fertility commune system may have worked. It is just that we need to keep in mind that, to them, the male played no role in reproduction. That means that the concept of fatherhood was still unrecognized. Descent was figured through the female line. The monogamous family system now so familiar to us did not then exist. There was no such thing as a "wife," no such institution as "marriage," and no such thing as a "father."

Actual family units formed within the separate rooms of the communal dwelling-clusters. In each such home, let us picture a middle-aged mother, her daughter and the daughter's children. Add a relatively insignificant male sexual consort to the mother and daughters and you have the Fem-Fertility society's basic "family."

In such families, the male consort may have typically shared himself with a number of such homes and their women. The more glib, self-confident, and appealing young male stud would have had no other status, none that was religiously sanctioned, and would have moved around frequently from one to another of his women's homes. His intent would have been to keep himself, as well as each of his bedmates, satisfied. Anytime he became overly annoyed by his male predecessor's playfully shrieking children, or became irked by one of his women's nagging, he would have moved on, taking up with one of the other women who flirted with him. The result was a hierarchy of status among those women serviced by the studs with the most seductive charm. The system resembled the chimp's minimally polygamous social order described earlier, and especially resembles behavior of chimps crowded in the zoo.

The Fem-Fertility society's younger, virile male studs would have taken no interest in work. Most of the work would have been done by women. The studs otherwise lived for the, by then, largely unproductive sport of hunting. To the male children in the homes, the frequent turnovers of mostly absent male consorts stood out as their role model, but the stable mother-daughter relationship was the role model for the girls.

In most of Fem-Fertility WV homes, he would be contending with the children of other Alpha males, those of the males who preceded him. The male juveniles among them would tend to be so disruptive as to be driven out of the home early and live a relatively homeless life along with the bulk of the sub-dominant men. Among such marginalized men, masturbation would have held no stigma and no reason to be hidden. Puritanism was necessarily conditioned in us later with the patriarchal systems' adopting of monotheism. Also, homosexual intercourse would have also been thought of as normal and probably openly practiced. The shortage of women available to the underclass would have led the bisexual's homosexual side to dominate and the subordinate heterosexual's nature to be adaptively inhibited. In general, the system would have brought out the worst in men with the males in general being describable as lazy and homeless "losers." The system's hyper-sexual and matriarchal way of life may have resembled that of the pygmy Bonobo apes of the Congo. It was just such "fornication" that later on, in the Old Testament, so antagonized the by-then monogamous and patriarchal Hebrew herding tribes.

Does such a view take liberties with the data? Perhaps, but then again, the social theory consensus has not used available data to present any other picture. Until data is available that conflicts with it, we do well to consider it. After all, it is not hypothetical. In China's Yunnan Province, the WV based non-mainstream tribal societies of both the Naxi and the Mosuo people resemble parts of it. Approximately a dozen other matriarchal WV-based tribal non-mainstream societies did or still do survive in the world in which the women dominate through their ideological control over public opinion. Indeed, as we shall later see, this became a definite phase of the decline process of all subsequent WV-based societies.

The Fem-Fertility agricultural WV System managed to spread as a technological revolution from one language system into another and across whole continents. After spreading early into Anatolia, it moved into Crete and Greece. The conversion to the agricultural Fem-Fertility WV System occurred all throughout and beyond Asia Minor into the central Mediterranean and north as far as the Dnieper River about 6,500 years ago.

The flourishing age of the Fem-Fertility WV system coincided with the full development of agriculture. People first came to live in village communes and to hoe till the land in a rain-dependent agricultural economy. In certain favored regions they adopted irrigation. They had developed pottery for cooking produce so the heat could break down the cellulose in starchy foods and release the digestible carbohydrates. People came to feed on the Earth's vast storehouse of concentrated food matter in seeds and roots. By 4800 years ago there was some cultural uniformity in prize quality bowl design existing in the Fem-Fertility WV system from Syria to the Indus Valley. People personalized the various other forces of nature, and the old mainstream animistic age began to develop polytheistic-age-like concepts. In Malta, its great age was between 3600 and 2500 BCE when large rock cut tombs were made, and communities were seated in them threshing communal grain before huge idols of the Mother Goddess.

In the Fem-Fertility System, as in the Hindu WV System later on, the cow was sacred because it represented the Mother Goddess principle. Due to the precariousness of weather and the power of storms, she was first depicted as a bovine of indeterminate sex so that her Fem-Fertility force could be interpreted by the shamanesses as a bull when the weather was stormy or when they were suffering from burning drought, and as a cow giving birth when the weather was good. The Fem-Fertility force may have seemed to them capable of being applied, through fetishes and magic, to almost anything and to make it grow, or be induced to return from the dead. They regarded the snake as sacred because, by shedding its skin, it seemed to them to be reborn, a belief they connected with the fem-fertility concept. This led to the snake or serpent later becoming the main symbol for their imagined Mother Goddess, the one who was supreme over their other goddesses.

The Fem-Fertility society had moved out of the animistic age into polytheism. The number of spirits worshiped in the mainstream had declined, thus making the agricultural WV system less inaccurate than the WV systems of the animistic age.

The fishing-based society, and the end of the Hunting Society.

Just as the Fem-Fertility WV System evolved from the Hunting WV system, so also did a new matrilineal but patriarchal society. The new one developed as an Indo-European-language-based WV-bonded society based on a fishing and shellfish gathering technology and way of life. More than six thousand years ago, the society resurrected the Gobekli Tepe Hunting WV ideal and began building rock tomb burial sites covered by earthen mounds. The new WV system began to extend itself along the West European Atlantic seaboard up the rivers to inland lakes. In Europe, it spread at the expense of the retreating Hunting/gathering WV System and its society. The megaliths were located as territorial markers for the society's village communities as well as for burial and altar use. By about 4000 BCE, this society, referable to as the Fishing & Megalith WV System, extended all along the European seacoast from Italy, southern Spain and Portugal, to the British Isles and north to the Danish Peninsula.

Both the Fem-Fertility and Fishing & Megalith WV systems spread at the expense of, and gradually replaced, the old Hunting WV System in the mainstream, and were absorbed into its proto-Indo-European language.

The by-then very old Hunting WV system had survived some thirty-five thousand years. All such mainstream WV belief systems since then have had much shorter life spans.

The social evolutionary process was achieving human cultural progress through the natural selection replacing of older WV systems with newer and less *in*accurate ones, ones that have been more technologically advanced and, hence, able to provide for the continued increase in human numbers.

With two fully functioning mainstream WV systems in existence, another social evolutionary process developed which we can refer to as *secularization* as defined in the Glossary. Upon the Fem-Fertility WV system's contact with the Megalith & Fishing WV based society, both systems adopted more "advanced" (less inaccurate, hence more practical) doctrines from the other. From later societies, we will find this process of societies absorbing more advanced doctrines from another WV system has played an important role in all subsequent human social evolution. In each such case, the new doctrines are definable as *secular,* and the process itself curiously reshapes, hence "secularizes" the society.

The fishing WV system evolved with the dolmen temple building ideal from the Hunting WV system's Gobekli Tepe temple development and, later, became secularized by adopting the Fem-Fertility system's agriculture doctrines, at least enough to add agriculture-technology-mythology into their WV and way-of-thinking. By 3,700 BCE, the Fishing-megalithic-building WV society had even begun "planting" their worshiped ancestors in rows in the cultivated earth of their megaliths and mounds. In turn, the Fem-fertility WV system secularized by absorbed megalithic WV notions from the Fishing & Megalithic WV System, such as the stone crypt burial of the dead. That helps to explain the necropolitic function of the great mausoleum in Fem-Fertility Crete, Sir Arthur Evan's so-called "Palace of Knossos." From Crete, the megalithic secular doctrine spread into Sardinia and Malta and later to the then Fem-Fertility communes along the Nile in Egypt.

After the secularizing, the Fishing & Megalith WV System and society began humanity's first great theocratic age of monumental religious construction with the building of tens of thousands of rock tombs covered by womb-shaped mounds built for the communal burial of their dead. Later on, after the doctrine of male fertility became more widespread, they erected large upright stone monoliths called "menhirs" as phallic WV system memorials to important leaders and great events. On the Karnak coast of France alone, 1,169 of these menhirs survive. The largest of them was 66 feet tall and weighed 330 tons. As the society flourished, the dwellings coalesced into hamlets and villages. Later, they began building large stone tomb necropolitic centers.

The Fishing & Megalith and the Fem-fertility WV societies had replaced the Hunting WV-based society, but both of them would, in turn, be replaced by the first patriarchal, male fertility doctrinal system and society.

six --- DEVELOPING THE FIRST PATRILINEAL SYSTEM

Prehistory to this point has been relatively simple. From here on, there is a noticeable increase in the amount of data available. That makes it necessary to shift from working with the data more to re-interpreting the way the social theory consensus interprets it, a task that is compounded by dissension and controversy within the social theory profession. It now becomes especially important to stay with the more accurate and functional definition of key words listed in the Glossary. More attention will also need to be focused on the rationalizing strategies listed in the Appendix. Among other things, our objective is to found out "how did Europe come to use agricultural-Fem-Fertility system words in Indo-European herder languages," and "how did the animal-herding WV Indo-European language users in Europe have DNA that traces to hunters." Also, "how did the language of the Indo-European speaking herders spread from Iran through Pakistan into India without any trace of an invasion by herders, and for what reason other than by being conquered would a people abandon their language and replace it with another? "

Answers to such questions are proposed below.

The domestication of animals made it essential for people of the vast Fem-Fertility WV system to take an interest in the animal reproductive process, but that presented a problem. Animal husbandry made it necessary to recognize that the male had to fertilize in order for the female to reproduce, a notion that was inconsistent with the whole Fem-Fertility WV and way of thinking. Yet, the development of agriculture did not mean that mankind could move completely away from meat eating. Up to four million years of upright evolution as an omnivore (finally leaning heavily in the carnivore direction) had made our line dependent on vitamin

40

B12 and the long-chain form of some of the fatty acids needed by our highly developed nervous system. Animal husbandry had to develop along with agriculture because these vital nutrients could then only be obtained from animal matter. Since people needed both plant and animal food, the success of agriculture depended upon the concomitant development of animal husbandry.

The Fem-Fertility WV System people could not, however, adopt the male role doctrine without corrupting the internal consistency and integrity of their whole ideological system. Besides, men had proved to be lazy and unreliable. They were easily induced to riot, became addicted to vices, wasted most of their time in unproductive hunting, gambled, and stole whatever they could. They had no interest in maintaining the placid peace so prized by the women, and were poor role models for the children. Because the men were relegated to a demeaning role in society, they were prone to random acts of violence. It was all unexplainable behavior to the women and reason enough for them to fiercely resist the belief that men had anything to do with fertility, that is, in the very creation of life.

The solution was for the Fem-Fertility society to obtain meat by trading grain for it from families that lived on land that was too dry for agriculture. Beginning, perhaps, just north of the Ural Sea by 7,000 years ago, these herding families began evolving a whole new and successful WV system based on nomadic-herding technology. By the time the Fem-Fertility ideological system-based society reached its zenith, the herders had abandoned the last of their Fem-Fertility WV and replaced it with a patriarchal, male fertility, way-of-thinking. It would ultimately develop into a type of WV system described as *barbarism*.

During most of the Fem-Fertility agricultural WV age beginning some 10,000 years ago and in the mainstream until about 3,500 BCE, the Fem-Fertility WV-based society was made up of peaceful farming women worshiping peaceful goddesses and guided by priestesses. There is some evidence of killing and warfare late in the Hunting based society and some human sacrifice and murders late in the Fem-Fertility based society such as in Crete, but before the advent of barbarism, the villages were not built on defensive positions and were not fortified. There is a scarcity of weapons in the archaeological ruins. All evidence points to the early societies as being peaceful. The natural, instinctive human inhibitions towards violence prevailed. Violence had to become religiously sanctioned before it could become a way of life.

Not being farmers, the dry-land herders in the pastoral regions saw the larger and more powerful bulls impregnating many cows, and then the cows bearing calves. They saw how the bulls were fierce, dangerous, dominant and *polygynous,* that is, "harem" keeping males. In answering the questions of the Four Questions Template, they subconsciously developed the concept of a universal male pro-creative force. What they were doing was evolving a fully self-consistent, new WV ideology, even turning the storm-fury, horned bovine manifestation of the Mother Goddess into what later became the Syrian male horned-bull god.

It was an ominous development. The bull came to be regarded as more than just a male animal. It became the very model of maleness. They had put up a polygynous, harem-keeping beast as the arch type deity for the wrenching process of family-structure change that they were undergoing. They were developing a harem WV belief system out of the free-love ways of the Fem-Fertility WV system. A destructive process had been introduced, one that evolved, step by step, into the first predatory WV based system and society.

The developing new belief system was first labeled "Kurgan" by archaeologist M. Gimbutas (1921-1994), and we owe her for much of the insight into their WV and way-of-thinking. Unfortunately, her work leads one to think of the Kurgans as an army of barbarians when the term should actually only represent what they believed, that is, their "herding-technology, male-fertility-god world-view and way-of-thinking." However, using such a long, compounded term is unnecessary when we can still use "Kurgan" as long as we keep in mind that it only represent their WV System and not a tribal army of a distinct race or ethnicity. It was only a WV that bonded people into a male-dominated herding-technology-based WV and the society it bonded, one in which most people spoke the Aryan, Indo-European language. The Kurgans were not primitive or barbaric people, just people with a barbaric WV system.

The Kurgan system was a male-developed ideological outlook that facilitated an aggressive, territorial-expansionist way of life. It over-conditioned the male hunting-instinct behavioral complex, the same instinct complex that explains why so many men love soccer, football, baseball, and other similar sports and why they like to hunt and fish. They (we) find pleasure in seeking out the "game," sighting it ("it" being, in sports, the *leather* encased ball), the chase, the catch, and the reward of "victory" (the "meal ticket"). The more predatory parts of the system were conditioned by the instinct-based aggressive drive characteristically involving "teams" or "war parties" aimed against other groups, a trait described earlier and characteristic of most primate group behavior. An example is that of the howler monkey. Even the concept of baseball's "home plate" and the "home run" comes from instinctive male hunting-gathering group behavior. The hunting/war team hunts out game in competition to other such group teams by moving to get the "game" (the leather ball) and return "home." The Kurgan system was heading in an increasingly male-oriented direction. The male sense of territory was being conditioned into a predatory, expansionist ideology, one that led them to raid Fem-Fertility WV-based communes and take what they wanted instead of trading for it.

The Kurgan system was shaped by human instinct, but it evolved to be increasingly patriarch because it became more successful as it did, and the system spread. In Kurgan mythology the land they grazed on became thought of as not just "special" but "sacred." They came to regard themselves as the only *real* people. To the Kurgan WV and way-of-thinking, all other land beyond their borders fell into "the dark, watery, and chaotic morass of the primordial abyss." Their own little world was under their exclusive and divine ownership and, to them, was the only real world. Its center was, to them, the literal center of the universe. Its most elevated area was, in turn, their world's most "sacred center," the navel of the world, with its umbilical nexus to the heavens. It was *their* world, the one which their mighty gods had created. Its borders were what "fell away" into the abyss, the region of death.

Essential to the whole barbarizing process was the doctrinal lowering of the status of women, a process that continued until the women's role became regarded as merely incubating a man's offspring. Their role was so reduced that they could no longer exert any of their earlier described instinctive ameliorating influence on society. They had become merely nameless females forming sexual groupies to men who were Alpha dominant.

The Kurgan WV animistic and racist concept of the "sacredness" of their life infused their weapons, and made them take on special "holiness," "sacredness," or "spiritual power." Their characteristic shapes became their art motifs. The Kurgans even gave personal names to their weapons, such as "Caladbolg" (Irish), "Caliburn" (English) and "Akenakes" (Scythian).

The earliest predations may have been caused by drought in their grazing grounds, but the Kurgan system chiefs were surely also lured by the tempting lack of defense of their Fem-Fertility WV system neighbors.

They discovered the ease with which gangs of them could raid the Fem-Fertility communes and steal their women.

The Kurgan gangs saw themselves as following in the footsteps of their warrior gods. If they could take other land, it was deemed to be rescued from the darkness of chaos. Battling for it earned them the right to the new territory by blood-sanctifying it. The Kurgan herder belief system people saw it as their sacred obligation to take over the land owned by any alien WV system and thus, to create new land from the chaos of its primordial lair. The people who inhabited those corrupted regions were not only regarded as unreal but also as "sub-or non-human." Everything about the "other people," their whole culture, was "profane," their way of life, "dissolute." Their very existence was felt as an offense to the Kurgan herder WV.

Not surprisingly, the Kurgan WV system was much older than 1,500 BCE when the earliest non-Old Testament scriptures, the Hindu epic, the Rigveda, was written. Most of the Rigveda consists of the Kurgans entreating two of their gods, Indus and Agni, to help them fight their enemies so they could obtain more loot.

The domestication of the horse had, by 4,300 BCE, brought mobility to the Kurgan herder WV system, and it expanded eastward across the Europe-Asian land mass, becoming increasingly more brutal as it did so. The system's herding WV-bonded people developed a way of subsisting on the endless grasslands northeast of the Fem-Fertility communes, and do so without need for grain. They learned to milk the herds, whether of goats, sheep, horses or cattle, and make fermented food products from the milk. They even drank the blood of their animals. When they ate them, they learned to eat the entire animal, entrails and all, and to break the bones for their marrow. We humans are capable of living almost totally on meat products, as the polar Indians have shown, and as nomads, the Kurgans learned how as well. They no doubt preferred to have more bulk and starch in their diet, but they were no longer dependent upon it. Thus, they could multiply and take over the whole immense plains of central Asia. As the Sarmatians, their polygynous herder WV system spread into the Ukraine and across the southern plains of Russia to shape the Slavs and give character to what developed as the Cossacks. The Kurgan WV System later spread to become the system of the Huns and still later the Mongols. As far East as Japan, the effect was to change the sun goddess, Amaterasu, into a male god during the Kurgan age.

The Kurgans mostly raided the smaller, more peripheral Fem-Fertility rain-dependent agricultural communes that were closest to them, not the great river irrigation systems where the Fem-Fertility communes had grown large. The smaller communes suffered through the Kurgan raids, but there is no archaeological evidence to suggest that rapacious Kurgan Indo-European speaking *armies* invaded the Fem-Fertility agricultural world. The Kurgan WV system society was no more able to organize and mobilize armies than was the Fem-Fertility society. It was a matter perhaps of eight to twelve men sized hunting-gathering type war-parties made up of Kurgan thugs who preyed on their Fem-Fertility WV believing neighbors. Like the hunting gathering WV system, the Kurgan WV system fostered small groups that were scattered over a huge area. Those that were not near any Fem-Fertility communes contented themselves by harassing and raiding each other.

What is proposed, and what has happened before in subsequent history, is that the raids on the Fem-Fertility believing communes became so disruptive that the communes began paying "protection tribute" to one or another of the Kurgan gangs so it would defend them from the other ones. As the practice grew, it helped to restore stability, but only by turning the Fem-Fertility WV-bonded communes into Kurgan run feudal manors. A Kurgan WV-dominated feudal age began, one that spread deep into the Fem-Fertility based society.

It is also proposed that the process continued to spread through agitation and conversion. Kurgan-believing and Indo-European speaking ideologues would have deliberately traveled to nearby Fem-Fertility communes to agitate the men to convert, rise up and take control away from the women. Thus, the more aggressive men within the Fem-Fertility communes would see it as a revolution. In this way, they could turn the Kurgan WV system into a sort-of "bully religion" in which Kurgan over-lords could rule Fem-Fertility communes. In any case, the Kurgan system did spread northwest across Anatolia and then clear across Western Europe towards the Western seaboard. The Indo-European language spread with the Kurgan system, moving through most of Europe without any mass migrations or invasions. In that way, the Indo-European language adopted the geographic terms of the Fem-Fertility WV system it came to lord over.

As the male-fertility Kurgan feudal system spread, even more extreme barbaric doctrines were filtering in from the plains of Central Asia. In some areas such as China, the Kurgan system adopted human sacrifice because that was thought to establish and maintain a personal, reciprocity relationship between them and their warrior gods. It more fully earned them their title to other people's lands.

Within the European Kurgan feudal manors, the bulk of the people kept their fem-fertility WV and did not convert to the Kurgan system.

To us now, the Kurgan feudal age was a strange world. We can even reconstruct a picture of what it was like and how it operated to weave together clues from ancient Celtic-Italian and Celtic-Irish epic tales, including ones that later became Christianized and associated with King Arthur. Here below is a general picture of what the Kurgan society may well have been like at its worst:

In each of their tiny 4,500 BCE European manors, picture the manor lord as living in a small fort-like enclosure with his aged father and his unnamed women and children, and, perhaps, a sub-dominant and/or gay brother and/or uncle. Living communally nearby would be his Fem-Fertility-believing serfs, and those of their teenage girls as the lord's mistresses, all communally tilling his land and tending his livestock for him. Each such domain had some eminence such as, often, a hill or boulder, a large tree or a spring which the lord regarded as his domain's "sacred center." By his WV system's warrior code, each such domain could be taken possession of only by someone approaching the site and slaying the overlord himself, the one whose role was to guard it. To attack the community instead was "sneaky," dishonorable, against their warrior's code, and hence taboo. The victor would then hoist his host's severed head on the top of a long "may pole" (hence, the later Swiss "hat-on-a-pole" legend) and take it triumphantly to the community to signal his sanctioned authority to replace their slain lord. Finally, he would kill or drive off all the male offspring of his predecessor. The "tossed out" or fleeing male juveniles who survived would have grown up to be the very beasts who, in searching for a domain of their own, probably did most to fuel the spread of the Kurgan WV System.

The immense Fertile Crescent agricultural communes and the more isolated colonies in Crete and the Indus/Saravati River region appear to have mostly escaped the predatory incursions. Even so, they adopted male-fertility notions which, by fully secularizing their Fem-Fertility system, enabled it to flourish anew. The Indus-Sarasvati River region of India/Pakistan experienced its greatest age from 3,500 to 2,000 BCE. In male-god secularized Fem-Fertility Crete, the system flowered from 2500 to 1500 BCE. It had a system of weights, an early Greek writing system, the use of money, and ships one hundred feet in length. During this peak period, Crete was ruled by ceremonial kings.

Fem-Fertility and fishing/megalithic WV systems in decline

As the Kurgan feudal system moved through Europe, it finally reached the Fishing & Megalithic WV System people along the Atlantic Seaboard. They were then building dolmen burial edifices covered by earthen mounds. The meeting of the two systems led to the secularizing of the megalithic society by the Kurgan animal husbandry doctrines. The Fishing & Megalithic WV-bonded people had already adopted the Fem-Fertility WV system's agriculture doctrines. They had come to institutionalize sky-gazing garden wizards who had begun engineering the Megalithic ceremonial centers in a way that helped them determine the seasons and know when to plant. In turn, the their tomb-burial concept was secularly absorbed by the Kurgan system and by 2200 BCE, had spread among them back as far as the Caucasus.

The adopting of another system's more advanced and practical doctrines always meant adopting doctrines that were necessarily inconsistent with their own closed WV system of thinking. That meant both ideologies had to be compromised so they could be made to *seem* to fit together and thus preserve what at least seemed to be a common, single, closed system of thinking. Otherwise, there would be no single, over-all ideology and hence no bond adequate to bind people together into a society. But fitting the incompatible together required a certain amount of rationalizing, a process that had to be done and has since been done often in the rise and fall of societies. Termed, here, "the accord process," it has been essential in the development of societies because older ones have to adopt new, thus secular, doctrines in order to keep a competitive position in the mainstream and continue feeding their growing numbers.

At Stanton Brew in the British Isles, Britons built tall timber temples about 3,000 BCE. By about 2,700 BCE, the less impressive, preliminary work at Stonehenge followed. It, in turn, was followed by the great monoliths erected about 2,500 BCE. The monoliths were then, in turn, topped off with the capstones. They seem to have been temples built to monitor the seasons and carry the buried remains of their local god-chiefs and some of his descendants.

By 2000 BCE, the Kurgan-secularized Fishing & Megalith WV society had blossomed into its Golden Era, but social problems were multiplying. The system then slipped into decline. As far back as 4000 BCE, extensive deforestation had begun in the European environment. The deterioration continued, and the heady days of both their coastal and inland European food abundance subsided. The Kurgan WV-system-run feudal system then replaced the old accord-compromised Fishing & Megalith WV society *in the mainstream*. Outside of the mainstream, the megalith technology doctrines spread to the world's remaining non-mainstream areas. By about 1500 BCE, the Fishing & Megalith WV system had spread south through North Africa. By about 500 BCE, it had spread to central Africa and through Pakistan ahead of the also spreading Kurgan Indo-European-speaking WV system. The Fishing and Megalith doctrines reached Dravidian-speaking Tamiland in southern India after 1000 BCE. By about 350 BCE, the doctrines had spread through Korea to arrive in Japan in the 7th century CE ("Common Era"). They reached northern Borneo, Polynesia and Madagascar before 1200 CE where they survived into the 18th and 19th centuries. They spread into Sarawak and survived there among the Batu Kitong who erected megalithic Menhirs as late as 1950.

The stone tomb crypt concept still survives to this day. Personally examined have been scores of Chinese Peranakan tombs in Malacca made early in the 20th century and apparently constructed of concrete that was molded into mounds the shape of the womb. Even to this day, megalithic-tradition lingers on in the little stone megaliths placed over the casket tombs within which the dead are buried throughout much of the world. It survives, as well, in the interring of bodily remains in communal tomb mausoleums that are located in necropolitic ceremonial centers called "cemeteries."

seven--- THE REVOLUTIONARY WV SYSTEM IN MESOPOTAMIA & EGYPT

By about 6,000 years ago, the Fem-Fertility WV irrigation communes had grown large and had outgrown the herder's meat supply. That led to the raising of livestock and, indirectly, to lowered resistance to the male-role-in-reproduction notion. It even managed to accommodate to the Fem-Fertility society's WV system as it filtered in. The women managed to see it as only natural that there also needed to exist a male creative force or gods, ones who mated with their goddesses. The result was that Kurgan male gods began to be adopted into the Fem-Fertility system. In turn, the role of the Mother Goddess shifted some from the "creation" of children to the "sanctity" of sexual activity. Their public role of satisfying the erotic was added to that of bearing babies.

Sub-dominant men in the large irrigation communes who had before dithered around in the fields only long enough to earn their next meal, then came to be seen as actually deserving a place in society because the secular male-god adaption found a place for them. What had been the male rabble soon began to labor hard in the fields to generate food surpluses which they could take to the temple shrines as tribute to the Mother Goddess. By means of such religious altruism, they could be "serviced" by fertile, sexually active priestesses, mostly likely in a heavily ritualized procedure mimicking the fertilizing of the earth and the sowing of seeds. Known as *temple prostitution*, the change must have been popular with the men and explain why it lasted thousands of years. Milder creeds survived well into historic times. Secularizing the society brought the men into the system, and created a larger and more productive labor force. Their offering of service and produce supported the whole female priesthood, enriched the temples, and enabled more elaborate ones to be built. Since the priestesses and temples were "the government," producing food for the temple offering was the original form of taxation in the mainstream.

As is always the case, secularizing the Fem-Fertility WV system necessitated an accord in which both female-fertility and male-fertility doctrines were compromised and then served together to be accepted as "the Truth." In the process, the female force lost its supreme role, and an age of artistic freedom and intellectual ferment was ushered in, especially in Crete. But even as the society experienced its last burst of prosperity, its patched up ideological system was spewing out diverse new sects. The social bond was dividing and by as early as 4,500 BCE, the male-secularized old fem-fertility WV-based society was showing signs of decline. One clue was a proliferation of animal goddesses. As we will see in later societies, falling back to the worship of animals or totemism appears late in the development of most societies and is a common sign of decline. Another sign was the proliferation of non-idealistic, abstract patterns in their art, a sign we will also see repeated in Part 2. Finally, the shift to the temple-prostitution doctrine was another clue since the "temple" part was declining, thus leaving the institution increasingly just "prostitution."

The Fem-Fertility WV system produced an agricultural abundance, but its WV emphasis on the supposed "sacredness" of fertility resulted in the usual pressure of numbers on the food supply. Periodic flooding and droughts inevitably brought periods of famine. The normal result would have been that the priestesses begged their goddesses for mercy, and since the privation generally persisted, we have a possible explanation for the beginning of human sacrifice. They were not doing enough to placate Her. As J. G. Fraser (1855-1941) explained in "The Golden Bough," it seemed natural to the ancients to appease their gods by sacrificing animals and children to them. After all, it would seem to them that the gods and goddesses needed to eat also. There is evidence of human sacrifice in the male-god secularized Fem-Fertility society in the Near East, North Africa, and as late as 1,700 BCE in Crete.

The most significant problem, however, was an increase in predation by armed gangs of male predators from nearby Kurgan manors. The only way to deal with so many such problems was to become organized. The irrigation communes had grown so large that it had become impossible for the people to come together to make collective decisions about what needed to be done. The priestesses were hardly more able to effectively run the commune than were shamanesses. Despite their attempts, they were unable to reach so many people and exhort them to effectively attend to the commune's important tasks. Crowding and their dividing ideological system were all undermining the whole egalitarian system, causing order to break down. Under such conditions, theft and selfishness typically grow. Another problem would have been the male juveniles. As mentioned earlier, chimp male juveniles hang around the periphery of the family-troop wishing for sex but kept under tight control by the adult males. In the fem-fertility system, this would have led to gangs run of male juveniles running freely with no dominant males keeping them under control.

Organizing was a necessary step, but it was also an unwelcome one. It meant picking representatives, but as Robert Michels (1876-1936) noted in more recent times, having representatives means turning over sovereignty to them. Then, the people are no longer sovereign themselves. Their "representatives" are called their "leaders" but become their *rulers*.

Even so, they had no alternative; it was just that mainstream representative government had never existed before. Achieving it was something no one could plan because no one knew how. The existence of the need was enough, however, and their ideological system evolved to meet it.

In order to deal with the raids by Kurgan gangs, it was only natural for the great Fem-Fertility communes to make ideological adjustments to in some way accommodate the men and inspire them to defend the society. Secularizing had already brought male gods into the system's pantheon and Temple Prostitution had become apart of the doctrinal system, but more needed to be done to meet the pressing need. Something else the men wanted and which the ideological system needed to provide was an end to the custom or institution in which the few charismatic male studs monopolized all the more desirable women. The male-woman ratio needed to be more even, that is, the women needed to be *rationed*. They needed to be apportioned one woman to one man.

Since the support of the men was essential, their wants dictated the direction taken by public opinion and, as always, the WV moved the society in a way that served its interests. The need for representatives and for a fair distribution of the women developed together, as also did the solution. In that age, illiterate, "spirit"-believing people reshaped their ideas, beliefs and doctrines in the old way. "Spirit"-based rumors arose and became what we now call *myths*. The one myth that accomplished the change arose in Sumer after 4,000 BCE, one which, for the first time, firmly established the principle, if not the prevalence, of monogamy in the mainstream.

The myth was what later evolved into the Genesis myth of Adam and Eve in the "Garden of Eden." In its simpler, original, early Sumerian Fem-

Fertility form, the Mother Goddess was known as, "Eloah." In the evolving process of secularizing, she became combined with the male element into a single duel-god, "Elohim," by adding the plural suffix "im." The Sumerian WV had shifted to combining the male and female creative, fertility, forces. In the early duel-god form, Elohim appears frequently in the four Judaic books of the Old Testament. The male gods in the old Fem-Fertility system were achieving parity with the goddesses.

In the myth's early Mesopotamian version, the combined god created the first human who then split into male and female halves in order to bring companionship each to the other. The goddess WV system was moving further away from its woman-emphasis into a balanced male/female ideology in order to meet the increasing Kurgan threat.

Later, when under rule by Babylon, the Kurgan Hebrew tribes evolved the myth into its more extreme patriarchal-monogamous Adam and Eve form, the one in which Elohim became the single Father God, Yahweh. Also, in the later Judaic version, Eve was taken from Adam's side to serve him, but only him. That was established as the new ideal family, that is, one man with one woman only. In the myth, Eve alone was to serve Adam, not two, three or more women, only one. As one of the Genesis accounts state, she became his "wife."

The more extreme Old Testament tribal version of the myth describes their male-fertility creator and father god taking the dominant role and giving "no-eating-of-the-fruit" orders to Adam and Eve. In defiance, the new, made-into-a-demon Mother Goddess, *as the serpent*, had Eve induce Adam to eat the apple anyway. That meant they had obeyed the female rather than the male god. By doing that, they had committed "the original sin." The tribal "God" had become the final source of authority and power. He subsequently cursed and banished them from "the garden" for their disobedience.

The "Garden of Eden" appears to have been the then-lush and sacred Gobekli Tepe area of the hunting WV mainstream. As mentioned earlier, the Fem-Fertility WV had originally evolved from the hunting WV system as it spread south down into the middle of the Fertile Crescent some 10,000 years ago.

The evolving more barbaric form of the myth was uniquely successful and was gradually adopted world-wide. It had laid the foundation in the mainstream for a whole new WV and way of thinking. What had been a new and more practical secular concept had finally been exclusively adopted as the answer to both the first (our origin) and the third (our moral means) questions of the Four Question Template. The old Fem-Fertility WV ways became "wrong," hence, insidious, even "evil," especially its more licentious aspects. By 3,000 BCE, the last remnants of the old Fem-Fertility system were exiting from the mainstream. A whole new mainstream WV had evolved in its place, one that bonded a new and very different society. The new one, unlike its predecessor, was able to mobilize armies of well armed and trained, nearly fearless, dedicated patriotic warriors.

The WV evolution of the Kurgan feudal system

As the Fem-Fertility system evolved secularly to meet the Kurgan threat, the Kurgan system itself also evolved. By 2,300 BCE, it had evolved along lines similar to the Genesis model. It also became a far more effective system. Instead of sending out gangs, it came to bond the herding-technological WV Kurgan thugs into a militarized society that built barracks, armaments industries and fielded well organized *armies.*

Each Kurgan ruled Fem-Fertility manor had been able to attack only other such manors with a war party gang composed of, at most, only the Kurgan lord himself and his cohorts. Certainly, each such lord sought a way to expand his small band of thugs into an organized army as the large agricultural communes were doing. Each feudal lord sought to steal from them or invade and loot the other manors. If the Kurgan chief could organize his still Fem-Fertility-believing serfs and turn them into an army to use between harvests, he could have the advantage he wanted.

But there was a problem. His Fem-Fertility WV-believing male serfs could not be induced to fight for their over-lords. Warring was, after all, what the overlords themselves were in effect commissioned to do for the serfs. Lacking status, the serfs also lacked courage. If they were pressed into an army, they simply fled from battle. The whole system was based on the premise that they slaved for the lords in order that the lords protect them. It was alright to the serfs if the lords ganged up on other gangs and stole their women and treasures, but only as long as they, the serfs, were not the ones to do it for them.

The system had been rigid, but it was ready to evolve. The feudal lords got into a competition for ways to induce their fem-fertility serfs to fight. They were forced to compete with each other in making ideological inducements that would tend to elevate the self-respect of the men. The chiefs adopted fem-fertility goddesses into their Kurgan male-god pantheon until they had achieved a balance. Then, begrudgingly, they gave up their "right" to all the women, at least whenever they wished. It was changed into a rare ceremonial privilege, one that survived thousands of years well into the Christian European Feudal Age. Over a period of centuries, such concessions in ideology form, gave the serfs new status and changed both classes into a single WV based society with a common interest and stake in the territorial ambitions of the chief. They could be worked up and ready to fight whenever he could induce them to believe another manor or the agricultural communes held easy riches for them.

In other words, both the Fem-Fertility and Kurgan ideologies were promoting monogamy and evolving hierarchies. The main difference between the two WVs was that the Kurgan belief system was developing into a new, Judaic form which still kept its hunting, warring and conquering mythology. It kept its "we are the only real people" and "our land is the origin and umbilical center of the universe" concepts. Retaining them ensured that their system's predatory barbarian nature remained. For convenience, the system in its new form is referred to here as the "mono-mate barbaric WV system." It was a less harsh, less brutal and a more effective predatory system because it enabled the chiefs to organize government, build arms industries, run spy systems, and field armies.

So it was that all Europe began to mobilize. Armies grew in size and dissolved into warring sections. By 1700 BCE, wall fortifications were being built around European settlements. Hamlets were constructed on hilltops for better defense. In Scotland, cylindrical fortresses of stone were built, forerunners of the later crude, castle towers of Medieval Christendom. In Maiden Castle near Stonehenge, an extensive wall fortification was built. With their crude, thunder and lightening mountain gods, they, as "Dorians," swept through Greece. Others, later on, swept into central Italy and, as their Roman myths indicate, stole their women from the other tribes. The better organized armies became the "barbarian invasions" often noted in historic times. Between 1700 and 1200 BCE, the system spread into the Mediterranean and across Malta and Sardinia. By 1800 BCE, Corsican Menhirs began sporting carvings of metallic weapons, and the Sea People incursions the Egyptians turned back in 1200 BCE were apparently migrating barbaric WV invaders.

The adopting of goddess had brought Fem-Fertility believing men into the new barbarian system, but the influx of powerful female goddesses threatened to over-feminize and weaken their patriarchal way of life. The barbaric WV system evolved to meet that challenge as well. Myths appeared that reduced the status and power of the new goddesses. In the early matrilineal mythology, the Great Mother Earth Goddess, Gaea, was supposed to have created the universe and have the Earth float on her amniotic-like waters. In the new adaptation, her role declined, and she was replaced by the Minoan goddess, Aphrodite, who then became merely the goddess of eroticism. The top god of Greece, Zeus, lowered the status of the goddesses by consecutively seducing or raping them.

Since the able-to-be-reborn snake symbolized the Mother Goddess, their transformed WV regarded all land that they did not occupy as being ruled by Mother-Goddess monster-serpents called "dragons," and myths about male-gods slaying them became common. The Hittite version of the WV system's weather god, Teshub, slew the sun-goddess, Hebat in dragon-form, and the Mesopotamian supreme god, Marduk, slew the serpent goddess, Tiamat, empress of the watery chaos in the abyss. Marduk was then credited with creating the universe out of her slain body. The early Greek god, Perseus, decapitated the mother-goddess, Gorgon, who also appeared in the form of a plumed serpent. Dragons are also mentioned in the pre-Hindu Rigveda.

The goddess-attrition process in the barbaric WV system continued only as long as it was needed, then it came to an end. The Celts, for example, kept the goddesses Danu, Anu, Brigit and Macha. One of the later ones, Epona, was the one the Celts mounted and rode, that is, the goddess of the horse.

The end of the Kurgan herding WV and way-of-thinking left us a legacy which, to this day, has served an important function in the subsequent human mainstream, the concepts of allegiance to the state and of property ownership. The new barbaric WV system had replaced the old Kurgan system in much of the world. It survived only in Central Asia and had its first resurgence with the rise of the Huns and the Mongols.

As it is with social evolution, all the change had been autonomic, coming about subconsciously. No one was aware that their WV had evolved. Instead, they always just believed that they had "finally found the Truth." It had all happened because human instincts are *conditioned* by the group WV ideology and it, in turn, changes in the direction of what is needed in order for the society to survive. Such changes come about by the natural selection process of social evolution.

The end of the Fem-Fertility WV system in the mainstream

In the large agricultural communes, male gods were added to the female goddess pantheon just as female goddesses were added to the male god Kurgan system, but in both systems, the humiliation of the female goddesses and the "slaying of dragons" served to shrink the all powerful nature of the goddesses. By 3,000 BCE the Sumerian agricultural communes had traded in their Fem-Fertility WV for a new monogamy-based patriarchal WV and civilization-building system.

The Mother Goddess survived but with less power. In the Old Testament, she is referred to as Asherah and Astarte or Astoret in Jeremiah 7:17-18, 44:17. Even in the New Testament times, she still lingered on as Diana in Acts 19:27-37 and who was known then in Ephesus as the Mother Goddess. Many of the goddesses survived as long as did the polytheistic WV system. The attrition of female deities has been an ongoing process. Even today, the mother-goddess survives. She just changed form and is now worshiped as the Hindu goddess, Shiva, the Shinto goddess, Amaterasu, and Christianity's Mother Mary prayed to even today by the Pope and Catholic Marianists.

The change of the Fem-Fertility system into the new patriarchal-monogamous WV was not uniform. In some regions, the fem-fertility WV survived and underwent religious regression, the process of abandoning secular beliefs and reacting back to the original WV system as it was. Indications are that is what happened in the Indus Valley Harappan WV system of Pakistan before 1500 BCE. The process undermined the system and disappeared from the mainstream. In its religious regression form, the Fem-Fertility WV spread away from the mainstream as a diminishing wave through parts of India, Burma, Indonesia, Indochina, and Siberia. The Japanese adopted their sun goddess, Amaterasu.

Traces of the matrilineal system still survive among the Khasi of northeast India and the Na people of Yunnan in southern China. It also continued in the still lingering culture of the Minangkabau of Sumatra whose culture survived the conversion to Islam. Personally observed and inspected have been matriarchal Minangkabau communal long houses built in the towns and cities of Sumatra as late as the 1930s or 1940s. Spreading close behind the old and by then regressive Fem-Fertility system was the new patriarchal-monogamous WV and way of thinking as if in pursuit.

Fem-Fertility cults and ethnic centers even survived in the mainstream. Some regressive cults, such as in Canaan and Carthage, practiced child sacrifice in a pageantry of pedophile-tainted infanticide. One version of the mother-goddess faith later evolved in Denmark that sacrificed the hundreds of men who keep being found well preserved in the Danish bogs. As late as the 16th century, matriarchal age shamanesses known as "witches" (a multiple-meaning term), were still supplying love potions to European women for use on their unexciting husbands, or poisons for philandering ones.

Old ways evolved and survived in the other WV systems as well. Even Megalithic WV system doctrines still survived as a European superstition cult. Their menhirs were used as fertility fetishes by Christian, Medieval European peasant women who, in the dark of night, rubbed their exposed bodies against them to enhance fertility. A part of the European goddess-farming sub-culture, the menhir cult survived into the 19th century.

In short, mankind had entered the patriarchal-monogamous WV system age. By a process of social evolution, the new type WV system had come to be the bond of all mainstream societies, as it has remained to this day.

Monotheism and the state

How could simply adopting a monogamous, patriarchal myth turn both the Fem-Fertility manors and egalitarian communes of a basically polygamous people into government-run states? How did that end them with organized, efficient, male hierarchal, well defended societies without any genetic change in behavior? The explanation lay in the Alpha male social instinct repertoire described earlier. The women-rationing ideal gave each man the right to earn his own single-woman "harem." It positioned men into the situation where each wanted to be dominant ("successful") in order to win the highest status woman he could earn. The number of women a man had no longer determined his status. Instead, having more might mean public disapproval or punishment. Ideally, what counted was how attractive was the one woman he did have. Women, in turn, competed with each other to be the mate of the man with the most status.

Each man was motivated to fill his single-mate "harem" by competing with the others to achieve a high status dominant role in the society, even if under other even more dominant males. The new system made the hierarchal system possible by exploiting the male-dominance instinct and calibrating it in terms of status. It did not work perfectly, but it did work. Compliance with the new monogamous ideal was appreciable.

Since their society was instinctively their basic hunting-gathering group, the way for even a sub-dominant man to rise in status and earn his woman was to gain male status, that is, "to show dominance" by contributing to the welfare of the "family-troop" (the society). Most men dream of achieving higher status or rank and ultimately dominance, that is, to be promoted, something that could more normally be achieved in a way beneficial to society only when it was strongly united and respected. The WV system was able to effectively bond them into a hunting-gathering group substitute-society. The alpha male feeling of reward was what men gained by exercising responsibility and authority over the lives and welfare of those comprising "his" society.

In short, the WV changes enabled the build up of a male hierarchy. In the academic world, the word used is "stratification" because their word seems less offensive to Western secular democratic and egalitarian doctrines or ideals. Nevertheless, all government is and has to be hierarchal. That includes multi-party representative constitutional government, those in which the people are ruled by representatives who preside over hierarchal bureaucracies and hold to legislatures in which members have different rank or power according to seniority. All legislators have their staff hierarchy, all of which are protected by armed service hierarchies, and monitored by law enforcement and court hierarchies. Without hierarchy, government and civilization could not exist. None of the prehistory mainstream societies had real, formal hierarchies, none had government.

Even though we are a mildly polygamous species as described earlier, the WV system's adoption of monogamy as an ideal still had immense appeal to people. It had a dramatically constructive effect on society and worked so well it almost seemed to be genetic. There is no reason to think that the people did anything else but revere their new monogamous system even though some wives did continue to be seduced by more dominant and already committed men, ones who were instinctively tempted to "stray" in loose proportion to their very success.

In order to help to reduce the tendency to stray from the monogamous system, the society's WV took on Puritan-like values in that sexual display and sexual feelings needed to be minimized. Sexual matters were then made to be private. The chaotic "free love" nature of the prehistoric societies, especially the Fem-Fertility WV-bonded one, had to be suppressed in order to help make the patriarchal-monogamous system succeed. Only later when the system began to break down in any society would the erotic nature of man publicly resurface.

In short, the whole new monogamous patriarchal ideological edifice needed to form a self-consistent, closed and unified way of thinking in order to bond a large society capable of substituting for the instinctively based family-troop. It also needed to be idealized and its sexual repressed nature reinforced. Without these supports, as we will see, the system was doomed to erode back towards polygamy and ultimately weaken the society enough that it would be invaded by barbarians.

During the early and theocratic age of the new patriarchal-monogamous WV system, adequate compliance with monogamy was maintained by peer-pressure. Judicial system enforcement only came about later during the secular age. The dominant male heads of households were not consistently loyal to their wives, but the one-woman concept had become the model. The better it worked, the more women were available to more men. Having more than one woman became risky and no longer boosted a man's public status. The more the people complied with it, the stronger, the more honest, respected, and more efficient grew the state.

As the origin myth evolved in Sumeria, the city states there became so well organized that they could and did mobilize armies of well armed, nearly fearless, dedicated, patriotic troops to drive off the Kurgan, and later, the mono-mate barbaric WV-based attacks. The new patriarchal-monogamous WV believing people organized armaments production, spy systems, and built fortifications. They also built infra-structural improvements, and stocked up on food for lean times.

What was adopted in Egypt was what had happened in Sumer. Both had started with large Fem-Fertility WV-based agricultural communes and ended with patriarchal-monogamous WV-base governments. Each man in a high-status, responsible position automatically provided status to those who worked for him and the most status to those who most helped him to better serve the society. Each individual felt the society was his and hence was his responsibility. As he rose in status, he had a natural Alpha male proprietary interest in his society because it effectively substituted for his instinctively familiar family-troop. It was what he and the other men would still feel was theirs if they owned it. Each wanted to protect and take care of it. The normally more than eighty percent biologically sub-dominant men had managed the greatest social revolution in human history. They became dominant, even if in a "middle management" level. Government that was organized around a single, undivided, closed, patriarchal-monogamous ideological system proved to be the only system able to effectively function with large urban masses of people. It was a vital and absolutely necessary mainstream social-evolutionary achievement made necessary by our ever growing numbers on Earth.

Social theorists do not consistently recognize the Sumerian and Old Kingdom Egyptian WV-bonded governing systems as bureaucracies. There was an absence of designated ranks, titles, formal chains of command, carefully proscribed areas of authority, regulations, qualifying educational degrees, and pay scales, all the fortifying embellishments that have since been added to keep the system functioning. Instead, capable men in the more educated classes were chosen to attend to certain national responsibilities. They, in turn, picked the men they needed who in turn chose theirs. They switched roles and were appointed to other tasks. Instead of being rigid, the whole hierarchal system was fluid, flexible, as are some of the present world's most subversive organizations.

The patriarchal-monogamous way of life also tended to foster feminine ways in the wife because it helped to develop courage, determination and planning-ahead propensities in her husband. This meant that in the early patriarchal-monogamous societies, her anxiety was reduced and she could focus more on taking care of the offspring. The father's responsibility to the children was primarily that of a role model and the final arbiter of dispute and punishment.

The one-woman limitation had restricted the Alpha dominant male's philandering style, but even he did not end up short in the social evolution. He still became responsible, and achieved as reward, a position of power over vast numbers of people spread out over a large region, much as the heads of major corporations do now. He had achieved far more power and control than he could have attained in the mere forty-member family-troop in which we evolved.

The Egyptian WV-based society was united into a single, large state. The sweeping in of the new social revolution arose heady feelings of power and dedication to its society-state because men had become able to work a direct, tangible, effect on their society. No society had ever changed so much so fast, had ever become so strong and so monumentally creative. The early pharaohs were sincerely worshiped. Gone was the feeling in the men of "uselessness" and, hence, of resenting the system.

In ancient times, tales were handed down from generation to generation, and in that way, people were aware of what the old system had been like. They knew how important a stake they had in their new system and felt subconsciously indebted to it. They appreciated it for extending opportunities that both the Kurgan feudal and Fem-Fertility systems had denied them. They were spurred on to exert themselves in ways that were constructive to all.

It took the new system to make military discipline possible. It was a system that brought responsibility to even men without status. Every army is built on gang-ship with the squad being the basic Kurgan "gang," or more fundamentally, the hunting-gathering group male hunting team or war party. Each army squad-member recruit has no status and no responsibility except to protect his fellow squad members and follow orders from his male dominant officers. The clear chain of command helps make this acceptable to him. He becomes aware that if he does well, he himself could gain status and become the giver of orders and have recruits under his command. In both the Egyptian and Sumerian WV-based societies, this encouraged men to have a prideful "fatherly," paternal, and protective feeling, one similar to what we now express as *espirit-de-corps* or patriotism.

The grandeur of their new society filled them with pride and awe. Men became willing, and in emergencies, even eager to fight and die for their country. By becoming dominant, men became courageous. The stronger their social bond, the braver the warriors. The assertive, challenging traits of higher-ranking males are the major sources of all aggressive behavior, including that involved in the building of strong, new societies, as well as the war and strife that helps barbarians tear down weaker, overly-effeminate ones.

The ability of human WV belief systems to institutionalize a hierarchy of dominance is not instinctively connected to monogamy. Hierarchy can even work in a celibate environment, as it has in the Catholic Church. A celibate hierarchy can function by attracting into it highly motivated, service-oriented people, including homosexuals, statutory rapists, and pedophiles.

In the new society, the position of the male juveniles improved dramatically because it brought ambition to them. Mention was made in earlier of sexual-inhibition in sub-dominant primates that is comparable in us to "shyness." Since most men are not dominant at puberty, most are sexually repressed in a strong society. In the two new patriarchal-monogamous societies, most young men felt a state of instinctive self-inhibition towards attractive women, an inhibition over which they had no direct control. They had the choice of humiliating themselves further by courting less attractive females, and even then, possibly being rejected, or they recognized that their state-of-being did not need to be permanent, that they could achieve eventual success by preparing for it. Adolescent non-dominant male youths who were not yet in the hierarchy were idealistically motivated to prepare themselves. They became ambitious and were motivated to learn, not to get a "degree" so they could get a better paying job but because they needed and wanted to know. They developed an intense and sincere *curiosity*. Learning became obsessive, it became the way to serve society, build status, and achieve the confidence it took to win a high-status woman. The reward they sought was not wealth but prestige and power, even glory. (In modern society, young men have lost most of that and continually changing and spending more on the educational system cannot re-motivate them).

Once ambitious but non-Alpha young men in the then new societies began to achieve success, they found that their intuition had been correct. The sexual inhibition did fade and the shyness did give way to confidence. Most male mammals are able to switch from being Beta to Alpha dominance under favorable conditions. Each man had the right and opportunity to deservedly court and win a more desirable, high-status woman for his wife.

Later on in life, as the men became even more successful, the more biologically dominant and heterosexual ones would tend to lose the rest of their inhibitions. They would be instinctively tempted to have other more desirable women as well. When the WV belief system prohibited it and the society was strong, such men generally resisted the temptation in order to preserve their status.

As we shall see later on, however, successful men in declining and weakening societies acquired concubines, harems or picked up mistresses, and monogamy began to break down. For a society to build civilization instead of tearing it down, the full potential of the male sex had to be exploited. That required the society to be based on an ideologically united, patriarchal-monogamous WV system.

The change was turning out to be the most important human social transformation ever experienced by the human race. By adopting monogamy, mainstream society had begun a daring experiment. Not being instinctive, monogamy could only be precariously imposed. Society needed to be strong in order to properly shape the human male's instinctive behavioral repertoire, something men have never understood and, in modern society, are secular social-theory-programed in a way that still keeps them from understanding it.

The patriarchal-monogamous system did not benefit just the men. It also appealed to the women because the home then became their "nest." Since it was protected by the dominant male, it stimulated in the wife the family-troop feelings of security, "belonging" and a sense of "coziness," all of which had been lost with the mainstream ending of the hunting-gathering family-troops and the beginning of the Fem-Fertility WV system. The patriarchal-monogamous WV had recreated the family-troop sense of "home" in which both the women and children felt secure.

The wife's worth in society rested largely on the status of her husband. If he took up with other women also, he would think and feel an elevation of his status and be tempted to brag to his closest male friends about his success with a new woman but mostly refrained from doing so because it was not socially approved. It would never occur to him that he was also lowering his wife's status in precise proportion to how his unfaithfulness had made him feel "good." It instinctively felt to him his just reward for his high status success, but to her, his escapade could only be a demeaning insult, one that reduced her to that of a harem animal. If a man was truly responsible and loved and cared for his wife, he would not want to hurt, even devastate her, just so he could feel "big."

The new system did other strange things as well. It even changed the nature of love. In the old polygamous Fem-Fertility society, the women were more "forward" in the mating ritual. In the hunting-gathering family-troops, a woman tended to turn on her charm and flirt with sub-dominant men. Girls learned to be sexually assertive in the old matriarchal society because competition was intense for the more charismatic, but system-decreed lower status, Alpha males. In contrast, the patriarchal-monogamous WV system women no longer had to be assertive with men. The dominant man, because of his high status, knew that a woman he picked would be responsive, and in the human family-troop they were. With his high status, the family-troop dominant male deserved his self-confidence. Even the more than eighty percent of men who were normally or physically lower in status acquired some level of dominance. The sub-dominant males gradually lost the society-imposed sexual inhibitions as they succeeded in the system and became nearly as sexually assertive as the old family-troop Alpha male. They became "virile." With more men being dominant, women no longer needed to flirt. A whole new era had opened up in the manner of courting. Courtship became more the man's role and the process took on the aura of "love" and chivalric romance.

Because Mesopotamian society had rationed one female mate to a family, it in turn needed to defend the family man's one-mate "harem" from society's alpha male interlopers. Government had to take on the responsibility of enforcing compliance because government itself depended upon monogamy to function. Men could not have the right to polygamy.

Having fidelity to a single woman had to be the major ideal of the moral system, and adultery became a serious crime, one that could not be left to blood feud and revenge. At first, enforcing monogamy consisted of persuasive religious exhortations and threats. Adulterers could be stoned to death. In the early and religiously idealistic theocratic stage of the society, religious exhortations and threats were enough. Later, religious moral codes came to be enforced by the clergy, perhaps even by the active police force in use by 1550 BCE in Egypt.

The new patriarchal-monogamous WV system also adopted what was then the world's most advanced cosmological understanding of the origin of humanity and the world and universe. By first splitting the fertility force into both female and male gods, people came to believe that cause and effect was determined by gods instead of ancestors or animist "spirits." Mainstream society had completed the leap from animism and ancestor worship to polytheism. This meant a reduction in the number of spirits people worshiped as well as a related, perceptible drop in the *in*-accuracy with which they understood themselves and the world. Both the cause and the effect was better technology and more people able to be fed.

Altogether, all the WV changes were essential in developing and sustaining government and civilization. World population, which had crashed during the late decline of the agricultural Fem-Fertility society, resumed its climb in the patriarchal-monogamous mainstream.

The formation of government had been so essential to human civilization that any ideology counter the patriarchal-monogamous WV became, by its very nature, anarchist.

PART 2 ---- HISTORY

eight--- THE MECHANISM OF CIVILIZATION

The development of the new Patriarchal-Monogamous WV system in the irrigation communes of lower Mesopotamia coincided with writing and the beginning of history. By 3,500 BCE, the new WV system in Sumer had built a society of city-states able to mobilize and fight off barbarian gangs. The recorded history of the Mesopotamian civilization began in Sumer and spread up through Mesopotamia to end in Babylon. In all its locations, the society was bonded by the same patriarchal-monogamous WV system, one built around the concept of a pantheon of gods of both sexes. The main goddess, Baba, was thought to oversee the economy by having her priests report to her. Though respected, the Mesopotamian king was not considered to be a god. He was at first only the supreme goddess' human male sexual consort. His rule was authorized and made legitimate by the sexual relationship he was thought to have with her. She and the other gods supposedly certified his authority and dictated the nature of his responsibilities. He was only their steward in charge of managing Earth for them in an efficient, productive, manner for the long term.

The people showed their enthusiasm for their new WV system and society by giving food to the priests as offerings to the gods. The gods, in turn, were thought to greedily and gratefully consume the food's "spiritual essence." The mundane morsels that were left were "depleted of the spiritual essence," but as the property of the clergy, they became wealth able to be utilized. They could be traded for other goods and services. It was the beginning of taxation in the patriarchal-monogamous WV system.

Communal living continued even after acquiring hierarchal leadership; the Mesopotamian city-states merely turned into hierarchal communes. All land, resources and everything people built and used in common was regarded as being owned by the gods and therefore held and used as communal property. The people of the communes worked, socialized and sometimes even ate together. Because of the theocratic idealism of their strong new hierarchal society, their communal system was able to plan and operate efficiently.

Written regulations helped. For a thousand years, writing had enabled the communes to keep track of economic matters. After 3,000 BCE, it also enabled the development of capitalism. Rules regarding marital fidelity and their enforcement had to be enacted, but laws concerning trade could also be passed and agreements recorded.

Developments in Egypt later followed along a similar course except that the whole Nile Valley was brought together into a single commune-state. This colossal achievement ensured that the ruler took on god-like dimensions. As the people adopted the new system, they willingly, even eagerly, set about building immense and beautifully gleaming pyramids for his use. Never before or since have a people been so enraptured with the greatness, grandness, and glory of their society.

As time passed, however, the ideals faded. Both societies weakened and their bureaucracies became ponderous and inefficient. Government can become a burden on the public when loaded with bureaucrats merely going-through-the-motions and interested only in "protecting their backsides." When a society's WV system divides, the society itself weakens. Dividing the ideology reduces the feeling of being in the family-troop, and the bureaucracy degenerates into "playing politics," nepotism, crony-ism and bribery. "Make-work" becomes common as each government minion seeks to obtain more funds with which to hire more subordinates. With all this, we in modern times, are intimately familiar. Bureaucracies tend to generate their own growth.

About 2300 BCE, the first successful barbarian invasion of the Mesopotamian patriarchal-monogamous WV-based society occurred. Its northern neighbors, the Akkadians, with their newly evolved mono-mate barbarian WV-bonded system and organized government, fielded an army and conquered the Sumerian city-states. In order to facilitate rule over them, the Akkadians needed to retain their system of government, but to do that they had to convert to its WV system. They brought into it a few of their own gods including their supreme male sun god, and forged the city states in southern Mesopotamia into a single state. They had begun secularizing the combined society, beginning the end of its theocratic age. The new king became one of the most powerful men on Earth, and the most creative age of the Mesopotamian civilization began.

In Egypt, the Old Kingdom period was followed by foreign invasions, then the Middle Kingdom period recovery occurred. It was, in turn, followed by more decline and then another barbarian invasion followed by yet another recovery and the the New Kingdom or Imperial period.

Why so many "periods?" The new patriarchal-monogamous type WV system had bonded a society that followed a strange, new, and erratic up and down, or cyclical, course. It was inclined to weaken to such an extent that it could be conquered by mono-mate barbarian WV bonded people. Then it would recover and become strong again; then weaken again. Human mainstream society had adopted a strange new pattern, one which would typically repeat itself endlessly over and over again. When the government or state collapsed, another government always took its place because no society could any longer exist without government. The patriarchal-monogamous WV system had been able to produce civilization by creating government, but that meant civilization had to depend upon government, and it, in turn, depended upon the unity of its patriarchal-monogamous WV system. Since monogamy was not instinctive, the system had an inherent, structural weakness. As stated earlier, by basing mainstream man's ideological WV systems on conditioning monogamy, mankind had been able to develop civilization, but it had also made its success dependent upon enforcing monogamy. The unrelenting growth of human numbers on Earth had made it necessary to *organize,* and to do that, humanity had been compelled to tinker with our instinctive nature.

Under Akkadian rule the Mesopotamian civilization grew large and prosperous. Astronomy had begun to develop as a science, and while the many Babylonian concepts of the universe and its origin were mystical and inconsistent, they had nevertheless laid a foundation what ultimately evolved into the then less-*in*accurate concept of "creation." It was the origin account that ultimately ended up in the Torah and the Old Testament.

Secularizing the Mesopotamian WV freed people from the ideological bondage of their closed system of thinking. That meant the development of capitalism and the decline of communism. Capitalism is instinctively-based on our reciprocity and division of labor. The women gathering and the men hunting necessarily made the sharing of food instinctive. It shows up as the giving of favors. The hunter is saying "I share this meat with you and leave you with the obligation to share with me what you have gathered." It was a matter of doing for others what they do for you, and meant we expect favors to be returned, something we instinctively feel is only "fair" and "just." It was simply an exchange, something in the capitalist system generally comes at the same time and is known as *the purchase*.

In the old family-troop hunting gathering communes, the Alpha dominant male imposed his own primitive system of justice. One had to placate him to protect one's self-interest. That worked well in the family-troop, but in society it was destructive and became known as *corruption*. In order to expand the size of our social groupings, we needed the ideal that the individual is entitled to use the exchange system to serve his own material needs but only in a way that also serves others and society. To achieve that, legal regulations were indispensable. When the individual cannot know most of the people in his society, he is not motivated to be so fair with them as in the commune. Regulations were needed to make people comply to the ideal. When people are not fair and do not return a favor, most of us instinctively feel they should be punished. Even chimps have been observed attacking another chimp who accepted a favor but did not repay it. In the communes, the reciprocity rules had been in the form of custom, and that was all that was needed, but in expanding the size of our grouping, the rules and laws of the capitalist system became necessary, rules that make the system fair. If a society cannot be viewed by the individual as being *just*, he feels alienated from it and demoralized; he no longer respects it and may, instead, come to subconsciously resent it. Subdued hostility builds up and the individual tends to subconsciously disregard its best interests, or even commit the deliberate harm, such as *crime*.

Capitalism also enabled the development of private property. The instinctive male territorial sense grew to be satisfied by the possessing of one's own, personal territory or *private property* (real estate). So "pride of ownership" developed. The ideal was for each man-led single-woman "harem" family to have its own house on its own land or, as now, his condo or even the inside of his leased rental unit. It became the "home," and "a man's home was his castle."

Then, the Mesopotamian civilization went into another decline. Government power weakened and a period of intra-regional warfare followed. Its growing ideological disunity was weakening the society and enabling still another mono-mate barbarian WV-based power, the Amorites, to invade about 1900 BCE. They also converted to the old Mesopotamian patriarchal-monogamous WV system. Since soil salinity had been increasing in Sumer, agriculture was moving north up Mesopotamia between the Tigris and Euphrates Rivers. Seeing the trend, the Amorites set up their new headquarters further north in Babylon. The city eventually grew to encompass some twenty-five hundred acres and was built within immense walls. Even such walls, however, were unable to keep out subsequent invaders. In the following centuries, the Chaldeans, the Assyrians, the Hittites, and the Kassites all invaded Babylon. Each such invasion ended with the barbarians converting to the Mesopotamian-Babylonian patriarchal-monogamous WV. Each time the conquerors rejuvenated its by then old society, its ability to be rejuvenated diminished.

Once the patriarchal-monogamous WV system arose and became a success, from then on it shaped all human society. It became the standard model for all subsequent WV systems.

In about 1500 BCE, Egypt ended two centuries of control by a Hebrew mono-mate barbarian herding people, the Hyskos, and ended their occupation. Evicting the legendary Moses and his disgruntled, fractious herders may have been part of the Hyksos expulsion and diaspora. Before that some of the Kurgan WV had evolved into Judaism, the most enduring of all mono-mate barbaric WV systems. The faction's myth that numerous and unrecorded-in-Egypt plagues caused their expulsion would have helped to soften their defeat.

The next decline era ended with new secular doctrines. The secularizing processes had broken down the Mesopotamian WV System's ideological unity and, hence, its closed system of thinking. With the end of its ideological restraint, the civilization was able to achieve new heights in both the arts and the intellect, but social problems were appearing. Mention was made earlier of the secularizing of society ending in more dividing of the WV, then social problems, and increasing stress. Both end in men losing their status and dominance. It is as if they feel abandoned by the dividing society because it has seemingly disappeared. They feel they no longer "own" it, that it has been "lost." That leaves them to focus their sense of responsibility entirely on their own family in order to better provide for it, even if at the expense of their society itself. To them, society had become the equivalent of "game" which the instinct-driven dominant male "hunted," exploited, for personal and/or family enrichment, leaving business and government corrupt and inefficient. The breakdown of monogamy combined to ultimately drive each historical mainstream society into its cyclical decline and leaving it vulnerable to barbarian invasion.

When society weakens, monogamy tends to give way to polygamy. In modern times, politicians, presidents, prominent TV-evangelists, and other "dominant males" tend to go directly counter to religious injunctions and risk their very careers in order to collect sexual liaisons outside of monogamous marriage. The "dominant male," as the successful business or professional man, instinctively feels he "has an inherent right" to have several mates in his entourage. He may have concubines, a harem or mistresses. Once, US President William Clinton had mistresses, even as also did some of the Congressmen who pushed to impeach him for it. It is no coincidence that women prefer the advances of the "dominant male," a preference for self-confident, successful men, especially ones who seem to radiate power. This instinctive force challenges the monogamous system and, hence, weakens society and threatens the civilization itself.

The new patriarchal-monogamous type WV system promoted hierarchy and entitled men to compete for dominance, but it did not provide dominance for them. There were always those still at the bottom of the hierarchy or unable to even fit in at all. Weakening society was hardest on them, on the man who is the least dominant. In our society now, even if such a man did obtain a wife, his lack of status may wear on him enough that he abuses her in a futile effort to appear dominant. In some cases his lack of status may lead to such depression that he beats his wife or children. Or, his lack of status may make him impotent. Lacking any role in the hierarchy, men form an envying, restless public which breeds most of the violent crime, forms gangs, and most easily turns into rioting mobs. When society is united, this subclass shrinks; when society declines, this subclass grows.

Assyrian-Mesopotamian sculpture and sculptural relief became the most impressive art that existed before the flowering of the Hellenic civilization. It was filled with barbaric symbolism in order to intimidate the weak and counter the over-humanism then dominating the old society. By dealing ruthlessly with over-indulgent Babylon's many and growing problems, the fascist-like Assyrians were well geared to prolong the old civilization's survival. They reduced the number of insurrections by relocating different ethnic factions in outlying regions and thus away from the Big City. They also ruled from their own capital in order to minimize Babylon's corrupting influence, keeping only a garrison there. The Babylonians still forced the Assyrians to retake the rebellious city some twelve separate times.

Beginning in the nineteenth century BCE, both the Egyptian and Mesopotamian WV ideologies took to adding more gods to their growing pantheons. Ultimately, they numbered in the thousands. In Mesopotamia, languages multiplied as well. Under the Kassites, Babylon became the lingual, Biblical "Tower of Babble." The proliferation of both languages and gods further eroded the WV system's ability to bind the people into its society causing the society to disintegrate into tribal, lingual and economic-social groups. Also, during the age of Assyrian control of Babylon, almost half the population consisted of slaves. As in Medieval Europe later on in the period of Church Decadence, it became the custom of rich women to wear the veil.

Egypt experienced its own social pathology. Animals became sacred and a man could lose his life for killing one. Animals were entombed and even mummified. In the Empire period, the mix of racial and lingual groups made it necessary to adopt tolerance as an ideal and, hence, to also tolerate abuse, crime, and corruption. The ranks of the Egyptian army shrank, the arts became coarse, and the scribes refused to further improve their craft even as alphabets proliferated in the rest of the known world.

To sum up what had transpired, both the Mesopotamian and Egyptian WV belief systems had begun as doctrinally rigid, closed and reasonably self-consistent in order to endure. For that reason both societies were resistant to change and had inherent limitations on their ability to do so. Because of population growth, however, change eventually became essential to their survival. It became necessary to upgrade the older WV systems with newer secular" doctrines. In each case, the result was a combined WV system, one that was no longer a single united whole. At first, adopting secular doctrines proved a powerful stimulus, but opening up of their Four Question Template core to change, always led to a proliferation of more beliefs that broke down the unity of the faith and its bonding power, creating social problems for both societies. From there, they went into a long decline.

When chronicling the civilizations, historians generally make short-shift of the decline phase, to the relief of the reader who may find reading it depressing. The problem with skipping it is that the decline in each society resembles that of the others. Studying the similarities is analogous to that of a geriatric physician seeking to better understand the normal aging process that humans undergo.

Near the end in both Babylon and Egypt, their societies could no longer bring the men the needed sense of family-troop security which had evolved in them. They were clearly no longer doing a good job. Naturally, and not without reason, women placed the social problem blame on them. The society needed help, so women sought to provide it by being more assertive in a subconscious effort to recapture the sense of security everyone had lost. In Egypt, men stayed home and wove while the women trafficked in the markets. In Babylon, the women gained the right to own property and to qualify as witnesses, things unheard of earlier.

Even so, conditions continued to deteriorate. People were so disunited as to feel "crowded" and subconsciously turned back to the older WV doctrines in hopes of recapturing the old sense of community. The people in both Babylon and, later, Egypt regressed back to their older beliefs.

A prosperous civilization creates prosperity-inducing epigenetic and/or microRNA-related mental and physical health problems. In all animal life, too much abundance ends in an accumulation of genetic-related defects. In other animals, this is culled out by natural predators. We have always been culled by micro-pathogens in the form of pestilence, as well as wars and famine as described by Thomas Malthus (1766-1834). Such Malthusian onslaughts worked to mitigate the epigenetic effects of mainstream society's profligacy and over-crowding, but they have never ended it.

The aging Babylonian civilization could no longer be restored by barbarian invasions. Star gazing science that had developed the usefulness of the zodiac for navigation degenerated into the superstition of astrology. Temple prostitution became just prostitution. Finally, the long and heavy demand for lumber caused the over logging of the regional hills, the "cedars of Lebanon." Erosion followed, then flooding, and the further salting of the soil. The slaves became the main workforce of the harshening capitalistic economy. The primitive jury system was abandoned.

The new system had at first made a place for most of the male bisexuals who were erotically more homosexual. They had mostly formed monogamous heterosexual families because the new system made sexual choice a "moral" issue. Civilization-building societies needed to maintain a single, patriarchal-monogamous culture.

But a society that excludes bisexual gays from the monogamous marital system, drives them into a polygamous counter-culture life-style, one which lends itself to the spread of venereal disease. Past societies met that threat by forcing bisexuals and homosexuals to submit completely to the dominant culture. By functioning heterosexually, there would have been a near total absence of homosexual-functioning bisexuals in the Egyptian and Mesopotamian population.

As with most social mammals, a certain small percentage of people of both genders are wholly homosexual, with about twice as many being males as females. There is also a rather small percentage who are Alpha-male-dominant and who feel nothing appealing about any physical aspect of their own gender. With the more dominant of the Beta male individuals, many have some admiration for some minor physical aspects of the same gender, a trait the individual is not usually even aware of. In the so-called "bi-sexual" ones, same-sex eroticism usually dominates, but in men in a normal society at least, it accompanies an otherwise alpha male-like affinity for a woman's closeness, affection, and for having a family and children. The bisexual-like male make-up tends to drive the arts. Artistic genius and the appreciation of art are more Beta traits and more a product of the skill and genius of sub-dominant men in a patriarchal-monogamous society.

Once in decline, the sexual choice character of the society changed. The blatant decline of Babylon pictured in the Old Testament may have been realistic. Before the establishment of the patriarchal-monogamous system, sexual preference had no religious significance. Homosexual liaisons would have been common in the Fem-Fertility society, especially among the disenfranchised, under-class males. Then, as the society matured, became divided, and weakened, a lax, tolerance ensued with the return of gay culture and the spread of venereal disease. Later, when the societies grew old and weakened, more bisexuals would have drifted back to brief and varied homosexual liaisons, and signs of gay-culture would proliferate. As there are far more gay men than lesbians, the enlarging number of unattended females would tend to break down the monogamous marital system and draw the society back towards polygyny. That, in turn, would tend to progressively weaken the society. With the decline of the Egyptian and Mesopotamian patriarchal WV system, homosexuality, pedophilia, and bestiality would have all become more public.

The biological sex-preference pattern of human beings never changes, but the condition of the WV social bond determines how most people live. Homosexuality is a product of survival evolution and exists in many other social mammals. It enhances the stability of the group by ensuring that most males are not ruthlessly competing for dominance. No family-troop, hence no society, could survive if all its males were equally determined to dominate as "Number One."

The old Babylonian city and empire sank to a mere shadow of its former self. After 500 BCE, its temples and idols were razed by their Persian conquerors as the people converted to the faith of Zoroaster. This brought the Mesopotamian civilization to its final end, the end also of the thousands of gods-based WV and way-of-thinking. In Egypt, the end came later with the conversion to Christianity, the end of the Hellenic age, and the razing of Egypt's "pagan" temples and libraries.

The monogamous, patriarchal, polytheistic new way of life had, by then, spread to China, Pakistan-India, Persia and Greece-Rome. The development of both polytheism and patriarchal monogamy had revolutionized mainstream society. The people had not discovered the eternal or final Truth, and their new WV and way-of-thinking was not the word of or product of any gods. It had came about only because the advances and lessons of the older societies had been, through the social evolutionary natural-selection process, re-formed into a more advanced, less *in*accurate, even though still "spirit"-based, WV and way-of-thinking.

In short, our climb out of the Fem-Fertility and the more barbaric systems was made possible by mainstream mankind developing a new and better society, one that was able to build civilization for the first time. The new polytheistic, patriarchal-monogamous WV system age had arrived through a mechanistic, evolutionary rather than "spiritual" process. The old belief in "spirits" was merely the expedient by which it was achieved. Out of the disorder and end of the animistic and matrilineal age, world population then resumed its growth.

nine --- THE HINDU CIVILIZATION

Fem-Fertility goddess idols have been found in parts of India dating as far back as the very beginning of agriculture almost 11,000 years ago. In Pakistan, the Indus Valley River system has a large number of archaeological sites of its early agricultural proto-Hindu Fem-Fertility WV-based society. From there, the Fem-Fertility system had spread south and had almost reached the lower tip of India by 3,500 BCE.

By 2,000 BCE, the system was in rapid decline in Pakistan. The Indus Valley people apparently spoke the Dravidian language, and the Indo-European-speaking cattle-herding Kurgans began raiding them after about 1,700 BCE, perhaps spreading among them by means of the feudal-"bully-revolution" described earlier. A personal examining at random of one-hundred and ten of their ancient Rigveda hymns revealed a simple theme: flatter the gods and promise them sacrifices, songs, dances, and their favorite nectar, all in hopes of getting their help in conquering other people and stealing their property. Also mentioned in translation are "maidens," "women loving their *man*," "heroes," horses, lances and arrows.

Later, the Kurgan WV system picked up Fem-Fertility WV system goddesses as it spread, ones which were often paired with their own male gods. In this way, two of the system's most enduring gods, Vishnu and Siva, were combined. In the region of the Indus and Seravati Rivers, the Kurgan system evolved into the mono-mate barbaric WV-based system. As it had done in Sumer, it gradually replaced the Fem-Fertility WV-based society. The Lord Indra god, for example, was credited in later scriptures with raping Ushas, the goddess of the underworld. The Rigveda also uses the anti-feminist symbol for the mother-goddess by referring to the "slaying of the *dragon*" (XXXII of Book 1).

Their WV continued to evolve and by 1000 BCE had developed into the Hindu patriarchal-monogamous WV and way-of-thinking, a system able and destined to create a whole new civilization.

The new WV system favored monogamy even though high status did entitle a man to have concubines. Governments were set up in northern India ruled by god-kings. Most of Northern India became a checkerboard of Hindu WV believing feudal kingdoms. Consolidating them involved considerable warfare with the blood that was spilled being regarded as sacrifice to the gods by both victors and vanquished alike. Each kingdom was ruled by the Aryan, aristocratic, hierarchy. The old feudal class system had become part of the Hindu faith and became explained in the "Law of Manu," their legendary first king and creator. Each class ultimately became a separate caste, each with its own version or denomination of the WV religious system. The most privileged Indo-European-speaking Hindu caste, the Brahmans, included a supreme deity in their polytheistic WV system. The beliefs of the more discriminated-against castes and the "untouchables" remained animistic.

The Hindu kingdoms were at first surrounded by no-longer mainstream, religious-regressive Fem-Fertility communes. This meant the better organized Hindu patriarchal-monogamous WV-based kingdoms became the center of cultural, political, and intellectual development. Their religious, scientific and artistic culture moved south without political control, spreading into the areas of, and secularizing, the Dravidian-Tamil speaking Fem-Fertility WV System.

The growing body of sacred Hindu epic poetry was being put to writing and a long age of great literature began. The Hindu WV itself became somewhat similar to what it is today. On the question of origins, Hinduism shaped various fantastically elaborate cosmological models, or admitted it was an unsolvable mystery, but to the individual, the reincarnation doctrine determined his own caste origin. The belief system's over all goal was for the individual to live *darma*, that is, with consideration, to live a righteous life with moderation and self-sacrifice in order to achieve a better reincarnation in the "next world." Thus, the doctrine of the "transmigration of the soul" was part of the system's moral formula. The goal was also to achieve "enlightenment" in the present world, that is to achieve what they tended to regard as "absolute reality."

The Hindu WV belief system had created a society that built a new civilization, one that had achieved economic growth, artistic creativity and then, finally, an empire-wrought political unity. Through military consolidation, a single bureaucracy was established by 320 BCE, one that came to preside over an empire of commune-communities under the sword of the Devanampiya Asoka dynasty. It grew to include all but the southern tip of the subcontinent.

The mysticism aspect of the Hindu faith increased, and intellectuals began to question, even to object to it. Kings began to resist the heavy and growing cost of promoting a largely idle Brahman class being supported at great expense just to perform rituals. A nihilistic, "free thinking" movement arose called *Carvaka*. Skepticism was growing, and in about 500 BCE, a less-mystical philosophy of life was proposed by Siddhartha Gautama who developed the popular "path" called "Buddhism." There were no gods in the Buddha philosophy and no soul was thought to exist outside of the body. There was no heaven or hell as its destination nor was he in favor of symbolic or magical religious ceremonies, the doctrines of caste, or of anyone being redeemed through another. He promised, instead, a state of enlightenment and blissful inner peace through righteousness and overcoming greed and self-indulgence. The humanistic philosophy of the Buddha began the process of secularizing Hindu society.

Building the empire had involved considerable cost and slaughter. Because of the many different languages, marital systems, regional and historical traditions, the path of the Buddha and other paternal-humanistic doctrines were adopted by the state as an ideological means of patching the diversity together. The aim was to help minimize intolerance and hence infighting. Even with the secularizing, however, the cost of maintaining an army large enough to maintain the empire became more than the state could bear. The empire and dynasty lasted less than 150 years. By 178 BCE, India had divided again into separate kingdoms. Then, the various Hindu kingdoms resumed their warring with each other. However, due to the humanistic influence of Buddhism, the fighting was less vicious and more ritual-like than before.

The Buddha's secularizing of the society ended its theocratic age. More traditional Hindus had regarded the Buddha's teachings as an affront to their faith and that the great variance between the two separate WVs came to undermine the ideological bond holding the society together. Jainism, in turn, arose out of the Buddhist-Hindu secularizing. Stress between the WV systems built up and the accord process began. As with earlier WV systems, these separate "paths" were all finally accord-worked, rationalized and compromised into a newer, more compatible two-part somewhat closed Hindu WV system of thinking which then managed to hold the society together.

With the breakup of the empire, the original Hindu states never again regained political control over the southern half of the subcontinent except under British rule in later times. The patriarchal-monogamous Hindu kingdoms of the North continued to be the centers of both cultural and intellectual growth, and their leadership in both science and the arts continued to work its way south into Dravidian-Tamil speaking areas where matrilineal descent still prevailed.

Then, the more central Indian kingdoms also adopted patriarchal monogamy into their WV. Soon, powerful kingdoms arose there that continued to resist imperial political expansion from the North. The Andrahan and the Kalinga empires even grew powerful enough to balance the Magadhan rule from the North for some four hundred years. The Kalinga Empire even invaded the North between 200 and 25 BCE and brought its Magadhan monarch to his knees before returning rich with spoils.

The Dravidian matrilineal Fem-Fertility WV and its Northern, Hindu/Buddhist secular culture spread from Tamiland into Ceylon. It also passed east into Burma and then Indochina and Indonesia ahead of the spread of the Hindu WV system there. As mentioned earlier, the crest of the matrilineal, Fem-Fertility WV wave was retreating from the mainstream in all directions to linger on into modern times in parts of India, Indonesia, and Southern China.

As with other civilizations, the Hindu WV system's secular age began the civilization's best economic and intellectual progress. Her greatest creative age had begun. The most advanced scientific discoveries and inventions appeared between 250 BCE and 550 CE, with the latter date marking the end of the second and smaller empire in the North, the Gupta Empire. During this greatest period, Hindu civilization traded with Imperial China, the Roman Empire, and the East African Bantu empire south to Zimbabwe.

Capitalism was adopted widely with the advent of the Buddhist and Jainist secular era and the end of the society's theocratic, communal age. The economy evolved to where factories were built in which goods were produced by numbers of people working on a primitive assembly-line basis.

Advances were made in medicine with the early doctors such as Caraka Samhita and in the 4th century, with surgery under Sushruta Samhita. At the same time, linguistics developed under Panini. In the 5th century, mathematics made great strides under men like Aryabhata, putting them then ahead of China. There were also great strides made in metallurgy. An extensive road system was built, and there developed an impressive golden age of the arts, including sculpture, literature, poetry, dance and architecture. Some of the most beautiful temples on Earth were built in India.

The secular-age creative flourishing of the Hindu arts and sciences came at some cost, as it does with every society. The Accord-secularized society enabled the growth of intellectual creativity and great art, but the dividing of the WV also worked to weaken the social bond until it became divided enough to bring the society's creative age to an end. Many Hindu doctrines became more extreme. Reincarnation doctrines became more unforgiving in such over-humanistic, animal-worshiping ways that eating meat of any kind became disapproved of. Jainists even worried about how they walked for fear of stepping on some "ancestor" who might have reincarnated as an ant. The saying grew that "the animal you eat in this life may be the one who eats you in hell."

In about 800 CE, di Shankara consolidated the divided Hindu WV religion, built monasteries and restored the aging faith to dominance. It was an effort to fight off decline by means of religious-regression. In the later Hindu WV, one could reincarnate as Brahmans and also attend Indra's heaven, or Yama's heaven where the god of death resides. The doctrine of reincarnation supported the caste system because it explained and justified whatever caste the individual had—that you, in your former life, determined your present caste by how righteously "you" lived your previous life, even though all people had the same caste as their parents.

The patriarchal-monogamous, secularized but religiously reacting Hindu WV continued to spread southward from the 7th to the 12th century. It reached the tip of the subcontinent, then, spread into Ceylon and east into Burma, as had the fem-fertility faith before it, then down the Malay Peninsula, and across Indonesia.

In northern India and then central and finally the south, the social bond had continued to divide as it had spread. The people had grown disillusioned with even their secular beliefs. Symptomatic of the early decline was the growth of the aging faith's renunciation movement. India became a land rich in "renouncers," that is, men of mature age who no longer wished to accept their responsibility to society, and took to what could be considered as dropping out of society. They took off most (or all) of their clothes, abandoned their friends, family, and jobs, and took to self-punishment, meditating, and living off food handouts from others. As a general rule, all renouncers sought "enlightenment" and "the meaning of life." Among them were "yoga" renouncers who focused on meditation. By numbing the conscious mind, they could toy with the breathing rate and contort themselves into unnatural body positions. The objective was to achieve "serpent power" so they could levitate themselves or even soar through the air. They also aimed for the ability to slow down the heartbeat and metabolism—something they thought was desirable.

Most characteristic of the system's animism-like, million-god polytheism was the belief there are various levels of "spiritual consciousness," "levels of reality," and "centers of enlightenment" in the body. Meditation devotees came to believe they could journey through the cosmos because the repetition of certain words was thought to impart "god-energy" to them. Rituals in praise of their many gods were performed by all castes. During festivals, the gods were even thought to "possess" some devotees.

Mention was made in the Introduction/Abstract of the need for objectivity in the way human ideological WV systems are examined. We are now examining the oldest WV system still surviving in the modern, mainstream world. Being the only polytheistic and thus the most primitive is not something made note of by historians and the social theory consensus, and what they write shapes the "World Community of Nations." Hindus would not be apart of it if the system regarded their multi-"spirit" doctrines inferior to the monotheistic WV systems. Nevertheless, such efforts to please believers makes poor science. No religion is "the truth" and all are more inaccurate the older they are.

The renouncers mentioned earlier had high status because "enlightenment" was such a prominent Hindu ideal, and, also, because Hindu doctrine enabled those who gave the renouncers food to achieve credit towards a better ultimate reincarnation. As a result, food was given to them generously, which tended to encourage their numbers. Hindu society became a haven for half naked, dusty, self-torturing, "dropouts" with bowls looking for free food and "enlightenment."

Westerners too easily assume the Hindu obsession with "enlightenment" means they seek to acquire worldly wisdom. The real, underlying agenda, however, is only the mere achieving of a *feeling* of attaining it. Those who seek it are high status and develop self-hypnotic skills in order to gain certain well-known feelings and sensations, such as that of "infinite understanding." They also seek feelings of "oneness with the universe," placidness, trances, visions, self-healing, and a sense of being able to float in the air.

Hinduism has been uniquely successful in achieving such "religious"-like or "spiritual" feelings. It should be noted, however, that Hindu mystics self-induce them by mental-physiological trickery, and then, only temporarily. Renouncer-mystics, for example, use such "meditative" or self-hypnotic techniques as constantly repeating a single mundane or made-up word. Since thinking depends on the forming of words, repeating the same word dulls the mind. That stops the hormonal "flight or freight" mechanism and enables the individual to relax. It also alters the electrical activity in the brain's temporal and parietal lobes, so that the sensations are felt. The feelings tend to replace normal consciousness, inhibit the sense of "self," of balance, of the self-protective pain reflex, and the cognitive ability to recognize one's own realistic limitations. Everyone has limitations. Flapping your arms will not enable you to fly. In other words, the changes tend to be pathological, especially if prolonged. They inhibit normal functioning in the normal world.

Some of the religious sensations are normal in mild amounts, even to be experienced all the time. For example, the feeling of "oneness with others," sometimes described as a feeling of "universal love," is the instinctive feeling of "closeness" and "sense of security" normal to being in the family-troop. In a society in its theocratic prime, the feeling of "oneness" is normal and mildly felt all the time by most of its citizens. We who are living now in the modern world have never experienced that. With Yoga trickery, a more extreme feeling can be briefly induced of "losing the sense of self," that is, of being separated from the body or feeling "a oneness with the universe." It sometimes arises naturally in the form of the so-called "after-death experience" claimed by some Westerners. In the so-called "out of body" experience, the individual has not actually experienced death because one's personality-identity is a product of the brain instead of the heart, and the individual is dead only when the brain is dead. When the heart has briefly stopped beating and the individual imagines himself floating above his own body, the still partially-functioning brain is using tactile, audible, and visual clues to create a mental view of his or her surroundings from above. The individual also has much the same hormone-free sensation of "total release" and placidness that Yoga trickery can achieve. This pathological state lasts at most only a few minutes. Consider, for a moment, how miserable would such a state be if it were prolonged, a state in which nothing is wanted, such as not wanting to learn, or to experience anything new and different, not even wanting world peace or the presence of one's loved ones. It is a state too much like death.

There are a few normal people who have sub-clinical temporal lobe epilepsy which causes them to see illusions, ones that can be mis-interpreted by them as "visions." This has tended to be one of the sources feeding illusions into all the old "spirit"-based WV systems. The modern-times version takes form as the seeing of "space aliens."

Another quest in the Hindu WV system is the feeling of "infinite understanding." The feeling is sometimes associated with grand mall epilepsy, but any well-trained renouncer with a quick mind and an enticing, beguiling personality can, and many have, induced the feeling in themselves, the feeling of having acquired real enlightenment in the *real* world. Once convinced, they come to experience "a high-status state of dominance." They become able to acquire a loss of fear and such undeserved self-confidence that, together, give them charisma. This enables them to set up Hindu-type personality cults in which their pronouncements all become dominance cues which attract to their *guru* a host of fawning, sub-dominant individuals. These synthetically-created teachers spread to their flock the same wondrous platitudes and empty promises which can now also be found everywhere in the many speeches and pronouncements of our modern political world.

All such Hindu meditative trickery was perfected after Hindu society had left its theocratic age and was in decline, that is, when people had lost the natural, theocratic-age feeling of "oneness."

The decline of Hindu society ultimately led to the doctrines of Darmashastra, the stultifying mass of rules governing how every household was to be run and which became solidified into rigid Hindu dogma. Girls went with bribes to be taken as wives. Then, some were burned to death to get another bribe for another bride. A wife who was not burned often lived under the cruel eye of her mate's mother. The husband would not tend to protect her from her mother-in-law because the system encouraged "mamas boys" who never "cut the umbilical cord" to their mothers. The wife's main goal in life was to survive the mother-in-law, have sons, and then treat their wives with the same arrogance and cruelty she herself had suffered. This is similar to the same sort of system that long survived in China. This regressive practice is based on an instinctive primate behavioral tendency in which upper status females will harass lower status pregnant or infant-ladened ones. Just the threat of the high-status antagonism tends to turn off the "presenting" impulse in the lower-status females. This is one of many evolutionary population control mechanisms in the animal world. The instinctive underpinning of this works for other primates but has a negative impact in human society. There are better ways to control population numbers.

Hinduism added another feature. If the wife survived her husband, she was, as a widow, fated to spend the rest of her life alone and in somber mourning, always wearing the same colorless garments without jewelry or makeup. Some preferred to throw themselves on their husband's funeral pyre. That tended to make the dead husband's relatives happy.

Even the old Fem-Fertility-worship doctrines resurfaced after 800 CE. A characteristic obsession arose involving the endless extending of the number of sexual positions, a subject that had been growing in the erotic secular literature. It had come to be a matter of one-up-man-ship to satisfy oneself and one's partner in ever more contorted positions. As regression set in, the literature took on cult dimensions and, by 1250, had become institutionalized in Shiva worship as a temple-prostitution cult known as *Tantrism*. More than a hundred Hindu temples were over-embellished with sculpture depicting the few normal sexual positions and hundreds of the supposed 84,000 unnatural sexual gymnastics they claimed to have imagined. The villagers, who now surround these garish temples, feel towards them a strange mix of both pride and embarrassment.

What had happened was that the "Great Mother Goddess" had returned to prominence. She was reemphasized in various forms, including as the cow goddess Vac, so that the cow became "sacred," and to this day, blocks traffic and is a nuisance. The Mother Goddess also appeared as the goddess of fertility and nurture, Para Devi or Maha Devi. As in societies before and since, the growth of feminine-emphasis accompanied decline,

In all their forms, the millions of Hindu gods were mostly all regarded as pleased to receive offerings of flowers, vegetables, fruit and incense, much of which was generally consumed by the priests and the rest doled back to the giver. But other Mother Goddess's incarnations were symbolized by horror and destruction and demanded blood, meat and alcoholic drink sacrifices to her, also semen. After the rites, the offerings were consumed, all of which was done at cremation and cemetery sites.

By the 9th century, growing social problems had driven people away from the secular ideals of Buddhist and Jainism and back to the older Hindu doctrines. People not only abandoned their more scientifically advanced views, but they also added to the complexity and mysticism of their aging faith. Astrology took the place of astronomy, and reincarnation regained its old standing. The secular age was over. Religious regression led to Gutama's original teachings being infiltrated by deity-worship, turning into the corrupted Hindu denominations it is known as today. The Buddha became just another Hindu god and Buddhism just another Hindu creed. In this altered form, his teachings later spread from India under the name of Mahayana Buddhism. Since Buddhism had been antagonistic to the caste system, Buddhism's decline enabled the total solidification of the system. The "untouchables" were excluded even from the religious rituals because they were deemed to have been born "polluted." Hinduism had the caste feature of racism.

Indeed, "pollution" became a big thing. A "high caste" man became "polluted" if he chanced to touch a "low" caste person. Women in menstruation were "polluted," as were people who were grieving, or eating meat. By becoming free of spit, fingernail clippings, and loose hair through daily "ablutions," one of proper caste could become "pure" and able to participate in the rituals. People also took to submerging themselves in "sacred" but polluted rivers to "purify" themselves.

Hinduism also absorbed Jainism so that it became still another animal-worship denomination of Hinduism. Earlier, the people had used animals to symbolize their gods, but the animals themselves finally became sacred. As with the goddess Vac, not only had cows become sacred but also a multitude of other animals including monkeys, elephants and even rats. All became objects of venen or worship. As also with Egypt in decline, the whole Hindu WV and way of thinking was regressing back towards totemism.

The erratic pattern of intermittent rise and fall characteristic of the earlier monogamous-patriarchal societies also characterized the Hindu society. Whenever the civilization became weak, it suffered invasions. The list of invaders includes the Persians, Greeks, Scythians, Gurjaras-Khazars, Kushanas, Hunas, Mongols and Turks. Each either left with spoils or converted to Hinduism and settled in. But after each such invasion, the civilization quickly recovered and prospered, that is until after the twelfth century. By then, decline was so prominent that subsequent recoveries never equaled the earlier age in cultural and intellectual attainments. Decline continued in the North until the Muslim invasion and the conversion of the people to the newer Muslim WV system in northern India beginning after 1000 CE.

One exception was the Punjab. There, the Sikh totally monotheistic WV-based society arose in the 16th century. It comprised both Hindu and Muslim-like doctrines but developed as a militaristic, and non-mainstream sub-society, one that still survives there. All male Sikhs must carry a dagger, but in practice, it can be rather small, even a mere two inches in length and thin enough to be kept in the wallet.

In the southern half of the subcontinent, the Hindu civilization continued to flourish economically until about 1500 CE. There, Hindu regressive regimes built another age of opulent wealth, but the golden cultural age had ended. Advances in the sciences and technology all came to an end. The whole civilization was in decline.

Much of Dravidian-speaking Tamiland below the 16th parallel remained matrilineal. Lineage was based upon cross-cousin marriage and survived in part of the region into the 19th century. The lateness of the Tamils' changeover to the Hindu monogamous, patriarchal system has isolated its people from ever fully identifying with the North.

Hindu Buddhist monks mounted an aggressive conversion campaign that extended the regressive Buddhist-Hindu WV to people outside of India. As they wandered into the outlying regions, they brought with them the culture, learning, customs and institutions of the, by then regressive Hindu system. The changes to Buddhism served to "spiritualize" it enough to enable it to be adopted by other societies as either a complete WV system or, in some cases, a secular one.

In Burma, the Hindu-Buddhist WV based civilization rose to its peak in prosperity from 1000 to 1250 with the building of the immense plain of pagodas in Pagan. The people of Ceylon converted to Buddhist Hinduism and developed a flourishing economy based upon a system of well-engineered canals and reservoirs during the eleventh century. Buddhist Hinduism also spread into Indochina which had been colonized by the Chinese with their own, *Shang* (see Glossary) doctrines and culture. Buddhist-Hindus then absorbed some Shang culture as well, and began building pagoda-like Hindu-Buddhist temples.

Indo-Chinese Buddhism then spread into China where more of its Hindu character was lost. Its presence there fully secularized Chinese society, all of which we will examine next. Then, Chinese Buddhism spread into Tibet, Korea and Japan, all of which modified it in their own way. In the former, it merged with Tibetan animism to become a more primitive WV system known as "Lamaism." Lamaism survives among the Tibetans even under the repression of the Chinese Marxist WV system. In Korea, it took Chinese-like form. In Japan, it barbarized into State Shinto.

Buddhist-Hinduism also spread from Burma, down the Malay Peninsula and then across the full length of Indonesia. Indonesian Hindu-Buddhism reached a cultural climax with the building of the great Borobudour Buddhist shrine in Java and the beautiful two hundred and forty-five Hindu temples of the Prambanan Complex, both in the 9th century. This was all followed by their abandonment and decline after the Eleventh century. During the height of Hindu civilization in Indonesia, its empire extended from Java to encompass much of Southeast Asia. To this day, Hindu and Western-humanist-secularized Bali carries on its version of Hindu society after most of the rest of Southeast Asia converted to Islam about 1500. Even modern Islamic Indonesia still retains some Hindu culture in Southeast Java, including the Hindu Fem-Fertility mythology of *Ratu Kidul*, the "goddess" of the Indian Ocean.

In Indochina, the Hindu-Buddhist WV based society built a massive system of dikes and canals to irrigate northwestern Cambodia. The city of Angkor was founded in the 9th century, and intense building activity began. Angkor soon became the largest Hindu city in Asia. The temple complexes of Angkor Watt and Thom comprise one of the most impressive and extravagant WV-system-based legacies in stone to be found on Earth.

The temple construction ultimately became too costly and the people rose up in revolt. This brought about a relatively sterile secular age in the twelfth century. The surprise sacking of the city by Cham armies led to the government switching over to the Buddhist denomination. Since Shiva had failed to protect their city, they would trust the Buddha to do it. The by-then over-humanistic Buddhist doctrines proceeded to undermine the whole basis of political power and began the decline of the empire. By 1300, the Chinese traveler, Chou Ta-Kuan, had observed that women were taking prominent positions in society, including those of professors and judges. State dogma had become pacifist, too much so as to be able to protect them from the Siamese who took away great chunks of the empire. Symptoms of decline typically appeared, including a liberal public attitude towards sexual matters with semi-nude public dancing.

As had happened in the Hunting WV system, there was an increase in the role of the women. It was, again, the instinctive primate response described earlier in which they undertake the task of placating the male leadership and become more actively involved in supporting the weakening society. As has always been the case, however, the society continued to decline anyway. By the 15th century, Angkor Hindu-Buddhist WV-based society and power had so weakened that Siam invaded to the very capital of Angkor itself, and looted it again of all spoils. The Cambodians then abandoned their great city during a drought and moved their capital a safe distance away to Phnom Penh. With that, the center of the declining Buddhist-Hindu society and civilization in Indochina shifted to Siam.

As a center of Hindu society, Angkor had all the makings of a fully developed civilization except creativity. Nothing was really new. It was simply an after-the-fact rehash of the same Hindu civilization in a new environment, one that could be efficiently exploited with the same old Hindu science and technology. The Hindu faith had become too old. In order for a new civilization to be built in the same area, it was necessary for a newer and better WV ideological system to arise and replace the older one.

Like all the others, the Hindu civilization was also cyclical and fell to barbarians each time it weakened. As with the other patriarchal-monogamous societies, it also tended to recover much of its strength with each such invasion, but as with the others, it also came to recover less each time.

The Muslim invasions began before 1100 CE. By 1500, the northern regions of the Indian subcontinent and Southeast Asia all converted and became part of Islamic society, much of it under Mongol rule. From then on, Northern India, Malaysia and Indonesia were no longer part of Hindu society and civilization.

After 1700, both Hindu and Muslim India became part of the worldwide empire of Western civilization. By 1800, Hindu society had begun an intense absorbing of Western Secular Humanism. This coincided with British efforts to suppress a number of Hindu doctrines, such as the caste system, suttee (widow-suicide), and thuggee (cult murders).

After World War II, the West became over-humanistic enough that the mild tactics of Mahatma Gandhi successfully nudged Imperial, but also humanistic, Britain to grant India her independence. Even though the people adopted much of the West's secular system, the secular ideology was not able to unify Hindus and Muslims into a single government and society. The country split into Hindu India and Muslim WV-based regional systems and governments in Pakistan and Bandgladesh.

Western agricultural techniques have enabled India to achieve a too-large population growth, a problem that India has not been able to control. The caste system was made illegal, but racial prejudice remains. During the 1990's, India adopted a socialist secular dogma with ponderous but useless efforts to collectivize her capitalistic economic system. The sudden collapse of the Soviet Union and Marxist East Asia's drift into capitalism, ended that reign of socialist thinking. By then, India had absorbed enough

Western secularism to begin an economic recovery. Thanks to her adopting the secular age capitalist economic doctrines, as well as with the help of her nationalism, India's universities have managed to turn out effective leaders in business and science. So now, the Hindu-based society is currently achieving an economic resurgence in a region already over-crowded and low in natural resources. She is even doing so while pushing against intense world competition. All such effort is to achieve her place in the culturally sterile, materialistic age of our now declining world civilization.

India is governed more by Secular Humanist, Marxist, Islamic and Brahmans than by the Hindu WV. but The non-Hindus work the constitution system to limit Hindu influence in order to have a government that manages to actually function. The long functioning government Prime Minister is a believer of the Sikh Dharma or WV. The Hindu faithful have been trying to bring back their old WV system to political control, but Hinduism's chaotic ideological disunity so enfeebles their efforts as to make them ineffectual. Hindu religious regression did have "its moment" in the 1990s, when Hindu crowds stormed the Ayodhya mosque, tore it down, and left it a pile of rubble.

Tearing down the mosque was a "success," but one that is unlikely to be repeated. It only leads to enough violent and bloody riots between Hindu and Muslim militants to threaten the very survival of the state. Repeated mosque-destroying would only induce a prolonged and bloody civil war in which neither side would win. Nevertheless, millions of regressive Hindus in Northwest India impose upon themselves a brutal, regressive "moral control" called the *khap Panchayats*, one that operates in the villages as a sort of Hindu Mafia. Both the regression of Hinduism and its caste system, as well as its multi-faith government are, however, gradually losing to the increasing spread of Marxist Maoism among India's Eastern provinces.

ten --- SHANG CHINESE SOCIETY

Hunting WV people settled into China during the last Ice Age. Agriculture built around millet cultivation began before 5,000 BCE in north China. Rice irrigation began later. The people were bonded into their society by the matrilineal-agricultural technology Fem-Fertility WV system. Later, as in much of the rest of the Euro-Asian landmass, they were surrounded by a spreading carpet of Kurgan WV feudal manors. By about 2,500 BCE, most of China was Kurgan feudal. Beginning in about 2,000 BCE and during the Shang period, the Kurgan Chinese WV began to ameliorate and turn into a patriarchal-monogamous system. Hieroglyphic clues even suggest the transition was facilitated by the same Adam and Eve myth as in the Near East. Four of the very earliest Chinese writing symbols were for "demon/devil," "secret," "man/son," and "tree cover." The four are all combined into one pictograph to represent "tempter" (The Discovery of Genesis, C. H. Kong & Ethel R. Nelson, CPH, St. Louis, p 2-3).

By 1,000 BCE, the patriarchal-monogamous WV based system had completely replaced the Fem-Fertility WV society. The new-dynastic Chinese society was bonded by the worship of a pantheon of gods dominated by powerful male gods, the more significant one to the state being, Shang Ti, the Force of Heaven. The WV also included an animistic world of ancestor spirits who interceded with the gods and demigods for the welfare of the individual and his family.

This old Chinese faith has no name. The people of China do not normally recognize their belief heritage as a *religion* or even as an ideology. They think of it as just "the Chinese cultural heritage." Rather than trying to deal with something that has no name, the word, *Shang* or *Shangism* is used here and is listed in the Glossary. It serves to represent the old WV system because the Shang emperor founded its first dynasty and because the "Force of Heaven" god is named *Shang-Ti*.

The society was a semi-feudal theocracy and the written records show that the economic system was communal, that is, communist. Starting as various theocratic commune-like kingdoms, this early prehistorical age had ended by 1800 BCE with the communes being amalgamated into a centralized empire controlled by the Shang emperor, the "Son of Heaven" and head priest. Evidence is that the WV was evolving from the Kurgan system and that human sacrifice on a grand scale existed from the very beginning of the Shang dynasty, and that thousands of people were sacrificed by being buried alive with the emperor upon his death. The WV bond ameliorated as the WV system evolved and, soon after 400 BCE, had become humane enough for human sacrifice to be largely eliminated.

As in any semi-feudal theocracy, the militarized Shang clergy ran and administered the state. The king acted as commander and chief of the armies that were also under control of semi-independent feudal lords. The Shang emperor represented "the Force of Heaven" only as long as he was able to keep its "Mandate of Heaven." To avoid making mistakes which indicate having lost the Mandate, the emperor consulted his soothsaying "advisory counsel" whose members juggled "magical" ox-bones and tortoise shells to legitimize their best, most practical (and, for them, the safest) advice. All state ritual was the centralized focus of their ancestor worship WV system.

As the Chinese WV ideology took shape, it developed those elements that enable us to understand what the WV ideological goal was of Chinese society. It can be summed up as achieving harmony, enlightenment, and contentment of the "spirits" of one's ancestors. It is also the preserving of the Chinese people's "central position in the world." The means to achieve those religious goals are doing right by others and following proper ceremony. By so doing, one is believed to enhance the status of one's family, one's ancestors, and the Chinese people as a whole. The obstacle to achieving all that is "the barbarians," that is, all people who are not Chinese. Shang society has long been obsessed with out-thinking, out-witting, and out-maneuvering "the barbarians." This paranoia-like obsession even now shapes the drive of the Chinese Marxist-WV System's nationalism.

Despite China's having to develop in relative isolation, it progressed at a pace that was unmatched anywhere else. Its bronze work, for example, remained notably the world's finest from the very beginning of the Shang dynasty.

The Chinese theocratic age continued until about 800 BCE. By then, the power of the central monarch had declined and the empire broke up into separate states that were often at war with each other. This was the age of contending states and was Chinese society's first great creative period, a period in which it began an unusually long process of leaving its theocratic age behind and becoming fully secularized. The first secular doctrines were fascistic and helped to secularize the Shang WV in much the same way democratic doctrines much later secularized the Christian WV and its society. Civilization was then as advanced in China as in India and the Mediterranean region.

About 200 BCE, the more barbaric WV of the Ch'in people absorbed the Shang WV. Its early-secularizing fascistic military-political doctrines led them to conquer the rest of China. They then built an empire that approximated that of Rome in terms of land mass. Under the subsequent Han dynasty, the borders of Shang society were enlarged to the point of equaling the size of present-day China. The emperor also had the whole written religious heritage of China destroyed.

Secularizing proceeded still further with the spread of Confucius' "path" in the 4th century BCE. The "path" of Tao also appeared. The semi-secular age gave way to the full secularizing of the society with the arrival and spread of Buddhism, the last significant secularizing creed or "path" until the arrival of Western Secular Humanism. Soon, the elite (but not the common people) had nearly forgotten the old gods, but the rituals and ceremonies of the faith continued as the old WV's last, tenuous bond.

Confucianism had supplemented more than contradicted the older doctrines of the WV system, a rare phenomenon that helped sustain China's unusually long secular age. Confucianism developed as a teaching of "the noble way," a mannered and gracious social and ethical code of conduct for the achieving of the ideal citizen and gentleman. It was a "path" that was adopted mainly by the educated urban elite.

Taoism teaches "a path" to a more "transcendental state." As a more sophisticated and mystical interpretation and elaboration of the old and metaphysical pre-Shang Fem-Fertility doctrines, it deals with the ancient animist concept of the "life force," a force which is thought to be concentrated in the embryo and to dissipate as growth and age intervene. The objective of much of Taoist procedure is to be so in harmony with "natural order" as to preserve the animistic "life force" and thereby live ideally forever.

By the beginning in the 4th century CE, Buddhism spread from India into China after developing a body of sacred texts dealing with such things as a code of monastic discipline, discourses on the supposedly previous lives of the Buddha, and the recounting of dialogs believed to have taken place with him. It also contained the doctrine that The Buddha had been sent to mankind in order to teach people "the right path to salvation." Among the Buddhist sects are those who worship Buddhist "saints," ones who purportedly delayed their well-earned reward of Nirvana in order to stay and assist others to attain it.

Most certainly much initial conservative-Shang antagonism had built up against the "paths of the Three Teachers" by the end of the 4th century CE. By diminishing the role of the old WV system, the "Teachers" had weakened the social bond. Those who adhered to the new creeds and those to the old faith necessarily had to come to an understanding so that the old and new could both work together and restore some harmony to the ideologically divided society. To do that, all the separate belief systems had to be surreptitiously compromised in order to restore a semblance of a closed system of thinking, something essential in maintaining the society-binding power of the WV system. An accord was rationalized into existence, one which turned out to be so successful that the Chinese secular age lasted to about 1300 CE, a secular age of more than 1,600 years and longer than that of any existing mainstream civilization.

With the end of the theocratic age and the full secularizing of the society, communal ways gave way to capitalism in the cities, although rural communes survived until after 200 CE. As with all the other mainstream societies, the secular beliefs never replaced the common people's ancient Chinese ancestor-worshiping WV system.

Between 700 and 200 BCE, women gained and enjoyed more rights and influence in society. Their position and role changed with each of the civilization's up and down cycle. During the last two thousand years, China managed to follow the same cyclical pattern as all the other patriarchal-monogamous "spirit"-based WV-bonded societies. Political decline and shrinkage in the size of the state would occur. Also, taxes would be raised, the gold standard would be abandoned and an inflationary printing of paper money would follow. Each such decline reflected a temporary decline of religious idealism, and a weakened three-part structure of family, justice, and state power. Each was also followed by another conquest and reunification by one of the more peripheral kingdoms still in the mono-mate barbaric WV state. Then the conquerors would adopt the Shang patriarchal-monogamous WV and way of thinking, rebuild enthusiasm and idealism and do away with its more impractical doctrines, institute reform. It would rebuild the infrastructure, and rebuild the empire. This pattern repeated itself numerous times. There is no need here to deal with the names and dates of all the dynasties.

The exception was the conquest of China by the Kurgan WV System Mongols. Their by-then alien Kurgan and uncompromisingly polygynous and nomadic WV system way of life ensured that the Chinese resistance to them was fierce. The size and sophistication of the fighting in the Mongol Wars dwarfed all other wars fought until modern times. Being the most inventive of all earlier societies, the Chinese invented gunpowder and the cannon, the mortar, and rocket propelled exploding missiles. In this all-out war, the weapons were mass-produced to keep up with the needs of the battling armies. The warfare was so fierce and devastating that the population of China was cut in half between 1193 and 1391.

The Mongols did take control, but this time the barbarians did *not* convert, so they continued to be regarded as a separate and hated tyranny, and the Mongols never achieved anything but a precarious hold on the society. After a mere century of Mongol rule, the Ming dynasty was established from an indigenous, fascist-type insurrection and revolution against the weakening Mongol autocracy, an event which resembles the indigenous uprising and driving out of the Hyskos in Egypt. In both cases, the triumph was achieved by rallying the public around "the cause of national liberation."

Despite the long length of China's secular age from the 4th century BCE on, the social bond had continued to weaken and social problems worsened with each dynasty. By the time of the Mongol conquests seventeen centuries later, social problems had become so serious that the people were deserting the secular beliefs and returning to the reassuring doctrines of their old Shang faith.

The Chinese course of religious regression resembled that of Buddhism in India. The secular creeds had their own administrators and, like a clergy, they fought to retain their followers by, in China's case, absorbing Shang-like doctrines. Thus, they took to performing the old Shang rituals and ceremonies as priests or monks in their separate public centers-turned-into-temples. In that way, they became denominations of the Shang faith. Then, the practitioners of the three creeds spread throughout the rural areas to partially replace the shamans of the Shang WV system. By taking this unique course, Chinese religious regression came to exert the least mind-control. It also enabled some intellectual-technological progress to continue. The denominations had divided the old faith in a way that prevented either from dominating.

But the consequences were not all beneficial. Since the religious regression was so limited, the social bond remained divided and weak. Social problems were not being reduced. After overthrowing the Mongols by 1382, the subsequent history of the Shang WV and its society and civilization was marred by intense social instability. China was plagued by frequent rural rebellions.

The Shang animistic-polytheistic WV lasted the longest of all other still existing patriarchal-monogamous WV systems for a number of reasons. Not only were the secular doctrines less disruptive to her original faith even during regression but, as well, the society's early stability resulted from its long theocratic-communal age. Another reason was the beneficial and enduring effect Confucianism had on the Chinese bureaucracy. And lastly, the Chinese protected their countryside. Rice was grown on the same land for thousands of years. The civilization managed to last long after the society itself had begun to weaken.

By the 15th century, loyalty to the Shang WV system and society was replaced by a loyalty-preference for one's family. Rural China reverted to the semi-monogamous so-called "family system" or "peasant mentality." The concept of *progress* ceased to be imaginable. In its place came the zero-sum peasant-mentality type belief that no individual or family could better itself without subtracting from the others in equal proportion. That is, "if you gain, it can only be at my expense." Villages came to center around a wealthy patriarch who resided with his chattel spouse and concubines to exert cruel leadership over his large, extended family and the peasants he ruled. Due to Western secular and Marx-Leninist doctrines, this system has since been mostly cleaned out.

China was still strong, however, and creative development continued in the arts. Chinese ships were used in colonizing and in trade throughout much of the Old World. Extensive commerce took place primarily with the Islamic, Hindu and African Swahili-Bantu-Zimbabwe society. Individual merit no longer determined a man's place in the hierarchy as much as did money and influence. The arrival of the Ming Dynasty brought about the last great age of the maturing Chinese civilization. By then, the Chinese empire reached its maximum extent. She even reforested by planting more than a billion new trees. Within a century, however, her trading empire had collapsed, Japanese pirates were in control of most of her seacoast, and she was ravaged by more inflation. The Chinese WV system had deteriorated into a mere patchwork of ancestor-worship-based beliefs. The feeling of being in the family-troop had been lost, and even conquering barbarians could not restore it. By the end of the 15th century, China's cultural creativity had slowed. After that, its civilization lagged behind that of Islam and the West. Accurate astronomy instruments in use before 1400 and superior to those used in Europe two centuries later were standing idle by 1600. No one any longer knew how to use them. Earlier, China had been most notable in the science of armaments, but Europe managed to overtake and become militarily superior to China by the end of the 16th century.

Even the Chinese civilization's long lasting and soundly based agricultural system developed problems. Western agricultural policies infiltrated China during the 17th century. Corn and yam agriculture spread into the more rugged and arid areas of western China bringing about an enormous increase in population. For the first time, severe erosion occurred. Then droughts brought on famine cycles. One of the worst such famine occurred in the 1876-9 seasons, causing the death of some thirteen million people.

Peasant rebellions became frequent. One of them in the 1850s was the most violent rebellion in human history. It swept across sixteen provinces resulting in the destruction of hundreds of cities and ending with the death of some sixty million people.

China's four hundred and fifty years of isolation persisted as European power built up around it. During the nineteenth century, China became a vassal state to the West. Even when faced with such humiliation, the academic elite continued to believe that China had a "vital energy" that maintained her as the nation "central to the world," the same animistic, and divine-land-umbilical-to-the-heavens concept common to the 4,000 BCE barbarian Kurgan WV.

During the first half of the twentieth century, China acquired a number of Western secular doctrines, imported Western technology, regained her independence, and began to recover. By 1950, however, rural instability had again surfaced, and the heretical Agrarian-revolution of Mao Zedong's Marx-Leninist non-"spirit"-based WV system had spread across China. Instead of establishing a "People's Republic," the Marxist WV believers established a single-party Imperial Marxist-Chinese WV-bonded state. The old Shang WV became too obsolete to any longer bind people into a society. It and its civilization had ended by 1950.

Why has the West misrepresented the once social-binding ideology of the Chinese people? The image of the Three Religions of China first arose in the 16th century when Jesuit missionaries were hoping to win over the government and the people to Catholicism. They made friends in high office by participating in the Chinese state rituals. Being Westerners, they erroneously assumed the state rituals to be secular because we in the West were beginning to see politics as secular. They saw Buddhist, Taoist and Confucian Temples and assumed the "Three Teachers" were the founders of "the three religions of China." It was an easy mistake because the Chinese religious literary heritage was totally destroyed about the time of Jesus, and there has been an aversion to putting it down in print ever since. It has been handed down verbally, from one generation to the next.

There are other reasons as well. One is that the old Chinese WV had neither a supreme "spirit" nor a belief-system-founder of any kind. Yet another reason is that the missionaries did not discover the importance of old China's WV system's main feature, its ancestor worship. The Chinese do not invite acquaintances or strangers into their homes, and their homes house the temple shrines to their ancestors. Meals and banquets are communions with their family ancestors and are performed for and by the family in the home before altars dedicated to their ancestors. Friends and guests have always been entertained in inns and restaurants.

The Chinese Mandarin elite also deserves blame for the error. They look down on and utterly dismiss as crass superstition all the mythology and other popular expressions of the old faith. They see the old and elaborate rituals and ceremonies as just being Chinese, not as functions of a WV belief system. When they look back through their entire history, the faithful can see only their one system of belief. So, to them, it merely seems to be their tradition and inseparable from their race and country. They do not even have a word in their language for "religion." All this is different from the Western heritage where people look back in history and note a series of different WV systems.

The "Three Teachers" only brought China three newer-to-them *secular* "paths." The three creeds were later absorbed into the Shang Chinese WV system during its age of religious regression. Buddhism came at a time when China was prospering and was open to new secular ideologies. This also explains why Confucianism and Taoism had also appeared by then. As mentioned earlier, Buddhism had been a secular faith in India before becoming part of the Hindu WV system when the old faith turned regressive. It helped secularize China as well. During religious regression, it then merged with the old Chinese faith. The "paths" of the Three Teachers became mere denominations of the Shang WV System.

To this day the multitude of ancient Chinese gods can be seen in the various temples wherever Chinese people live. Among them are Huang-Ti or Shang-Ti the Creator, Tou Mou, or Mother Nature, K'uei Hsing. Personally seen have been many of them represented by idols, some with as many as fifteen heads and eight arms. Some can also be seen hanging from taxi rear-view mirrors and in household shrines. When asked their names, the Chinese have learned to translate them the easy way, that is, as the Buddha.

Scholars tend to believe religions are what is represented in temples, churches, mosques or the "sacred scriptures." Functionally, however, they are whatever the people believe and follow in their daily lives and which is often very different from what is found in the temples and scriptures. A Chinese opera, for example, is an offering of entertainment to reward their gods for a bountiful harvest, even though it is not performed in the temples. Shang Chinese worship their ancestor spirits in home shrines, not in temples. The idols in the temples are reserved for bowing to and the burning of josh sticks.

Still another unacknowledged characteristic of the Shang WV is that its "spirits" evolve. Over the millennium, they transform. The Earth God, for example, was originally named "She" and had immense power, being second only to the God of the Heavens who mandated power to the emperor. During the Chinese faith's 4,500-year plus history, the "She" changed names, changed appearance, and changed position. Ultimately demoted and turned into a mortal man, he became known as the legendary Zhang Mingde. In more recent times, Mingde became an almost forgotten, excruciatingly humble old man with a long white beard.

Moreover, as Catholicism spouts "saints," the Shang "spirit"-based WV similarly spouts new gods. Among them is the Marx-Leninist-renegade ex-emperor, Mao Zedong. The archaic worship of one's ancestors and demigods did not come from the enlightened minds of Confucius and the Buddha.

Other defining characteristics of the Shang Chinese WV system include the way the Chinese endeavor to reward and entreat their gods and how they ward off the troublesome ghosts which they believe seasonally surround them. These ways include Lion Dancing and long and elaborate funeral processions to threaten away lone ghosts who they imagine arise from their ghostly prison. There is also divination, making annual food offerings to the "hungry Ghosts" burning phony money for them to spend when they return to their dungeon, and the curling up of building cornices into sharp points to keep demons from sitting there. All these and more are, to this day, expressions of the old Shang Chinese WV.

So, briefly, the founding and mainstream WV system of China that had developed some four thousand years ago, later absorbed the "three paths" as "denominations." The total combined but divided Chinese WV and its civilization came to an end in the mainstream in 1949. It was replaced then by the troubled Marxist patriarchal-monogamous WV-based society. The obsolete, old polytheistic "spirit"-based WV then ceased to be mainstream. It became the cult that now serves only to help bond such Secular Humanist WV-shaped nations as, South Korea, Singapore and Taiwan.

Under the Asian heretical version of the Marxist WV system, the traditional care with which China had previously attended to its natural environment lessened. Multi-millennium-long practices were reversed. Marshes were drained and plowed up. Many dams were built, coal smoke began to choke the skies, and population congestion led people to move to where water was scarce. Desertification is increasing and the Gobi Desert is approaching Beijing. Yet, with the world's overgenerous corporate financial assistance, she managed to industrialize and build up her military forces. The Orient has been very adept at utilizing Western technology.

The Westernized corporate business world was only interested in building factories there to use her cheap labor. Whether or not China observed "basic human rights," or observed worker safety, was of little concern to the stockholders. To justify the betrayal of their own Secular Humanist ideals, Western business interests took to claiming that "trade and investment with China would bring her into the Community of Nations. The Baathist-Muslim WV based regime in Libya seems to have taken that path, but such a risky model has not yet been tested on many other regimes, and it certainly failed to bring Hitler's Third Reich into the "community of nations."

Until at this writing, the Chinese and Indochinese people generally accept the present version of the Marx-Leninist WV system, but the younger and urbane generations have at present little interest in Marxist ideology. They have, so far, also ignored their old Shang faith in favor of Western secular nationalism, just as Western planners had hoped. Thus, there is a destabilizing, long-term, ideological tug-of-war going on in China between Marxism, Shang heritage nationalism, Christianity, and Western secularism.

The collapse of the Marxist system in the Soviet Union has been almost equaled by the transition of the system in China to capitalism, a transition that looks suspiciously like *secularizing*. The Chinese Marxist system has also ceased to be a revolutionary movement and adopted the Western secular concept of the national state. Then China went on to conquer rather than bring about a revolution in Tibet. It even threatens to conquer Taiwan. The adopting of Western secular concepts makes the system little more than an ideological facade for the racist-chauvinism inherent in China's still-surviving old Shang faith. Instead of "workers of the world unite," the intent is to "extend China's borders over all people of the 'Chinese race,'" meaning to them, Tibet, Indochina, Taiwan, Singapore, Bhutan, Korea and Japan.

The retrogressive barracks-state, Juche, God-King, personality-cult WV of North Korea is a form of heretical Marx-Leninist religious regression. China prefers to prop up the economy of its thuggish ally, and use it as a surrogate troublemaker for the West. China conveniently dodges blame for supporting it as an intent to avoid being overwhelmed by refugees.

eleven --- THE GREEK-ROMAN SYSTEM

During the 3ʳᵈ millennium BCE, the Hellenes-speaking Kurgan WV-based society and it's feudal system spread from the Balkans to colonize both Italy and Greece. As it did, the evolution of its WV was influenced by the mono-mate barbarian WV beliefs of the two regions, such as that of the Etruscans in Italy. The philology work done on Pilos A indicates the society's early theocratic Hellenist WV based economic, social and divided political system consisted of feudal military garrison-state communes, ones that were led by an efficient bureaucracy and a respected military class. As the system spread, it adopted Fem-Fertility WV-based agricultural doctrines and goddesses. Before 1000 BCE and by means described earlier, it had brought down the number and power of the goddesses to end in a slimmer pantheon than of either Egypt or Babylon.

As traders and pirates, the Hellenic society could pick and choose the agriculture, mathematics, and writing technologies of Egypt and Mesopotamia without having to invent it. At the same time, they ignored the old and corrupted Babylonian and Egyptian doctrines of temple prostitution, animal worship, astrology, the building of necropolitic palaces, and the mummification of the dead. Also, instead of adopting the cumbersome old Fertile Crescent's writing systems, they adopted the Minoan alphabetic script. They made practical choices because barbarians have always been practical.

After 800 BCE, trade with the Mesopotamian and Egyptian civilizations led to the WV system developing the monogamous family system in both its Greek and Roman communes. The feudal system broke up and was replaced with city-state monarchies which were, in turn, replaced by oligarchic rule of the nobility. The Kurgan WV militarized, polygamous mind-set had evolved into a mono-mate barbarian WV system, one which included the deification of Mt. Olympus and the Homeric-

Hesiodic mythology as well as, in Italy, the origin mythology surrounding the birth of Rome.

The system then moved out of its theocratic age as the old gods came under attack by freethinking Greek philosophers. Utopian secular ideals and other new and secular beliefs appeared which divided and weakened what had finally become an Olympian-based patriarchal-monogamous WV system. Individualism and humanism were growing, but the society and its civilization were able to flourish because the old and the secular were accord-rationalized into a WV that could sustain the social bond.

Dictatorships were set up in the name of the disenfranchised masses while, in reality, the tyrants represented the interests of the growing merchant class. By 500 BCE, most of the city-state dictatorships had, in turn, given way to rule by assemblies of the free minority, and the power of the commoners replaced that of the nobles. The political ideology of "democracy" fully secularized the society, and the greatest creative age of the Hellenic civilization began. The arts flowered and an intellectual age appeared which towered above that of previous ages. Sculpture was developed as a Greek art form that was not equaled or surpassed anywhere in the world until the Western sculpture of Giovanni Bernini some 2,000 years later. (To worshipful Classicists excited by the undraped form, Greek sculpture is still the best).

Production techniques were developed as well, ones that enabled objects to be produced in batches for large numbers of consumers. Euclid, Aristotle and others made great strides in the early development of the scientific method. There were also far-reaching advances in architecture and engineering as well as new developments in the fields of painting, poetry, philosophy, medicine, and mathematics. This was the golden age of the Greek-Roman civilization.

The society's transformation to democratic secular doctrines did not occur uniformly. In more conservative, rural areas of Greece, such as in Sparta, the process lagged. There, the popularity of the loose, secular system of the Republic was not accepted and change came to an end. Religious regression ensued with the adopting of militaristic doctrines. The barracks state commune system of earlier, feudal times, was restored, including its communal mess halls. Monogamy survived, but men could not marry under the age of thirty and all male citizens served in the army until middle age. An "iron curtain"-like set of restrictions descended; travel was prohibited. The fascist-like Spartan League became a closed society, and a time of conflict between Sparta and Athens followed.

The Greek Republic was narrow-based, being built, as it was, upon a mass of slaves and other non-voting, non-citizens who made up approximately 87% of the inhabitants. There was virtually no middle class. During the 4th and 3rd centuries, Greek society developed all the problems that go with being governed by democracy-promoting ideologues, and no political system is perfect. As Alexander Tytler, wrote in 1787, "a democracy is always temporary in nature; it simply cannot exist as a permanent form of government."

The society finally turned into a sort of "mobocracy." In its "jury system," a citizen could accuse a richer businessman of wrong practices, bring up heresy evidence, share in the decision to convict him, and then be rewarded with a share of the fine that was paid.

The Greek world of entertainment came to include the production of bawdy comedies in which, for example, Socrates was lampooned as fouling his clothes. The Parthenon, which began as a temple to Athena became merely the nation's gold-reserve repository. Women became more assertive. Of all the symptoms of decline, however, most important was that Athens and her league of similar cities had weakened militarily. The Athenian League was hardly able to defend itself even from the Spartans.

However, as it turned out, Greece's Macedonian mono-mate barbarian neighbor that invaded and conquered her. The conquering Macedonians then adopted the Hellenic WV system, including the society's artistic cultural heritage, but not its democratic doctrines. They were replaced with a centralized and authoritarian, fascist system. Then, Greece-Macedonia set out to destroy the Persian Empire. In doing so, it create the first empire of the Hellenic Imperial Age, one that was significant in spreading Hellenic WV and culture to more distant regions of the then-known world.

The Greek-Macedonian Empire and Rome had both expanded from about 350 BCE, but it only took a few decades to build the widespread Hellenic Empire. As its more Eastern parts broke up over the next several centuries, its citizens mostly returned to their old WVs and cultures. As they did, the civilization's more Western parts were absorbed into the expanding Roman Empire. The civilization's second and last imperial age began only during the first century BCE. The empire of Rome grew at a much slower pace. As it grew, her neighbors took up arms to defend themselves which, in turn, was each time interpreted as a threat by the Romans and, each time, justified the Empire's next advance. Conquered people were required to adopt its secular Greek-Roman Hellenism and could still continue worshiping the thousands of "spirits" in their own, older, WV systems. In such ways, the Latin speaking part of the Hellenic WV system managed to spread the civilization into much of the then known world, and to set up an era of relative peace and free trade.

The Greek society and civilization the Romans had taken over and adopted had already moved out of its theocratic age, became secularized, and had already passed most of its Golden Age. The Olympian priesthood had become powerless, and capitalism had replaced the last vestiges of communism. By then, the Romans had also passed through their theocratic and republic stages, and had, as well, undergone regression, just as the Greeks had experienced Spartan fascist-regression. Rome had replaced the secular political system of Sparta and Macedonia with its own cult of the emperor, its own form of fascism, both of which successfully welded together the societies of the Old World.

The pattern of the patriarchal-monogamous system had continued with the Greek-Roman WV system. Barbarians conquer civilization, convert to its WV, rejuvenate the society, create an empire, and then spread the civilization's culture to others. The Macedonians and the Romans had spread advanced Hellenic secular age art and science to the rest of the mainstream Mediterranean World.

The material wealth of the upper classes throughout the Roman World was partially the result of continued improvements in production techniques. Concrete was used widely for the first time. A great road system and many aqueducts were built. Slave labor-based industries flourished. The adoption of Roman secular, Hellenic and imperial doctrines, had brought about a mild rejuvenation of the other Old World societies. Robbers had been cleared from the roads, and pirates, from the seas. The same coinage was good from Egypt to Britain. A reign of near-universal peace had been established.

Probably the greatest scientist of this Hellenic civilization was Aristotle; but only Roman "armchair theorists" who disdained "vulgar experimentation" followed. They would not get their hands soiled, not even to prepare manuals on how to apply the science that they had developed and much of Greek-Roman science was never put to practical use. Their scientists figured out the basics of the steam engine, but only the lowly craftsmen would put their hands to building one, and they were too ignorant to know how. By 300 CE, science was in decline in both Greece and Rome.

During the course of the Hellenic WV-based society and civilization, Greece and then Italy were denuded of their forests. They had to import lumber for their building material and for the fires that stoked their kilns, foundries and baths. During the latter days of the Empire, Rome was importing wood from as far away as Britain, and then to the extent of even denuding the coastal areas of southern England. After the deforestation of Italy, the sheep over-grazed the hills. That, in turn, led to erosion that spread to much of the Mediterranean. The over grazed hills could no longer absorb the rains so the water rushed off in torrents to leave the land dry and barren. Areas around Rome received some of the overflow and ended with malarial swamps. Worse yet, farms throughout Italy suffered a labor shortage as workers migrated to the cities. Farms were set up using inefficient slave labor and much of the food consumed in Rome and the resort cities was import in the form of tribute.

In the face of worsening male leadership, the pattern of women becoming more assertive repeated itself towards the end of the third century CE. The position of women had improved first during Greece's golden age. In the WV-system's late Roman age, the status and influence of her women continued to improve, all of which only enabled the men to blame them for society's growing problems.

Under emperor Diocletian hyperinflation occurred between 200 and 344 with price controls being employed in futile attempts to limit rising prices.

There were also many rich tourists out to see the world of prostitution resorts. In some of the grand villas, ornamental phalluses hung like good luck charms, and people copulated in scenes painted on the walls. Amidst their masses of slaves, the rich men of the city lived opulently, with both their devoted wives and numerous brothels to serve them.

As with the Greek Republic, there was no middle class. The free citizens of Rome had once mostly been free farmers, but they had gone to Rome where they could be fed and entertained free by the government to keep them from rioting. The land they left was replaced by commercial farms, each run by the villa-lord who used slaves from the Empire to mine the soil with for a quick return, all in order for him, his family, and his fawning retinue could lavish in the resorts during the appropriate seasons. Much of the grain consumed in the cities came not from the villas but was imported in the form of heavy taxes or tribute from the Empire.

Religious regression in the Greek-Roman society had first appeared in Sparta when it reacted back to its semi-Kurgan WV system. Later, Alexander took the Greek secular political ideology and turned Greece from a republic to a fascist autocracy. The Romans evolved a political form of regression, but their WV system could not again react back to their old polytheistic WV. Throughout the civilization, the thousands of gods people once worshiped no longer inspired people. The world had outgrown the polytheistic age, making religious regression of the Greek-Roman WV system more unappealing than in the decline of any other civilization. Instead, the Roman world became a sea of assorted cults all vying for the allegiance of people, ones who were desperately seeking belief-relief from the disintegration of their ancient multiple-god WV systems. They began converting to monotheistic-like WV systems as the old gods began settling into their graves. For the first time, a WV-based civilization was without effective religious regression, and heading into the "behavioral sink."

The old society became so pathological that its collapse was not only anticipated but masses of people actually looked forward to its end. All over the Hellenic-Roman Empire, people were hoping for "the End Times." Many of the cults were no more than left-over vestiges of the polygamous matriarchal age. Some flourished by fostering decadent doctrines of older eras, such as of the erotic indulgence involved in the orgiastic ceremonies of the Baal, Attis, and Dionysus cults. Some were mere vehicles for the justification of brutality and near-pedophilia, such as the Phoenician god's demand for human (child) sacrifice. But the age of dualistic, good-god evil-god, near-monotheistic faiths had arrived. Less ancient near monotheistic cults such as Mithraism and Zoroastrianism, as well as the ones of the Essenes, Gnostics, and Judaics attracted followers, but the most successful form of WV was the near-monotheism of Christianity.

The key to Christianity's triumph lay in its tie-in with mono-mate barbarian WV system of Judaism. In contrast to the general breakdown in moral values, the obedience of the Judaic WV believers to their "Laws of God" had gained respect and made them stand out from others. A large body of Judiacs arose called "proselytes." They were people who were not circumcised, Hebrew-speaking, and unable to claim descent from Abraham but who nevertheless believed in Judaism and its patriarchal, communal way of life. However, Judaism was doctrinally only a tribal federation united by a WV system centered in Jerusalem. Its ethnocentric doctrinal limitations meant it was not the answer to the troubled times. It was petulantly seclusive and even given to unrelenting strife between its many factions.

Since so many people still wanted Judaic doctrine, a real but unexpressed need for a Judaic-like WV system arose. In answer to that need, a Judaic sect appeared which deemphasized the Abraham-tribal-circumcision and tribal/racist aspect in preference to its god being the savior of *everyone* who believed in him. Since people desperately wanted better times, a Greek-Judaic apostle-activist of the sect, Paul, spread the rumor that just such a better world would follow. He credited the "good news" to "Jesus," an executed leader of a militantly Judaic sect, one who had promoted himself as "the Jewish Messiah." Jesus had been a "healer" and a militant rabble-rouser against both Rome and the Temple leadership (Math: 10:14). Because he was regarded as "anointed," he was considered by his followers as "the Christ," and was called "Jesus (the) Christ." With his armed followers (Luke 22: 36), he is depicted in the Scriptures as starting a riot in the Temple. The implied hope was that it would spread into a general insurrection against Rome and its puppet Sanhedrin.

Since the movement had begun as a Judaic heresy, it was still tied to the system's old lore, including its then-superior, thought tribal, moral code, its then-more-viable explanation of the origin of the world, and its then-oldest and latest account of a single, all-powerful, Father God. Being Judaic-based, the new Christian faith held an unrivaled edge over all the other cults. The need for a Judaic-like WV system had been satisfied.

Afterwards, the Church began to collect the circulating sea of letters of revelations, recollections, testimonials, and apocalyptic visions. It all had to be sorted and evaluated. Many of the collected scriptures, probably the most dubious ones, were ultimately cast out of the collection. The different stories about Jesus' life, and other works which had influenced them, including Revelations, were all added to older Hebrew scriptures like the Torah, to produce the Christian Bible. Among the ones kept were the four Gospels with each subsequent one picturing a more supernatural, miracle-ladened Jesus, one performing miracles that resembled those described in the Greek Septuagint version of the Old Testament Book of Kings, Psalms and Zechariah. The later Gospel authors had apparently reasoned that since Jesus was their Messiah, he also had to have performed miracles similar to those in the Old Testament, ones which the Messiah was expected to also perform, a process Biblical scholars call *intertextual*. It might also be noted that scholars often try to find natural cause explanations for the scripture's "miracles" when the whole reason they are there is to impress everyone that their gods can do things that cannot be explained.

There were questions about the Book of Revelations and its horrifying and brutal amplification of the 200 CE Book of Daniel and the anticipations of the Essenes found in the Dead Sea Scrolls. There was confusion over whether "the beast" represented Satan, the anti-Christ, the persecuting tyrant, Emperor Nero, or "licentious" Babylon. Whatever it was supposed to be was to be ultimately destroyed by the Holy Ghost-God-Christ so that Heaven or Heaven-on-Earth could arrive and (only) the faithful be saved. Along with the other sixteen supposed prophetic books of the Bible, it forms a hand-wringing emotional perception of what the coming Fall of Rome would be like. In it, the stars fall from the sky, immense "beasts" rise from under the ground and battling armies bloody the Earth. All was written in allegorical word pictures that are not, cannot, and never have been taken literally even by those who claim them to be "the inerrant Word of God." What is written as "a beast," for example, is never interpreted by the faithful as being simply just a beast as it says.

Also in Revelations, God is not the serene, confident, assured and peace-loving one in the Sermon on the Mount. Instead, he is shown as a desperate, Savior-God engaged in an amplified version of Zoroaster's 500 BCE all-out, climactic, war between "good and evil," the one in which a vicious, vengeful God wages a last-gap struggle-to-the-death against the "Spirit-force of Chaos and Evil." No wonder Revelations was first excluded from the official cannon by a number of early Bishops. It was retained, even so, because it taught mass salvation, thus supplementing the faith's goal answer to the second question of the Four Question Template. Also, its graphic horror and torment served to threaten those denominations that were thinking of abandoning the common, and therefore, "official" line.

In brief, then, the scriptural picture emerged as a recounting of the Semitic, before science origin theory of the world, man, and his history, as well as a New testament-updated account of the Hebrew God. In the New Testament, the old vengeful tribal warrior-god seemed to have been generally replaced by a nicer one. This new one taught that, instead of slaughtering non-believing tribes (such as in the Torah), men should "live in peace and turn the other cheek to their persecutors." The newer god was one of love, kindness, compassion, and forgiveness. Unlike brutal old Yahweh, however, this new god, "God," sadistically damned the "souls" of those who did not love him to where his evil minions could torture them in "a lake of fire forever" (Matt. 25:41).

Not only was Christianity a new WV and way of thinking but, as well, it was a new type of belief system, a monotheistic-like, non-tribal one which taught the universal brotherhood of all believers. Its successful spread among non-Judaic-believing people led the emerging fellowship of believers away from the Chosen People's exclusive, racist, doctrine towards the unity of all mankind. By a process of Darwinian-like survival of the fittest among competing religious cults, not only had a popular near-monotheism evolved but, as well, the model for a whole new class of WV systems. It had evolved into the first great, universal-brotherhood type WV system, and a type that was destined to become the most successful of all. It had not only brought about the mainstream end of the old polytheistic faiths but had also answered the Four Question Template in a way that brought a loose unity to many different people over a larger area of the globe. The theme of this newer "spirit"-based WV system was that Jesus had come to save *all* of mankind who believed in him from the imminent, destruction of their (Roman) world.

The Christian concept of a single God was part of the "new wave" way of thinking for the times. The concept of monotheism had been taught both by Zoroaster in Persia and Amenhotep IV in Egypt by 1,350 BCE, but the concept was still controversial. Conservative intellectuals and scholars believed that a single and abstract God without either an image and human weaknesses was an extreme form of "intellectual materialism." To them, the Christian God was so formless and abstract as to be "non spiritual," even "irreligious." Christians were even accused of being "atheists" because a god without definable image or form seemed about the same as no god at all. In contrast, more "spiritual" or "spirit"-filled polytheism was regarded as the very foundation of society. More conservative people saw change as threatening the very survival of civilization.

The new Christian WV system appealed not only to progressive intellectuals but also to the Roman poor, the women, the beggars and slaves. From them, it spread among the urban poor of the Empire, the poor and desperate masses who everywhere resentfully looked forward to seeing the climactic end of the over-bearing old society, their own personal escape into Heaven, and the arrogant, greedy rich being left behind to be consumed in Hell. That was the promise and the goal that Christians were to live for.

The people had grown to hate the fascistic, overly patriarchal Roman rule. They looked back at the more permissive mother-goddess age and welcomed the embrace of the "Virgin Mother Mary." Jesus had even admonished his men to reject their fathers for him as in Matt 8:21-2,10:37, and Luke 12:51-53. As the early icons all show, the people of the late Eastern Roman Empire pictured Christianity in icons as the bigger-than-life "Holy Virgin Mother Mary," the great reformed, angelic, and no-longer-sexual, Mother-Earth-like goddess. In the West, even her face was regarded as too sacred to be painted from a model. She was usually depicted with the long-nose the ancient Celts had imagined characterized the face of the gods. Christianity's first fifteen hundred years of icons all showed an almost overlooked, cadaverous, and unlovable-looking little baby Jesus sitting awkwardly, and seemingly forsaken, on the lap of the awe-inspiring, larger-than-life Mother Mary. Her dominance survives even today when the Pope himself publicly pleads with Her to intercede for him.

The early emphasis on the Mother Mary helped to wean people away from the old temple-prostitution and secularized Fem-Fertility goddess WV in which the mother's role was just to be fertile and produce babies. It was a switch in emphasis from the sexual to the nurturing role, to the immaculateness of motherhood, that is, to childcare and "family values." The idealizing of a nurturing motherhood was part of the patriarchal-monogamous family package. It was part of the long religious evolution away from the polygamous matrilineal system because the new way had become essential to the forming of government and the success of society and civilization in general.

While Christianity began during the first century CE, it had taken until about 350 CE before half the people of the Roman Empire had converted to it. With the opportunistic conversion of Constantine and the imposition of the Christian faith on the whole Italian Peninsula, the earlier Christian ten percent of the population swelled to a majority. The mere appearance of Christianity did not, therefore, end the Greek-Roman or Hellenic civilization. It ended with the conversion of a majority of the people and their takeover of power. That is the defining point when the cult of Jesus became a mainstream WV system and the beginning of the new society and its civilization.

After the conversion of the majority to Christianity, the old Greek-Roman temples were ordered torn down as non-Christian polytheists rioted in protest. The minority upper Roman class dwindled in number and wealth. Just before 500 CE, the last remnants of the class disappeared during a final wave of rioting and looting. The Greek-Roman WV system fell to the status of a minority cult. Its society and civilization had ended.

twelve --- CHRISTENDOM

From the very beginning, and as the world's newest, mainstream WV belief system and society, "Christendom" became split into two ideological parts to become what developed into the Catholic Western half centering in Rome and the Greek Orthodox Eastern half in Byzantium. The divided society was not reunited until Western arms had, by 1700, recovered the Eastern part from Muslim WV-based Ottoman Turkish control.

We first take up the Western, Catholic Christian WV-based part of Christendom that had begun about 350 CE. By about 500, Christianized Rome was no longer able to sustain the Empire, and was overrun by Normans, Goths, Vandals and other mono-mate barbarian WV-bonded people. As had happened in Egypt, Mesopotamia and elsewhere before, the barbarian conquerors converted to the patriarchal-monogamous WV of their subjects. The barbarians liked the brutal god of the Old Testament's first books and gained prestige by taking charge of "His" mighty empire.

In the early centuries, the barbarians merged their ways with Roman custom and law. Even so, Hellenic art and most science died with the decline of the Roman aristocratic class during the 4th and 5th centuries. The artistic culture established during the civilization's Formative Age largely grew from the mono-mate barbaric WV system's folk culture. The barbarians learned from the Roman Catholic clergy, but absorbed and modified it to suit themselves. The new society did not even adopt any of the Hellenic WV system's cultural heritage until a thousand years later.

The Roman Empire had been united, but Christianity was not. In the 3rd century, the Church was mired in such disunity that even Rome itself had two separate Bishops, each in charge of his own Christianity. By the 4th century, Bishop Epiphanius of Salamis, Cyprus, listed and described eighty different Christian heresies. By 350 CE, under Emperor Constantine, the Roman Church aggressively restored unity, but in the next forty years, in those parts of the Near East over which the Christian-secularized mono-mate barbaric WV-bonded tribes had no control, the dividing of the Christian WV had turned into a shambles of about a hundred and fifty-six heresies all launching vile verbal attacks against each other and conspiring with lies and intrigue to steal members from each other. Wherever it spread in the rest of the Near East, each ethnic group reshaped it to produce yet another heresy. There appeared the Iconoclasts, Nestorians, Donatists, Coptics, and the Samaritans as well as the Montanists, Chiliasts, Pelagians, Arianists and many others.

In the Near East and outside of barbarian control, the diverging, squabbling Christian sects were evoking derision among believers of the other faiths. Even in an age of warrior kings and father-gods, the too-tolerant clergy of such a disjointed and effeminate faith had no way to forge unity out of their system's debilitating diversity. The Near East Church could not help a dividing and decaying world because it could not even help itself. For more than five hundred years, the divided Christian WV in the Near East barely survived as a society.

The barbarians had no understanding of writing, no concept of employing accounts, planning and investing in agriculture. They were not familiar with written law and land title. Church influence was essential, but the Church was not in control, and the barbarians were slow to learn from a Church they considered to be too effeminate. The breakdown of Rome's "brutalized" society had turned the masses of people back to the various new fem-fertility-like cults, including Christianity, ones tainted with the less harsh brush of the Mother Goddess. Unlike the brutal Old Testament Judaic tribal god, St. Paul had gone out of his way to picture a loving god who wanted his people "saved" by "turning the other cheek." His vision of a suffering Cross-crucified, nurturing Christ-God who preached humility, love and compassion was a vision that appealed to the masses. It was the old Gnostic concept of the Mesopotamian WV system and of the aesthetics' original "Paradise State" in which mankind was created as uni-sexual beings. Before the barbaric conquests, Christianity had regressed so far back to the fem-fertility-like WV way that priests had taken to wearing dress-like, emasculating, garments, and so many men were castrating themselves that the practice had to be outlawed by the Council of Nicaea in 325.

Understandably then, the tough and brutal barbarians adopted the Roman political system and disdainfully left the clergy in charge of morals and belief. They jealously guarded their political control as being the "nobility whose rule was ordained by God." The Church was never able to gain complete control of society. It later managed to come very close, however.

Learning to deal with the barbarians was not the Church's only problem. Another was that so many of the scriptures were unclear. One author recently compiled a list of 5,500 puzzling doctrinal questions that frequently come up. In another reference, the editor compiled eleven questions from Genesis alone to which the scripture gives both "yes" and "no" answers. Intelligent people wondered why an all-wise and all-powerful God made "His Word" so confused, so inconsistent, and unclear.

From the very beginning, the early Church struggled with the inconsistency problem. The Bible had so many of them because there were so many different books by so many different authors. There were thirty nine-separate Old Testament books, plus some thirty-eight more that were ultimately rejected by the church. There was also a proliferation of New Testament gospels. The task of integrating all that mass of material in a logical and reliable way was beyond Church ability. The total had risen to more than two hundred and twenty separate gospels, epistles, and acts composed by a bewildering number of separate, often unknown, authors. Out of all that, they had to decide which should be included within their Catholic Bible. In 1943, more than fifty Christian gospels were found in Nag Hamada, Egypt. Not one of them was in the Bible; they had all been rejected.

An even worse problem was what to do with the scriptural pieces that were left. From one book to the next and from one end to the other, there were inconsistencies. More than 175 of them came close to being direct contradictions.

In order to be regarded as "Truth," WV systems need to be at least somewhat self-consistent so the WV could reasonably pass for a closed system of thinking. To that end, the Church tried to reduce the inconsistencies by excluding the more inconsistent, hence more spurious, gospels from the official list. The more it excluded, the fewer inconsistencies were left, but they could not remove all of them without eliminating the Church itself. More than one hundred and fifty-four of the gospels, acts and epistles were eventually eliminated from the official canon with only the remaining eighty being incorporated into the Catholic Bible. Fourteen more books were removed later to become the Protestant Bible.

Yes, there are different Bibles. Besides the Protestant Bible, there is the Catholic Bible, the Eastern Orthodox Bible and the various Coptic Bibles.

Even so, there were still too many inconsistencies and unanswered questions. If everyone got different answers to questions about the faith, a host of important questions had to be left unanswered. Why did the Old Testament's tribal god, Yahweh, do such a poor job creating us that we had powerful temptations to do things he did not want us to do? People wondered why the world did not end and Jesus did not return soon as he said he would. Why do the scriptures show Jesus' descent from King David through Joseph when God was supposed to be his father through his mother Mary? Does the Virgin Mary respond to prayer as if she were a personal, omnipresent Goddess? And if we are to "turn the other cheek" when struck, why did the Apostles wear swords as the gospels indicate? Did Adam and Eve have navels? How did Moses manage to describe his own death?

The questions seemed endless and the answers even more so. Some of the questions could not even be given "yes" or "no" answers. No unity would have been possible if everyone had been allowed to have his or her own interpretation. The only solution was for the Bishop of Rome to become the "Holy Papa" or Pope, and mass enough power to become the infallible judge of what the Holy Scriptures meant to say. So, the Bishop of Rome did became "the Pope," and the one alone who decided what the Bible meant. ("The Roman Church has never erred, nor will it err to all eternity," Pope Gregory II). From then on, the Church actively discouraged ordinary Christians from reading it. The Orthodox Church, centered in Constantinople/Istanbul, consists now of only one seventh of all Christian believers.

The Pope also had another reason for taking the Bible away from the people. Was everyone *really* supposed to wash each other's feet (John 2:1-11), drink wine (Mark 16:18), play with snakes (Mar 16:18), and drink poison (Mark 16:18)? Moreover, Church authorities discovered that there were tales in the Bible about Abraham pimping for his wife to save his life and making so much money from it that he became rich (Gen 12:11-13:2), about naked and drunken Noah being seduced by his daughters (Gen. 9:20-24), the offering of Lot's daughters to be raped by a mob, the erotic songs of Solomon (Sol 7:2-7), references to "piss" and defecation (1 Kings 14:10 and 11Kings 18: 27), the rape of King David's daughter by her half brother (2 Sam.13), devil-worship (Rev. 13:4), goddess worship (Jer., 7:18, 46:17-19, 25), grotesque threats coming from God (Zech. 14:12-13 and Deut. 28:53-55), seductions, fertility rites, child-abandoning, and human and animal sacrifice (Deut. 13: 13-19). Although these stories often involve significant parts of Biblical history, they were really not fit for Sunday school or to be read from the pulpit. Later, one 15th century Pope even set out to sanitize the Bible by censoring it!

He was replaced because it was unnecessary. The Bible had been taken away from the people.

There were still other problems. Both Judaism-believers and "pagans" alike were ridiculing Christians for claiming their faith was monotheistic. To deflect this criticism, Church elders began a several-century-long metaphysical effort to resolve the "three-god problem." All their intellectual machinations were finally concluded by the end of the 4th century when a consensus was reached that there was only "the One God essence." It was supposedly made up of "three persons," one being Jesus, the second being the Father (of Jesus) and the third being a God who was not Jesus or His father and who was called "the Holy Ghost." The faith's failure to be a true monotheism did not deter the commission from officially concluding that they had "solved the problem." So it was "officially" declared that the faith was a "monotheism" and, in that way, the faithful were satisfied.

The rest of the world, however, still asked how three gods could be one, especially since there were actually *four*. The Old Testament had transformed the Persian "force of chaos and evil" into "Satan," even referring to him as a god (II Corinthian 4:4). Also, there was the Virgin Mother Mary goddess who was believed to be omnipresent and to at least intercede in response to prayers. Praying to her was an important function of the Pope. The four gods consist of Mary, Jesus, Jehovah, and Satan if we just skip that ephemeral entity, the genderless "Holy Ghost." The reincarnating of various gods into a single one does not make a monotheism.

Even so, Christianity was still far less *in*-accurate than the old polytheistic WV systems with their thousands of gods. Islam is also less than a monotheism because it teaches the existence of Satan, angels and demons. Moreover, Mohammad, was claimed to have made a visit to heaven and of being "perfect." That warrants his stature being labeled at least "divine." Nevertheless, Islam is, of course, the least polytheistic of the old "spirit"-based mainstream WV systems (Judaism and Sikhism are not mainstream). In order to be as accurate as possible, the mainstream WV systems of the Christians and Muslims are generally referred to here as "near monotheisms."

After the break up of the Charlemagne Empire, Europe disintegrated into an amorphous mass of small, independent, agricultural communes. Lacking effective government, the rural communes were vulnerable to the deprivations of Kurgan-like gangs of lawless thugs. By the ninth century, the farming communes were no longer willing to put up with the constant incursions. During the following generations, all proceeded to submit to the authority of one or the other of the gangs in exchange for protection. Thus, egalitarian communes became manor communes under warlord control and the Formative Age ("Dark Age") gave way to the Feudal Age.

In the Feudal Age, a farmer could point in any direction and know he was pointing towards another manor controlled by a group of brutal rapists and killers. He knew that his own gang was the only protection he had from them coming over, raping his wife and stealing his tools and food. In order to keep his own thugs there to protect him, he was resigned to regularly turning over to them a large share of his communal labor, his respect, and his obedience so they would stay and protect him. In such a way, feudalism was instituted because it was better adapted to the conditions of the time than the egalitarian communal disorder it replaced. All social-political systems arise to serve the purpose needed at that time, and all of them change when new needs arise. There is no ideal system, and no system is better than the others except when it is needed.

The Western feudal system arose about 850 CE and came to acquire the full support of the Church. The rule of the new military caste became "decreed by divine right." A ladder of allegiances developed from the farmer on up to the top man in the military caste. This incipient chain of command later grew until there existed a monarch in the Roman style, that is, a king. Thus, there was a king of the Franks, a king of the Goths, of the Ostrogoths, Visigoths and the no-goths (my apologies). In the feudal manor, the lord controlled the communal lands, the wine press, bridges, the bake-oven, the mill, breeding bulls and even the communal mess hall where the people ate. Feudalism had instituted manors, but the manors were still communes. The Abbeys were also communes. The manor lords "owned" everything in the same way that "the gods" owned everything in the Sumerian city-state communes. In other words, a feudal hierarchal military caste system was superimposed on the communes, but the European feudal system's Formative Age still remained communal, hence *communist*.

Social theorists do not refer to the Marx-based WV systems as "religions" or even "secular religions." For social scientists to refer to the Marxist system as a world view (WV) or religious system instead of an economic system would antagonize and cause dissension with their

Marxist colleagues. Marxist scholars idealize an egalitarian communal society and cannot accept that communism has to become hierarchal in order to function in large systems. So, to avoid controversy, the European Feudal economic system is designated as *feudalism*, not communism, while the feudal term is otherwise used for *social-political* systems. Also, because Marxist ideology had idealized communism, people took to calling it "Communism," not Marxism. That enabled Marx's philosophy to exist in an "ivory tower," well separated from the practical application Lenin and Mao were desperately trying to make of it. In all such ways, Marxist scholars were placated and the turmoil between them and the capitalist economic consensus has been minimized.

Feudal communism still had one serious flaw. It gave the lords a vested interest in keeping alive the constant threat of war. Even so, the system did encourage each member of the feudal commune to feel loyal to the manor and its territory, and to help defend it. It was the same territorial-type loyalty that would later be broadened and transferred to the national states during the Crusades.

In such a brutal world, the effeminate Church strove to gain more power. To do that, it had to harden itself to the way of the barbarians. The meshing of the incompatible, of Christian pacifism with barbarian militarism, took a full millennium. It started in the 5th century when the Bishop of Rome recognized that killing in battle and executing were legitimate undertakings of the Christian state. Thus, there came, in time, the bloody conversion of the Saxons, the emergence of Charlemagne's empire, and the Crusades with each being sanctioned by the clergy.

The temporal power of the Church increased along with its ruthlessness. By 880, the Roman Pope had his own national state, also his own army and navy. Papal justice was, as elsewhere, brutally harsh, with serious offenders being tortured and and then pulled apart by horses. During the Crusades, the Pope had his own Knights Templar, an international expeditionary army of conquest that was under his direct command, an army which once even conquered Byzantium. All over Europe, people were traveling to the Papal Court in Rome for decisions. The Guelph Party of the Pope came to exert political influence and sometimes control throughout all of Christendom. The Pope even grew able to remove the "grace of God" from any individual, including kings, and, by placing an anathema (curse) on them, deprive whole regions of all intercourse with the rest of humanity, a practice even worse than the modern imposition of "economic sanctions." The drive to acquire barbaric power was succeeding.

The Papal state built up in size until it comprised all of central Italy. In the 16th century, it was ruled by its warrior Pope, Pope Julius II (1503-1513 CE). In full battle armor and with a sword in hand, for example, he led his troops through a breach in the fortified defense of French Mirandola, then under siege by the Pope in a war for the Papal empire. The Pope of Christendom and Christendom itself had by then attained their peak in barbaric power.

As the Crusading armies poured out of Europe, the exposure of the Christian barbarians to the much-more-advanced Islamic civilization hastened the social evolution of Christian society. A European intellectual-cultural infusion occurred, and Europe became ready for civilization. The creative flowering of civilization, however, finds hard going when held back by feudal political and communist economic institutions. Old institutions had to change.

Because of the Church's ruthlessly enforced unity, direct contact with Islam made the European barbarians conscious of being part of a single Christian people in a world of overly humane, pleasure-loving "infidels." The kings gained power as they helped to gather the feudal lords together and lead the Crusading armies. In that way, the Crusades expanded the territorial horizon of all classes. They also served to increase Church power, but the real payoff was to the society. The Crusades changed the people's vision of their family-troop-world by moving the mentally perceived borders of their little manors to the mental perception of their vast single-language kingdoms. Their perceived borders then came to expand further, even to extending around the whole of Roman Catholic Christendom itself. This all meant an expansion of the size and strength of the Christian WV ideological bond to the point of binding the whole of Catholic Christendom into a single, though politically amorphous and politically decentralized, family-troop society. The tight family-troop system of the barbarians had finally been absorbed by the Christian faith and turned into a militant and aggressive (barbaric) universal-brotherhood WV belief system. That meant that Christians had expanded their sense of territory into a single, whole society housed in what then became the world's prime breeding-ground domain, all of which was headed by the Pope.

A vivid characteristic of the theocratic, Formative Age was the building of great cathedrals in Europe. These amazing edifices compare in significance to the great pyramids of Egypt, Sumerian ziggurats, the mosques of Islam as well as the early temples of China, Indochina and India. They were built by free men freely giving their labor in a cooperative effort directed by respected leaders. Indeed, nearly all the great monuments of the human race were begun by societies during their theocratic age.

The direct result of the Crusades' strengthening of the social bond was a precipitous drop in the frequency of feudal wars. As warfare diminished, communications improved, leading, in turn, to further political unity and the increased power of the kings at the expense of their feudal warlords. The decline of warfare, in turn, facilitated all the accouterments of civilization. Trade routes grew, villages became towns, and towns became cities. Feudalism was on the way out. Population growth accelerated between 1100 and 1300. The Crusades played an essential role in establishing internal peace, increasing agricultural production, and the subsequent growth of population.

Europe was still communist except for Spain and the Italian city-states. Even the building of towns did not at first bring an end to communal ways. The towns themselves became communes. Even after the town communes were broken up, the crafts still had their own labor and management communes known as "guilds." Thus, communist ways persisted even as capitalistic ways spread. Economic and social institutions evolve slowly as the need changes. Every system is the "best" when the shape of society changes because it needed to change.

The old cultural ground areas of Italy and Spain had been capitalist from the days of the Roman Empire. They gave leadership to the rest of Europe in the ways of the "newer" economic system. The clergy adamantly opposed the expansion of commerce because, even after more than a thousand years of waiting, the Church was still expecting the imminent Return of Christ. Economic growth occurred anyway.

After the Crusades, a lethargic slump set in. First, Europe became aware of a threat from the East where the armies of the Kurgan WV Mongols were advancing. The Mongol army invaded the Ukraine, conquered Kiev and slaughtered its citizens. Then it moved on Vienna. The Mongol armies were set to conquer and ravage Western Europe, but the timely death of the Khan changed their plans. Western Europe was saved.

With the end of the Mongol threat came the Black Death. The dramatic increase in the population of Europe reversed and, by 1350, it was plunging. The bubonic plague so ravaged Europe that the population dropped by more than a third. This led to a mass pilgrimage to Rome. The throng hoped to atone for "their wickedness" so that their god would remove his bubonic retribution. "God," of course, ignored their prayers, and the plague continued. His failure to heed the frantic prayers of a pleading Christianity and Jesus' failure to return as promised served to erode the morale of the clergy. Frustration and disillusionment spread throughout the whole society.

With the collapse of morale, the Church became corrupt. Titles and Church offices and indulgences were all for sale. The clerical consumption of wine was enough for obese and drunken monks to be caricaturized. In 1409 there were three "infallible" Popes all disagreeing with each other. One Pope, Gregory III, brazenly set out to even rewrite the Bible. Although the Popes were considered infallible, he was finally convinced to abort the effort.

Between 1350 and 1550, there arose a bizarre mix of specific decay staining one of the most noble edifice of all Christendom, the magnificent buildings of the Vatican. Great inspiration and progress hopelessly intermingled there with decay and decline. The stain-of-decay part can be detected in the Sistine Chapel scene where Michelangelo painted Adam reaching out to grasp the apple. Adam and Eve are depicted in it as being interrupted from an act of fellatio. The Sistine Chapel was also decorated with the homosexual pornography of the painter and criminal, Caravaggio. In the lower right-hand corner of the Sistine Chapel's "Last Judgment," Satan is depicted as copulating with the Mother Goddess, she in the form of the snake. Even the pagan, Greek-Roman Sun God, Apollo, is depicted in the Chapel.

The short-lived social-moral-cultural decline of barbarian Christendom continued into the sixteenth century and was well expressed in the demonic paintings of Hieronymus Bosch, Jan Mandyn and Pieter Bruegel. Ladies wore masks in public to hide their identity, as do gunmen today. Moral decay was also evident in such great cynical and/or ribald literary classics as Gargantua, Don Quixote, Gulliver's Travels, Canterbury Tales, and the Decameron.

Shortly after 1500, the corruption of the Church led to the Reformation. Martin Luther's protesting against the Catholic interpretation of the Bible broke down the ability of the Church to any longer maintain the society-wide unity of Christian doctrine. The Pope ceased to any longer be the head of all Christendom. Without an official interpretation of the Bible, people were once again free to interpret it in as many ways as they wished. Christianity split into Catholic and Protestant sects and the latter began splitting into other sects. As Catholicism then underwent Jesuit reform, the gross corruption of the Church ended, but the multiplication of Protestant Christian denominations continued, even accelerated.

By 1600, European civilization had taken the lead over the civilizations of Islam, India, Indochina and China. By then, they had all passed their last creative ages and were in decline. An acceleration of European science followed, including the development of the arts. By 1700, there was no other place on Earth as advanced as Europe.

By 1650, Christianity had divided into one hundred and eighty separate sects or heresies. Inter-denominational wars were threatening to tear up Europe and break it down again into a plethora of tiny kingdoms. France, for example, was in danger of being split into a Calvinist kingdom, a Catholic kingdom, and a Lutheran one, each with its own monarch and army. New political doctrines were needed that could bridge the religious gap between the states and prevent the impending political disintegration of all Europe. There needed to be a separation of church and state. It became essential for the European "kingdoms" to become "nations," that is, to become non-religious entities.

The biggest obstacle to church-state separation was the doctrine that the kings ruled "by (God's) divine right." "Not so," Niccolo Machiavelli (1469-1527) stated, pointing out that power actually arose from the machinations of princes. The legitimacy of "divine right" was weakening and the rule of kings could begin to be seen more objectively.

Along with the developing of national states came the reawakening of the old Greek ideals of the Republic to replace the monarchical system, and representative republics began to replace the rule of the king. In some cases, such as with Napoleonic France, the sovereignty of the lower classes was represented by an autocrat of the people, but the trend was towards secularized governments constituting a balance of powers, that is, with the president balanced by the legislature, both balanced by the judiciary, and, later, all watched over, at least theoretically, by a professional, independent media. It was a system that tended to restrain any single individual or faction of a divided society from gaining complete control.

As always, the change entailed a trade off. By its nature, a "balance of power" facilitates the unrelenting expansion of bureaucracy. It also leaves an emotional vacuum because the instinctive primate affinity for strong family-troop leadership is poorly satisfied, especially in time of threat when people lean towards a powerful leader. Otherwise, they subconsciously feel insecure, a sort-of emotional deficit, which they tend to sublimate into a common, doctrine-based railed against "kings," and then against "dictatorships," even as kings are kept as figurehead rulers.

In a society rent by division, a concentration of power in the hands of one man had, indeed, becomes dangerous and rarely beneficial. Dictators have generally become corrupt because, regardless of their speeches, and the platitudes in them that replace substance, such leaders in a badly divided WV system no longer feel an adequate sense of responsibly for the welfare of their country. Living in a large and divided community entails the loss of the deeply longed-for family-troop feeling of "oneness" with one's vast brotherhood of fellow believers.

At least, some of the loss could be compensated for. New ideals arose to bridge religious differences, ones that needed to be regarded as "eternal truths." It was largely John Lock who achieved that by proposing "freedom" and "rights," even the right of rebellion. As with most ideals, it had its limitations. Later on Vilfredo Pareto (1848-1923) pointed out that "freedom" and "rights" balance each other out. An example might be that if you have true "freedom," then you have the "right" to smoke even when others have to inhale it too. No society could ever exist in which people have the "right" or "freedom" to do anything they want.

Since the unity of the religious beliefs had been lost, the more selfish, relative worth of the individual became what was next idealized. "Individualism" and "free will" then became part of the newly developing secular ideological system. The ideal of "democracy" became the paramount goal with the rise of the United States, even though it was a republic. During the Constitutional Convention, James Madison specifically stated that their objective was "to protect the minority of the opulent against the majority." Not until the 3rd and 4th presidents, did the underclass manage to gain enough power to protect its own interests. It has been referred to as a "democracy" ever since. In 1787, Alexander Tytler wrote: "a democracy will continue to exist up until the time that voters discover they can vote themselves generous gifts from the public treasury . . . with the result that every democracy will finally collapse due to loose fiscal policy, which is always followed by a dictatorship."

Even as the secular nation concept caught on, the disunity of Christianity's WV was still building resentment towards those who interpreted the Bible differently. For all to live and cooperate within the same nation, still other doctrines were needed so that resentment could be kept minimal. The solution was for being humane and tolerant to be idealized. In all such ways, the denominationally divided nations of Europe managed to idealize a path to survival, even if not always peacefully.

With the help of Adam Smith (1723-1790), capitalism had long since fully replaced Feudal Age communism. Implied in their new economic system was, again, the doctrine and ideal of "serving the needs of the individual in a way that also serves others." Later, Marxist ideologues waged a century-long struggle to reverse course and bring back communal living, but it was a call to regress. Marx did, anyway, succeed in making capitalism a controversial subject. So, in difference to Marxist ideologues, it became expedient to avoid the term "capitalism"and use such flattering but cumbersome designations as "the free market," "individual initiative," and "free enterprise systems."

In the end, the list of secular doctrines came to include those of "rights," "equality" individualism, humanism, tolerance, freedom, democracy, the "free enterprise system" and science. The whole list was worked together into a nearly closed ideological system. The development of the secular system was subconscious because no one wanted to know they were creating a new ideological WV just to solve European political and social problems. Later, the secular ideology sometimes came to be referred to, appropriately, as "Secular Humanism,"although the term makes most people uncomfortable. People would rather feel they were discovering "eternal" or "self-evident truths." After all, since all the "born-again" Christians claimed to have "the Truth," so scientists could hardly admit they did not have it. Even though abstract truth is a totally unreal concept, the science-minded made the scientific method and the "laws" of science into "truths" and added it to the other secular doctrines. Thus, the new ideological system came to be regarded as "the Truth." "We hold these Truths to be self-evident . . ."

The scientific age

Secular Humanism had ended Christianity's supreme role as the total bond of the society, bringing the Christian theocratic age to an end. The old faith was beginning to show its age, and science was playing the major part in doing it. Science had arisen from a movement of nobles to explain what Christianity did not explain. It evolved into a whole new manner of thinking in order to correct even what Christianity did explain.

Science became so successful that science-minded intellectuals even came to believe science secularism could replace Christianity entirely. To that end, from the 16th to the 19th centuries, notable intellectuals used the light of new scientific discoveries to attack old Christian doctrines. By 1725, the attacks had reached a crescendo as Christianity experienced the withering assault on "God" and the faith by Voltaire (1694-1778). This was the "Age of Reason," the "Age of Enlightenment." With each such assault, Christian scholars counterattacked with a barrage of publications that were supposedly based upon the "scientific body of knowledge" itself. Still, the role of "God" in the world continued to shrink. After Machiavelli had already shown the way nations were ruled, Giovanni Battista Vico (1668–1744) pointed out in 1720 that even society was created by man, not "God."

The dissension continued. In the 1730s, atheist Denis Diderot led a "truth-seeking" movement to base Western society on a new WV faith of humanism and rationalism, ideals which he and his followers hoped would replace Christianity. The hold of the churches and the European monarchs who ruled through "divine right" had weakened but not as yet been broken. An earlier such attempt by Descartes had also failed, just as did the efforts of Diderot.

People such as Edmund Burke (1729-1797) and, later, Gustav LeBon (1841-1931) worried about the effect the scientific revelations were having on their society. They had seen the bloody aftermath of the French Revolution, including the massacring and actually even some *eating* of the nobler members of the cultured classes and the bloody work of bomb-throwing anarchists during the century that followed. They had also seen how the American colonies had the effrontery to revolt and create their own nation, a process that could seemingly lead to the disintegration of the West's whole imperial system. The two grand shocks caused fears that Europe might lose its world-empire and collapse into bloody revolution and anarchy. Astute observers concluded that the battle between secular-science and the church was playing havoc with the very structure of society. It was enough even for non-theist-thinking emperor Napoleon Bonaparte to publicly oppose all efforts to replace the old WV system.

In response, the Christian apologists took courage, and in 1845 they began another vigorous exchange of publications in an impressive defense of their by then ancient faith.

The last climactic blow came around 1850. Auguste Comte brought out the most progressive threat of all to the church. He unveiled a new set of doctrines which he regarded as "the center of a universal system . . of moral, scientific. . .poetical aspect" which he called, *Positivism*. In his work of some 838 pages, Comte attributed a first stage to religion, then metaphysics and finally, his science. His aim was to replace Christianity's big, confused Bible of some 1100 inconsistent pages and usher in . . . a whole new epoch for mankind."

Again, it was hoped, or feared, that the old Christian faith was about to be dropped into the dustbin of history. But could scientists really take over the immense responsibility of operating society without trashing the purpose of science and corrupting its means to achieve it? Besides, the Age of Reason was not seriously altering the common people's devotion to their ancient faith. So, even those who were most friendly to Positivism thought they had better keep their agenda more limited. The result was the move to Positivism failed to achieve significant momentum.

The lack of momentum, in turn, doomed Comte's effort to replace the old faith. Confidence in his effort waned, then the dwindling effort collapsed entirely. It was subconsciously felt that the stakes were too high and that the better and safer course was for the two belief systems be somehow reconcile. In that way, the stage was set for the Western Accord. Public opinion shifted away from attacks on the old "spirit"-based WV system. In turn, the religious community intuitively responded by accepting government as having full secular political (but not moral) authority. This was all made possible by means of a number of subconsciously-made, unspoken compromises. There was no official agreement and nothing was put down on paper. Not being put to writing, it has never been put into our history books. Even so, the Accord is one of the key events in the entire history of Western civilization, as it was to every civilization.

The Accord had come about because it was necessary. So, anything that violated the Accord came to be regarded as "mean spirited," "confrontational" and "in bad taste." Scientists would continue to make discoveries, but lack of verbal restraint between scientists and the church had become taboo.

The effect of the Accord was to shift the focus of social theory towards reconciling science and the old WV religious system. Subconsciously, social theorists were motivated to rework both into a single closed system of thinking, and do it so well that their effort could seep into public opinion without ever being noticed. This meant that the differences between the two needed to be minimized even though the "miracles" in Christian doctrine had ceased to be compatible with science centuries earlier. Reforming the old faith by removing its "miracles" would remove much of its ideological substance. All the Accord could possibly achieve was the illusion of compatibility by compromising both Christian doctrine and social science.

For Christianity to accommodate required it be "liberalized." The result was the creating of "liberal Christians," those mostly of the upper and middle income classes who were skeptical of "miracles" but who, even so, worshiped Jesus in their Methodist, Lutheran, Episcopalian, and other such mainline churches. They eventually came to comprise about half the US population (with the other half almost evenly divided between Fundamentalists and non-theists). By compromising the faith that way and secularizing Christianity, social theorists stripped the "Holy Scriptures" of their supposed inerrancy, and turned the old faith into a pallid, diluted thing. This served to further weaken the social bond, demote its moral authority, and encouraged the growth of materialism, sensualism and crime. For almost the next century and a half, Fundamentalist Christianity was left out of Western public opinion or public discourse.

What the compromising did to the old faith was no worse than what secularizing had forced the social theory consensus to do to science. In order for the social, biological and natural sciences to appear reconciled with even a liberalized Christianity, social theorists had no other recourse than to use the twenty-one stratagems listed in the Appendix. No social scientist wanted to know he was compromising science, so the effort had to be surreptitious; it had to be entirely subconscious.

The Accord's reconciliation process continued for the next century and a half. The social theorist/secular and the old "spirit"-based WV and way-of-thinking were both seemingly fitted together. The illusion-building process successfully enabled both Christians and science-secularists to have a common public opinion. That, in turn, enabled society to operate satisfactorily as a single "group." The rationalizing had managed an accord even though the two main factions held different, even totally incompatible, beliefs.

The process had been done so skillfully that the compromised secular system even proved capable of also accommodating all other old WV religions of the world. Consensus social theorists had managed to shape the secular ideology in such a way that it could expand across the globe. During the last half of the 20th century, it's spread enabled secularized government to be established in most nations. By taking over this way, the secular WV minimized, but could not eliminate, the world's other WV systems and their inherent divisiveness, nor could it eliminate the burdensome drag on the progress of science inherently connected with the older "spirit"-based WV systems.

The artistic age

The very early sixteenth century beginning of the secular age had started on an ebullient note. Its beginning had meant an escape from what had become the narrow, closed, confines of Christian thought. Escaping from it enabled culture and science to flourish. While the corruption of the church still affected the arts in the more still-barbaric parts of Europe, old-cultural ground Christendom south in Spain, Portugal and Italy reached its short-lived but effervescent Renaissance peak with the sculpture of Bernini, the frescoes of Michelangelo, the paintings of Raphael and the building of the magnificent Saint Peter's Basilica in Rome.

Southern Europe was also at the forefront of both trade and exploration and in the lead, at first, in the conquests and colonizing of Asia and the New World. Later, Southern Europe would be the first, also, to turn regressive and lag behind as the Western Golden Age of Culture spread north and swept across Europe. Its geniuses included, Beethoven, Mozart, Shakespeare, and many others. This four-hundred-year long cultural sweep across the continent finally ended in peripherally Westernized Russia, and there, to die out with the Marx-Leninist Revolution.

As noted earlier, creative, golden age art portrays beauty, elegance and idealism because they expresses the pride and confidence felt by the citizenry. Every mainstream patriarchal-monogamous society has had a creative age beginning when it became secularized. Social conditions have to work on individuals to cause them to be the most creative. The prerequisite is a deep if unexpressed devotion to, and respect for and pride in one's society, a subconscious territorial urge that, both together, enabled people to expand or breach their society's mental and artistic borders. We are territorial animals and when the individual feels himself to be an inviolate part of society, more outstanding people need only to have the freedom to be creative. The Alphas have their political-economic territories; but society's non-alpha genius shows up in its science and artistic creativity.

Our territorial intent is an instinctive-emotional and marginally-more-male intent to feel fully oriented within the group's (society's) borders and want to breach or extend them. The actual border checkpoints on maps are only the "officially" recognized physical borders or territorial limits. Breaching all the society's borders and expanding them is an instinctive more-male intent, a sort of spatial tool intimately connected not only to war and private property but also to creativity and instinctively connected with *curiosity*, with the desire to learn. It is a mostly-male-minded sense of wanting to learn "where the something is which limits who, what and where we (society) are." When acutely conscious of their society around them and being part of it, they sense every and all physical and intellectual limitations and borders to it as challenges to be overcome, even to wanting to hurl themselves against them in order to push them back. So it is, that with power, curiosity, creativity, courage, determination, and self-less integrity, mankind has pushed forward his cultural heritage by progressively pushing against every conceivable border in every possible direction by whatever means it takes.

Thus, mankind's territorial nature is not limited to the conquering of new lands, but more importantly to the breaching of such other borders as those to human understanding and artistic creativity. In united, healthy societies, more men become dominant and, hence, they feel a deep and sincere sense of responsibility toward their society. They become ambitious to make it dominant by extending its limits or borders, including those that separate the old arts from better art and the the old and less accurate "science" from more accurate science. Each such male territorial-sense-caused step in improving our understanding, both of ourselves and the universe, is a break through that border, a breakthrough that pushes back the dark, primordial mist and murky chaos separating what we think we understand from what we need to understand. True scientist-barbarians have the Kurgan-like will to extend human understanding beyond what the reactionary faithful still fill with imagined chaos and old-religion "spirits." Science is the supreme human achievement.

None of this is exclusively male because all traits are shared by both sexes, but each sex has an edge over the other in the many and various human traits. There is no equality between either individuals or the sexes; all are different. It is just that all people deserve equal opportunities, also that both sexes, including the little differences in the way men and women think, are both equally important to the survival and future of the human race.

The empire

The expansion of Christian-Western imperial power was not the pallid thing conjured up by the word "colonialism." Even the so-called "colonies" in the New World were merely extensions of the Western Civilization's Empire over subjugated indigenous people. Besides, Europe did not colonize much of its empire. Europe controlled the world, but every powerful mainstream civilization in history conquered other people. The Western Imperial Age differs from the others only in its immense size, having ruled over all the other old mainstream societies. The possessing of empires has not been something "bad." They all served the vital function of spreading the creative age advances of one civilization to the older ones that had stopped progressing. Western, Christian, civilization has been particularly effective in that.

But civilization follows a cyclical pattern. Christianity was losing what was once its barbaric vitality as it regressed back almost to the original and overly feminine WV and way-of-thinking of St. Paul. The continued dividing and weakening of the social-ideological bond led to the end of the great classical-romantic age in the arts. After the Russian Revolution, the West's newer grand-style music became dissident, painting became impressionist, sculpture became abstract, poetry became petty, architecture became functional, and literature evolved from quality to quantity, all of which was welcomed because people were losing the pride they once felt in their society.

The aggressive American expansion into its frontier ultimately served to invigorate the whole WV system and its civilization. The US replaced France as the center of the new secularized society and everywhere people became oriented to the US Constitution and Bill of Rights, to the hallowed "sacred scriptures" of Secular Fundamentalism. The nation's growing wealth and power also tended to add appeal to its secular enforcement, all of which made the US the revered "sacred center" of the civilization. Being able to bond with all the other unscientific "spirit"-based WV systems, the US secular WV formed a common unifying thread connecting all the other religions and forging them all into an adequately united whole in the form of the "Global Community of Nations," the United Nations, and the multinational corporate world economy. All over the world, businessmen learned to conform by wearing business suits, and (ideally) following the same business rules. Everywhere people learned to sit in chairs, shake hands, eat with metal tools, use flush toilets, and speak English.

The Christian WV has, even so, also expanded around the world, especially in places where their own faiths were more primitive. In Vietnam, regressive Christianity spread as worship of the Virgin Mother Mary Goddess. In India, it became a faith that freed people from the karma of caste and directed them on to Nirvana. In Sub-Sahara Africa, more than thirty-three thousand different Christian denominations sprang up, each led by a charismatic leader who had "talked personally with God." In the Chinese world, the role of Jesus was to protect worshipers from "ghosts." Christianity has become whatever people want it to be. Even the Catholic Church gave into "Saint" inflation, and canonized more people in the last quarter of the last century than in the whole previous two thousand years.

With the help of its old-religion adaptive secular ideological system, the United States had managed to replace the European empire with a world organization which it dominated with the help of its European Allies. The US dollar currency came to dominate the international economy, but instead of setting up an obvious empire, the US established a sort of world commonwealth from which, unlike an empire, she seemed to extract no tribute or taxes. However, decades of trade in which she accumulated a huge debt from an imbalance of trade made it uncertain if she would ever be able to repay it in dollars of approximately equal worth. If, as it seems likely, it ultimately turns out that she cannot, the world would all eventually turn out to have been "taxed" and, hence, Western civilization's Second Imperial Age.

thirteen --- ISLAM

In the 7th century, the Byzantine Empire's vast, over-civilized Near East and Mediterranean world was languishing in a state of overpopulation, pressing upon badly managed agricultural systems, cleared forests, over grazed land and depleted soil. Everywhere, Christians were divided into a multitude of sects whose talk about the brotherhood of man was all mere platitude. Their disunited, squabbling world had already experienced more than three hundred years of economic, social and scientific-technological stagnation. The arts had long since slipped into uncreative opulence for the few who were rich. The poor and downtrodden had been promised "salvation" with "The End Times'" climactic termination of the old Roman world, but it had ended three hundred years earlier, and no "salvation" followed. Conditions were miserable, and people were disillusioned. In despair, they rioted whenever they had any special excuse.

In order for the Near East to progress, the people needed to be united; but how could that come about? In the past, barbarian conquests had been followed by conversion and then recovery, but the last sweep of the barbarians had only turned Europe into a mass of hostile Christianized tribes divided into tiny communes and manors. What was needed was a Judaic-based Christianity-like universal brotherhood WV system that was militant enough, like the barbarian WV systems, to be able to impose itself as a sort of revolution on the diverse and divided people of the two continents. It could not work if it were a backward, racist, tribal faith. It needed the barbarian-type, revolution-ability to convert, unify and take control away from a corrupt ruling class so it could bring honest and responsible people into government again.

If such a new WV system could be militant, barbarian-like, and aggressive, it could improve upon the Christian model. It could repress all homosexuality, be more monotheistic and be more consistent with Acts

17:29 in not dealing with idol-crucifixes and all the other depictions of God son-incarnates, saints, and Mother Mary. Such a world-view could be advanced enough to attract people and enable them to bond together into a new, family-troop society. Such a faith would appeal to people enough that they would leave their older and more primitive WVs, such as did the people of Arabia.

Such a faith's Hebrew-tribal-nomadic heritage and its brutal God would help ensure the interest and militancy of the men of Arabia. It would not even be forced to compete with a sea of other less attractive but look-alike cults, as had Christianity. Indeed, it would seem like having no real competition at all. The developing new Muslim WV would need some of the superior parts of the Hebrew heritage and be as group-moral and cosmologically advanced as Christianity was in the 7th century, but without the Church's effeminate and overly-humanist monastic doctrines. From its very beginning, Islam was motivated to distance itself from the chaotic and effeminate nature of Near East Christianity. There, icons of Mary were proliferating, priests were wearing emasculating diadems, men were castrating themselves, and there was not enough discipline to bring about unity.

In short, the need was for a new WV that was able to spread among a people, unite them, and be militant enough for them to conquer old societies and revitalize them, one that needed to be militant enough to be a new form of barbarism, a *non*-racist universal brotherhood form. After all, barbarism had proven to be a major factor in the social evolution of the human race. The civilized Christian world had become decadent and in need of a barbarian rejuvenation, but the then shrinking society had grown small enough that its age of constructive influence was declining. The need was for a universal brotherhood WV type of barbarism that imposed its own system on its conquered people and converted subjects instead of converting to their old and more effeminate beliefs and ways.

Where there is a sociological need, an answer or a supply naturally follows. Just such a WV system did indeed arise in seventh century Arabia. The prevailing belief there, at the time, was a polytheistic, idol worshiping WV system controlled by shamans. Some three hundred and sixty idols representing assorted tribal gods were kept in or around a small cube shaped stone temple situated close to a lone spring *(Ayn Zubayda)* in the middle of the barren desert. The center of the stone temple, called "the Kaaba," was regarded as the compass-aligned most holy umbilical nexus to the heavens and was believed to be guarded inside by a snake, the symbol of the Mother Goddess. Still embedded on one of its outside corners is a dark colored rock, apparently a meteorite, one that was credited with having been sent from "Allah," then one of the ancient WV system's two most powerful male gods. His emblem, the moon crescent, had originally been a representation of the Goddess while the main male god had been represented by the sun. Sharing power with him were three goddesses, including all powerful *al-Uzza*. That was before the combining of both Fem-Fertility and Kurgan gods described earlier.

Apparently, the old Arab WV was in transition. The moon's crescent came to stand for Islam, and the Kaaba became the most revered but least elaborate of all Muslim temples, the new faith's "holy center" where the believing throng mill around it once a year kissing the Kaaba's stone corners. The kissing includes the corner in which the black rock is embedded and which has its prominent oval cleft exposed within a metal frame. The cleft had once widened and then finally split in two. It was subsequently glued and wired back together. Kissing it is an endeared ritual of the Muslim faith. Only out of subconscious tradition has its significance survived so long. Its split is the still-surviving cleft which, in prehistoric times, seems to have represented the Goddess' vaginal entrance.

Both Judaic and Christian beliefs had been seeping into the towns of Arabia, and the people were open to a new and better WV and way-of-thinking. So a new, militant, universal-brotherhood faith did appear, one which was announced as "Allah's message" by an obscure heretical Judaic sect. The heresy belonged to one of Arabia's mono-mate barbaric WV-believing brigand bands, robbery and plundering, as well as trading, still being universal among such nomads. Their Judaic heresy was that of the Hagarites, a Judaic sect that traced its descent from Abraham through Hagar. Its claim to Abraham and hence, to Judaism meant that the Muslim faith, like Christianity, would be based on the old Mesopotamian-Hebrew-speaking tribal legal, cosmological, and historical heritage. Also, as with Christianity, it would develop as a whole new WV belief system.

Among the Hagarite Judaics was a man who stood out from the others and who later grew to be a brilliant administrator and military tactician. Muhammad (570-632) had been a bright, precocious but illiterate youth who had grown into adulthood well aware of the prevailing religious ferment. He first became known as a poet "of great spiritual depth." Later in life, as "Allah's messenger," he passed on numerous and poetic messages that were scribbled down by others on loose scraps of paper. All together, the voluminous exhortations provided people with a system of guidance.

A generation after his death, they were gathered together in some sort of rough order. Known as the Quran, it developed as the new, and updated version of what the Judaic and Christian god wanted with us. But, strangely though, what the "messages" said the god wanted was as different from what the Christian's god was said to want as both faiths differed from what the Judaic god was supposed to want. Unlike more primitive Judaism, its over-all message was for *all* races and people and would spread as a new mainstream WV to bond together the society of Islam.

The Qur'an underwent constant change from the beginning. We know this from a 710 copy, the oldest full copy known. The dot-like parts of its script were absent, leaving many words open to as many as thirty different meanings. As a result, the Qur'an has been translated into the many North African and Near East dialects in a chaotic sea of confused meanings. The process is still going on with, for example, a recent Saudi Arabian-system-backed Wahhabi (Salafi) anti-Western mass produced and jihad-promoting translation which was distributed all over the world at near give-away prices.

The Muslim answers to the Four Question Template mirror those of the Bible, with mostly the same Creation, goals, moral axioms and obstacles to achieving the goals. Like Christianity, it built upon the before-science Judaic foundation of the Mesopotamian civilization's then still-relatively less inaccurate account of the origin and development of the human race. To the Muslims, the old god of the Hebrew-speaking tribes had been so badly misquoted that it took Mohammad to "get it straight." Mohammad had adopted the same stratagem as that of the Christian Apostles in making use of the Judaic WV to the effect that "only I have God's last and correct word." Even in modern times, "new" WV faiths, such as that of the Rev. Moon, are still being turned out based upon this same time-worn formula.

In regard to the "goal(s)" of the Muslim WV, the Qur'an is dominated by *Yawm al-Qiyama,* the "End times" and the "Resurrection," even more so than is the Christian Bible, as in Surah 75, ll.102-7, 43.61, etc.

Dominating the moral means is that people come into the world without the ability to control their own destiny, or to even understand it. As slaves to fate, people needed guidance, and the Muslim scriptures provided it. The good moral axioms and the brotherhood aspects found in many of the Muslim scriptures are pointed to by Western scholars as the reason for the society's thirteen centuries of successful civilization. Rather, the development, spread, and success of Islam was due to human nature when ideologically united, not the integrity of its founder and its "god." Islam sees itself as the correct Judaism by being for universal brotherhood instead of Judaic racism. An objective examination of the Islamic "Holy Books," however, reveals both Allah and Mohammad as being unprincipled killers as in *Sahih Moslim* 3371, 4345 and *Ishaq* 426, 459, 653, 676, 981, etc. Both Allah and Mohammad are shown to be as ruthless as Yahweh and the Abraham, Moses and David "prophets." Moses, for instance, is described in Genesis through Kings 2 as having directed and supervised the enslaving and mass slaughter of some forty tribes, not just the men but their women and children as well. Abraham is pictured as pimping for his wife. His and the other's only virtue being their described obedience and loyalty to Yahweh.

The Muslim faith's obstacle to the good life is supposed to be the same Christian heritage Evil Deity known in the Qur'an as *Iblis* or *Al-Shaitan* (Satan) and a vast multitude of his demonic helpers. The faithful are also directed to oppose "infidels."

While Mohammad was passing on messages proposed by "the one god, Allah," Christians were praying not just to their god but also to Jesus, even to the Mother Mary. They were even beginning to pray to "saints." Muslims saw all that as regressing back to polytheism and were unimpressed with the "explanations" that Christians gave. To the Muslims, it was a betrayal of the Old Testament while Muhammad's messages were perceived as a reform, a "return to a true monotheism."

The first Muslims to convert were other Arab nomadic brigands. They destroyed the old totems at the center of Mecca, tore away the old tribal idols, and covered the ancient polytheistic Black Rock temple, thus preserving it as their "sacred Kaaba." Wherever they were, no matter how far away, they were to face Mecca and the Kaaba, and fearfully grovel on little carpets over the sand five times every day humbly humiliating themselves before awesome Allah.

Islam was motivated to avoid Christianity's weaknesses but in some ways it moved too far. It became a universal brotherhood faith but "brotherhood" did not include "sisterhood," and the women lost most of their ability to influence public opinion. In one of the faith's early battles, heavy losses resulted in a shortage of men. They adopted their four-wife policy as an expedient, one that they should have later abandoned, but did not. They had betrayed the very nature of their own Qur'an which clearly did not propose or authorize more than one wife.

Muslims regard their WV belief system as beginning with Abraham and, therefore, older than Christianity. Yet, Islam's calendar year "one" begins with neither Abraham nor Mohammed's birth but with the latter's takeover of Medina. This is consistent with our use here of the term, *society*. Mainstream societies begin when they have gained *territory*, such as the Muslims did of Medina. That means that their faith before the Medina takeover was, to be literally consistent with our Glossary definitions, only an heretical, Judaic, sect or cult, not a mainstream WV system. It became a mainstream society only during the lifetime of Mohammad, not Abraham. Despite Muslim belief their faith is the oldest, the Christian WV-based society is older because it began, as we define the terms, with Constantine and the conversion to Christianity of the Roman majority some three hundred years earlier.

With the Arab desert brigands converted and in his army, Muhammad and his successors spread their new "spirit"-based WV and way of thinking across the lower part of the northern half of the then-known globe. The Islamic empire grew because it was as revolutionary as it was militaristic. Defending armies were often two to three times the size of the invading Muslims, but the defenders were disillusioned and apathetic, sub-dominant social outcasts, anarchist conscripts, slaves and mercenaries who were no match for the Muslim WV-system's united and inspired warrior-followers.

With the Near East and the rest of the Mediterranean divided by a ferment of almost polytheistic, competing, over-feminist Christian sects, and the "Chosen-by-God" racism of Judaism standing against them, the Muslims swiftly took over and, barbarian-like, rejuvenated the old society. They did not adopt the older civilizations' by then antiquated, multiple "spirit"-based WV systems. Instead, they converted people to their own united new, non-racist, and universal brotherhood faith.

As their system expanded, the Muslims subconsciously recognized the need to ameliorate, to mildly secularize, their WV so it could more readily spread among the people they had conquered. They emphasized their sacred scriptures' brotherhood aspects and ignored the barbaric and more bloody Scriptural parts such as Suras 9.29, 47.4. The Muslim WV system had evolved into a model civilization-building tool.

Persia was one of the Islamic society's first conquests. There, the Arab Muslims picked up the advanced Persian culture, adapted it, improved it, then reimposed it on the rest of the peoples they conquered. (The Persian mainstream WV system has not been covered in this project only because the Persian civilization offers us few new lessons).

Then, the Muslim armies took Palestine away from its Judaic WV-believing people. Because the Arabs considered their faith to be the only true Judaism, they figured that not only Medina but, as well, Jerusalem, were both their "Holy Cities." They built two mosques on Judaism's most "holy" Temple Mount, the elevated "center-of-the-universe-nexus to the Heavens" platform on which once stood the real Temple of Judaism. In one mosque on top of the Temple Mount is the slab of rock Abraham was supposed to have stood on when the Judaic and Christian god(s) supposedly spoke to him. The slab is also what non-deity, Mohammad, was credited with having flown from in order to reach "Heaven" for a visit with Allah and the others.

The Qur'an does not prohibit the use of pictures, even of Mohammad, but Christianity's extravagant use of Mother Mary icons and the many crucifix-idols of Jesus all led Muslims to make such regressive practices anathema. That, in turn, coincided with a fervent iconoclastic movement or reform in Christianity, but one which failed. Islam, however, took the iconoclasm doctrine to such extremes as to seriously impair the civilization's whole artistic heritage. The lack of paintings, pictorial reliefs, and sculptural works, even dance and music, severely limited the civilization's artistic attainments.

Harsh justice was employed to stamp out corruption and crime. The inequality of wealth was reduced and the common citizen had the rights of every man even though non-Muslims were not given citizenship. Successful land reform was undertaken as, for example, in Spain. It also helped that the faith forbid women to display themselves, literally translated, "to draw their garments to themselves," and in that way, keep Islam's male subjects from being too erotically aroused as they have since become in the West. The effect was to constructively focus Muslim men to more idealistic, social, and less sensual ideals and goals. As usual, however, extremist militant fanatics misinterpreted its literal meaning and took to incarcerating women in little tents.

So, hope returned, and the men saw a future ahead and worked together to make Islam strong. It was a new version of the old process of barbarians conquering the declining dynasties of the earlier civilizations. They had "smelled the odor of (social) decay," had invaded, conquered and imposed reforms. Although they were brutal, uncouth, unsophisticated and uneducated, they were, even so, hardy, intelligent, fearless, and eager to learn. Though impressed with the "enlightenment" of the earlier, older civilizations' secular achievements, the Muslim barbarians nevertheless noted the waste, the rank sensualism, and the obsession with material wealth. They also noted the addictions, softness, fearfulness and the "protecting your backside" government way of doing things. It disturbed them and made them feel the need to reform the system they had taken as their own. It was a typical alpha-male way-of-thinking when not negatively conditioned by having to grow up in an over-humanistic, multi-divided, belief-bonded system that had gone effeminate.

In Egypt and through contacts in Spain and Byzantium, the new society adopted what Greek-Roman science had survived. Without setting out to do so, the Muslim faith built a new civilization, just as had all the other patriarchal monogamous mainstream WV-based societies.

Neither Jesus nor Mohammad had given any practical doctrines as to how their society was to be governed. Upon the death of Muhammad, Islam was left without any political plan or formula, without even a means of designating his successor. This ultimately enabled the most significant schism of the faith to occur, the one between the Sunni and Shiites. Since the split ended up dividing Persians from the rest of a more backward Islam, its real cause was more ethnic than political. Because of their rich cultural heritage, the Persians became Shiites, and have always proudly emphasized that "they are not Arabs." So, even from the beginning, militant Islam was unable to maintain total political unity. Since then, many other sects have also arisen. Some Muslims believe in "temporary marriages," a doctrinal regression which honors brief assignations with prostitutes and makes a mockery of even their regressive four-wives Muslim form of "monogamy."

A "religion" is only what its believers believe, not necessarily what its scriptures say. The Qur'an, for example, does not promote slavery, the chewing of addictive khat leaves, "female circumcision" (the mutilation of young women's genitalia), or more than one wife, but all are openly practiced in Islam.

In spreading across North Africa into Spain, Islam converted the Berbers of North Africa, the "Moors," and began a process of conversion that worked southward over the following centuries deep into central Africa. It was unable to spread at first into Pakistan because Hindu civilization was still vigorous there. In Europe, the spread of Islam was halted by the growing strength of barbaric Christendom and by the Balkans-Greek-Christian refuge in Byzantium. It also made no important headway among the Chinese because their civilization was also still strong and creative. None of this was coincidental. The geographic limits to the spread of every civilization were where people still had an effective ideological system of their own. Only when a people's aged WV becomes divided and obsolete do they discover the "truth" in a newer one, all of which explains why all the "spirit"-based WV systems of prehistory had given way to the more advanced patriarchal monogamous ones of Egypt and Mesopotamia, and why all the old polytheistic WV system except terminal Hinduism have also now been replaced in the mainstream.

The Islamic WV and its militant society had a natural aversion to effeminate over-humanism. Due to Christianity having an emasculated clergy, Islam countered by trying to do without a clergy. It's Mosque clergy at first bore no titles, wore and still wear no vestments and are often referred to as "the lay people running the mosques."

Islam was hardly a century old when a secular-type doctrine arose, *mutazilah*. Its acceptance between 750 CE and 950 ended Islam's semi-theocratic age, the shortest one of any mainstream society. An accord was then established that served to prevent a more serious shake up of the society. What followed was a flowering of the art of calligraphy, literature, poetry, architecture and the sciences.

Soon after the secular age reached maturity, the seeds of regression were planted. The earliest sign of religious regression was the appearance of a specialized clergy, the *ulema*, whose function was to codify. They took the injunctions of the Qur'an and turned them into a theocratic legal system. They established the principle that all laws should come from the Qur'an. Since other laws were still needed anyway, the "codifiers" proceeded to make more laws based upon the life of Muhammad. Thus, the number of "sacred laws" proliferated. When they ran out of more laws to make from the life of "the Perfect Messenger," they began collecting them from his successors. Finally, the proliferation of supposedly sacred and near-sacred texts and laws threatened to shamelessly overshadow the Qur'an itself. The proliferation of "sacred laws" was then wisely brought to an end, but the doctrine still persisted that all law should be sacred even though no more such laws were added from the 9th century on. Since new laws were still needed as society progressed, the secular leadership and a secular legal system still survived.

The Golden Age of Islam was from about 700 to 1150 CE. During that time, Islamic society absorbed and improved upon Greek science and Persian culture. The circumference of the Earth was accurately calculated, and it was widely accepted among the educated that it was globular. Ibn Alsatia even developed the Copernicus solar system model two centuries before Copernicus managed to do it. Islam grew to excel in medicine, philosophy and in the science of history, especially under the historian, Ibn Khaldun. Islam also became eminent in geology, mathematics and chemistry. Thousands of fine hospitals were built and beautiful mosques were constructed.

Thus, a new and flourishing civilization arose from the very ashes of the old ones of Egypt, Greek-Rome and Mesopotamia. While Europe was still barbaric, Islam created a civilization that towered above the earlier ones and pushed forward the stock of human literature, architecture, science, and intellectual understanding, all to new heights, as was, also, still happening in China, Indochina and India. In the ninth century, Islam was of such universal power as to demand and get tribute from lesser lands, including from the Pope in Rome.

The first center of this great age was Baghdad. Built beginning in about 750, it became the great metropolis of the world. As the civilization prospered and creativity continued, the political leadership of the men in Baghdad weakened, causing women to feel insecure and needing to assert themselves. In the Quran, women are given the status of prisoners of war and beating them for disobedience is advised, such as in Sura 2.288 and 4.34, but during the eleventh and twelfth centuries, women grew independent and assertive enough that the Arabic word, "naashiz," came to stand for "unbearable womanly disobedience." Due to their pressure, women came to possess more freedom than they have ever attained since, except in some of Islam's more Western-secularized nations today. Nevertheless, a woman's position in Islamic society changed very little in comparison with other civilizations. The four-wife-provision for the wealthy meant that four-mate entourages proliferated as wealth grew. That rapidly undermined the foundation of Islamic society. The lessening number of Baghdad women available to men in the lower economic classes in the 12th century helped create a resentful, restless male under-class which used every flood or fire as an excuse to riot, loot and burn. In this sense, the populace became almost sovereign. Gangs of thieves, a criminal organization of assassins, and poorly disciplined mercenary civil troops competed with each other for control of the streets.

After the 10th century, Cairo grew to compete with Baghdad in learning and prosperity. After 1100 CE however, dissension and division had so undermined the Islamic social bond that both cities fell into decline. Decline spread across the whole of Islam. The rich were living too lavishly. There was extravagant waste and corruption. Social problems were multiplying. The signs of decline become serious enough to cause people to turn back again to Islamic orthodoxy in order to avoid more disorder and collapse. Intellectuals, such as Abu Hamid al-Ghazali, attacked human reason itself in order to restore the swiftly aging faith. The era of intellect, culture, and science passed away.

With the regressive return to the "sacred" fundamentals, it became accepted among Muslims that the mere 77,034 words in the Qur'an were all the language and vocabulary the world would ever need, thus, that the "sacred" texts constituted everything that anyone ever needed to know. Religiosity grew until dogma had regained total mind control. "Higher education" consisted of committing the "Holy Text" to memory. Not only did scientific discovery slow to a crawl, but much of what had been learned was shelved away back in the dark and dusty corners of the mosques where it was forgotten, and where much of it rests to this day.

Barbaric Europe grew aware of Islam's growing softness and weakness. The decline was attracting the predatory nature of the barbarized people of Feudal Age Christendom. The year 1100 began a century of the Christian Crusades. They cut into Islam's trade routes and stopped the flow of badly needed lumber, causing serious economic problems. In those days, almost everything was made from wood. It was also the only fuel Islam had for cooking, heating and smelting, being as important as crude oil is now.

Europe could manage such forays into the Muslim world only because the savage thrust westward by the Kurgan WV-believing Mongols had been diverted away from the destruction of the Slavs to the destruction of Islam. The huge and pompous Muslim armies which set out to turn back the "barbaric hoards" consisted of their then apathetic, woman-less, sub-dominant, resentful and indolent male underclass. The smaller Mongol so-called "hoards" sliced through and slaughtered them.

The Mongol conquests of Islam began about 1220 and continued for the next half century. After that, the parts of Islam under Mongol control warred with each other. Then, in the 14th century, the invasions began again under Tamerlane. Cities were left in smoldering ruins, and great libraries and hospitals were gutted or leveled. In some areas, the barbarians left mountains of skulls. They were trying to kill everyone and turn the land back into the prairies they were used to. They finally gave that up because there were just too many people.

The destruction was so severe and lasting that no significant recovery took place until the fifteenth century. The fact that the Mongols were not a seafaring people helped Egypt and North Africa to hold them off and escape the devastation, but decline had set in there, anyway.

After the scourging and pillaging had ended, a fascist resurgence began with the Islamic empire of the Turks during the 16th century. Turkish Islam expanded into the southeast reaches of Christian Europe and took the Balkans, while Islam lost Spain.

The Turks had taken control of a corrupt and divided society. Soon, they were lamenting that the flow of opportunists from the rest of Islam to their capital, Istanbul, was "filling the city with trickery."

Another new center of recovery for Islam was in Hindu Pakistan. By the 16th century, it had been conquered by the finally-Muslim converted Mongols or "Moguls." Islamic society had taken five hundred years to penetrate deep into India. Only in Northern India, the Indus and some of the Ganges River valleys, had the Hindu WV declined long enough to enable the newer Muslim WV to take hold. The newer society and civilization of Islam spread across only that part of India that had been Hindu the longest.

The spread of Islam by Arab warriors had ended, but Islam still continued to spread. Traders brought it to Southeast Asia where it had replaced Hinduism by 1500. There, it was a less militant form of the Muslim WV because the people of Southeast Asia rejected the system's austere desert-nomadic legacy while keeping some of the richness of their own Hindu cultural past.

Under the Ottoman Turks and the Moguls, Islam experienced another prosperous age even though one that did not equal the achievements of her Golden Age. In Islamic Mogul India, as in Hindu-Buddhist Angkor and in Rome, great building activity took place. Civilizations prosper as they move from a region of old cultural ground to another, but by the time the Mogul dynasty was established in Northern India, Islamic society had already suffered more than three hundred years of decline and religious regression. Even though Mogul India was prosperous, its cultural achievements compared poorly to those of either the Muslim or Hindu WV system's greatest age.

After Baghdad and Cairo had finished their five hundred year rise to supremacy, the scientific, cultural advancement of Islam could no longer be maintained in any region more than a few centuries. Decline began in the Ottoman Turkish Empire in about 1650 and had spread to Mogul

India by 1750. Each time the society's core moved from one region to the next, it lost creativity. Muslim religious regression had brought the despotic character of fascism to the whole society.

During its later age, Islam continued its expansion southward in Africa. Beginning in the eleventh century, it had spread peacefully into the western Sudan where it built the empire of Ghana. Muslim north-central Africa reached its peak of affluence and learning outside of Egypt in the city of Timbuktu. It had spread throughout South East Asia by 1500, but by 1650, even the more recent parts of Islam were in decline. The tide had run its course.

As the civilization of Christian Europe extended its commerce worldwide, it entered its Imperial Age and began taking over and subjugating the rest of the world, including Islam. Along with the spread of Western rule went Christian missionary activity. In parts of the Old World where animism and polytheism survived, the missionary activity was often successful, but three hundred and fifty years of Christian missionary activity in the Muslim world only achieved a partial success in a few regions. Being only marginal successes, such lands proved to be most marred by conflict between the two WV systems during the 20th century, that is, religious conflict that is always been referred to, secularly, as "ethnic conflict."

The modern government of turkey was constituted in 1923. A seesaw of Secular Humanist reform and restoration began, but the principle of separation of mosque and state became firmly established in Islam. Largely because of US pressure, Europe enabled the rest of Islam to regain its independence. The Western concept of the secular nation took hold enough to enable the different tribes and kingdoms to rise out of feudalism and be bonded into nation states, with Turkey setting the example. In much of Islam, however, the American model gave way to long-term, single-party, rule.

Iraq, Syria and Libya adopted a fascist, welfare-state form of secularism. Such systems successfully promoted a fine Western type educational system, but their less-than-impressive secular political doctrines failed to inspire people, making it necessary for their Ba'ath Parties to employ police-state tactics in order to keep control. Even a bond between the three Ba'ath governments proved impossible.

The US-aided-liberation of Islam from the European Empire had brought about a buoyant period capped with the blatantly secular rule of Gamal Abdel Nasser from 1954 to 1970. Subsequently, US support for Israeli and her policies slowed the secular development of Islam, largely ended the faith's short secular recovery and, in some nations, re-accelerating the eight century-long religious regression decline. Some nations have periodically locked themselves totally out of Western secular influence and into the most extreme distortions of historical Islam. This has, each time, frozen them into a form of primitive stasis. They became like prisons, without progress and hope. Women became uneducated and shrouded in little mobile tents. People became slaves to ritual, to the washing of their feet, sinking down on the floor, and muttering the same praise to Allah five times every day. This down-on-the-floor self-degrading ritual is so confining that in the Six Day War, Israeli planes wiped out the whole Egyptian air force while its pilots were "presenting" themselves to Allah. Moreover, throughout all of Islam, business and industry sink for the whole lunar month of Ramadan as people fall asleep on the job because they are up half the night eating and drinking in anticipation of the next day's fast, some even gain weight. In the deserts and tropics, they abstain from all liquids all through the long hot day to "purify" themselves while their sweating bodies accumulate uric acid and other poisons from lack of fluid.

The best that regressive Islam can do with science is to collide with it. Over eight hundred years of Muslim-reacted religiousness has come to mean that anything Western, such as its science and technology, has had to be apologized for. The people believe all their thoughts and actions to be "the will of Allah." It all helps to explain why Arabic lacks even the fundamental terms needed for effectively applying modern science. Lurking behind every effort is fear of being "sacrilegious." Cause and effect become the equivalent of "Intelligent Design." Even though scientific-technological progress is needed to support Islam's irresponsibly burgeoning numbers, most Muslims are more attuned to dismissing science than dismissing their old, pre-Islamic, and animistic superstitions. In July 7, 2001, for example, the Boy Scout's National Committee of Muslim Indonesia hired sixty-five shaman "psychics" to negotiate a peace with the "evil spirits" who, they claimed, inhabited their site.

All the civilizations before Islam began with a long age of theocratic communism and had survived for up to 3,000 years. Islam was the first civilization to spread over old cultural ground and absorb only old and dead civilizations, ones which had, typically, long over-exploited their natural resources. In that, Islam paved the way into the modern world. The whole world is now an over-used and over-crowded landscape filled with ideological enemies with long memories. Islam did not have a two to three millennium growth from a solid base of theocratic communism. It could take over only old cultural ground. And its having the regressive four-wives provision, all explains why its WV had barely a four hundred and fifty-year rise to its peak, and a decline already extended enough that the loss of its society-bonding ability is foreseeable.

PART 3, THE PRESENT ERA

fourteen --- BARBARISM AND MODERN TIMES

Western, Christian WV-based society entered the 20th century with a civil war known as "World War I," a war that led a quarter century later to "World War II," the one that destroyed the world's two latest mono-mate barbaric WV systems. Like Islam, both Germany and Japan had militantly aggressive WV systems, but unlike Islam, they promoted racial superiority, not Islam's WV of universal brotherhood. Western society defeated both racist resurgences of the mono-mate barbaric WV system.

A more significant example of a new aggressive (ambitious) WV system was the successful development of the economic philosophy of Karl Marx (1818-1883) into the first barely barbaric, non-theistic-based, WV system, one which inspired a Revolution and the 1918 takeover of the massive and diverse territory of Russia. Like Islam, the new society's WV was based on a universal-brotherhood form of barbarism, but from the very beginning, its WV was afflicted with defective doctrines and the lack of a number of important ones. These defects ultimately led to the collapse the Soviet and the theocratic-like age of the Chinese Marxist WV-based systems and the establishing of the present system in Asia.

Briefly, the Marx-Leninism's theology answers the Four Question Template as follows:

(1) The answer to the origin question, is that "society began with feudalism."

145

(2) In answer to the goal question, Marx opposed the very basic economic structure of human civilization and proposed a return to primitive, egalitarian communism. The East Asian Marxist WV system still adheres to such a goal even though there is conclusive evidence that huge human populations cannot form and live in such a system. For example, as mentioned before, behaviorists have discovered that most human individuals are unable to have a relationship, even to know or recognize, more than a couple hundred people. People feel more sincere compassion for an abandoned and starving dog than for tens of thousands of foreign civilians killed in our wars because we are biologically tuned to be hunting-gathering size groups. People in "the other groups" were ones we had, and still have, little sincere feeling for. We lack motive to work for their mutual welfare, the welfare of any huge mass of people. The only way the individual can relate to the rest of society and its members is to share with them a common, united ideology, one that can bind them together. Even then, they will tend to break up into hunting-gathering sized Alpha led church groups, clubs, associations, etc. To hold it all together so the whole mass of people can get along and work together to achieve a common purpose, there has to be a common ideology in order to hold it all together. There also has be be government based on that common ideology.

The most important "cause" people have is self-defense. It took patriarchal-monogamous government to enable egalitarian Fem-Fertility system communes to escape from barbarian feudalism. In the same way, Western society needed government in order to prevail over Nazism and Imperial Japan. Without government, such primitive mono-mate barbarian WV-based government would again arise again and re-taking control of mainstream society.

One of the functions of the government is to see that the economy runs in a way that compels the individual to serve his part. The communal ways can only survive when a society or nation is united and run by a respected theocratic-like (single-party) government. When the binding ideology divides and weakens, the communal system also weakens and a legal system is established that enables the individual to serve his own economic interests in ways that benefit the rest, in other words, capitalism occurs. As the ideological division of the society continues and finally collapses into ideological regression, the capitalistic system also fails and becomes corrupt and exploitive.

Socialism and Marxism, or so-called "Communism," are both WV ideologies based on Karl Marx's unrealizable communal goal. The difference is that the Marxists in East Asia have temporarily abandoned the "egalitarian communal" goal. It was discovered after the 1918 Soviet Revolution that the Party could not depend upon the people to cooperate and conform to Marx's ideal even when they were free to do so. Indeed, they failed to even when they were told to. Eventually, the Party discovered that they would not conform to Marx's ideals even when gulaged, starved and "liquidated." To the Party's surprise, the Russian people still wanted to think of their own interests first. Between 1932-33, the Soviet Marxist government tried and failed to communize food production, the most basic and most important industry of all. From seven to eleven million people starved to death or were executed during the experiment.

Unwilling to learn, Mao Zedong (1893-1976) attempted to communize agriculture in China from 1959 to 1962. His failure cost some thirty million more lives.

Socialists, watched the unfolding spectacle, and finally concluded that the communist egalitarian society goal was not achievable after all, so perhaps it could be *near*-achieved with a lot of compromising. Instead of an egalitarian, government-less society, they would accept a "representative democracy." And since the people were divided and still had no interest in living communally, the socialists would just impose their democracy on a capitalistic economy. Thus, "socialism" became nothing more than a capitalistic, parliamentary ruled, welfare state governed by socialist ideologues.

After the humiliating failure of both the Soviet and Maoist agrarian experiments, the Chinese Marxist Party finally came to realize in the 1990s, that they might possibly need to make some changes. Capitalism didn't seem be so bad after all. They saw how Marxist Lee Quan Yew in tiny Singapore had adopted it and transformed Singapore's economy into a vibrant success, and he still managed to keep his Party in control.

The Chinese Marxists decided to do the same. They adopted the political-economic system developed in Singapore. The Party kept its same old unattainable Marxist egalitarian communal goal, but adopted the Singaporean capitalist system as if they could use it to someday reach their Marxist goal. However, they were not inclined to admit they were adopting the very system Marx expected them to rise up against, so they called their "transition-to-communism" form of capitalism, "socialism." Such a subterfuge was not entirely their fault. Even the whole Western world avoids the "capitalism" term because Marx had succeeded in converting enough people to his Economic Imperative doctrines as to make the "capitalism" term unpopular. So, from then on, capitalism became known as "the free market system," "the market economy," and "the free enterprise system."

However, Lee Quan Yew, the Party head in charge of Singapore's success," recognized that capitalism was so effective that he, his Party, and the people of Singapore all lost interest in Marx's pie-in-the-sky ideals. Singapore has long since ceased being a Marxist state.

As the present time, Cuba has the only Marxist government run communal based system. It survives only because of outside threat, the threat of a second US invasion. The gradual subsiding of that threat has made it necessary for Cuba to allow the Church back in and to increasingly introduce capitalist changes in the system. If the perceive US invasion threat is going away, the eroding of the Marxist WV binding power would ultimately end Cuba in a Chinese-Marxist or a non-Marxist Party Singapore type capitalist system.

(3) In answer to the third question, the means by which the people are to work together to achieve the goal, Marx-Lenin and Mao provided their WV system with absolutely nothing. All they could concentrate on was "power coming from the end of a gun" so "the working people could rise up and overthrow the capitalists." That did not well serve as the basis of a society's moral system. Rather, it seemed to promote the idea that "the end justifies the means." At least, that is the way it was often applied. Even the Cambodian Marxists used "the end justifies the means" in yet another innane attempt to apply Marxist theory to agriculture. In the process, the little country took a loss of from one to two million lives. A system that regards its most needed people as "the capitalist enemy that needs to be overthrown by force" tends to subliminally promote violence. Marxist governments can set up legal systems, but if the WV is not based upon a moral code or principle, the citizen has no society-wide moral standards he can use to judge such laws. Legal systems are necessary, but they need to be based on the WV system's moral code, not in place of it.

Perhaps "free love" might be considered a possible Marxist moral means to reach its goals. A "free love" family code system was actually adopted in Russia in 1918. There followed some controversy over how far it was to go. The ideal was proposed that the communal movement should do away with privacy, even of the individual's own body, that it *also* be communally owned. The whole controversy had ended by 1935 with the total restoration of the classic monogamous marital system. Unfortunately, there is no record of how damaging the seven year reign of "sexual freedom" was to Soviet society. Certainly, the thought of taking sexual license during a time when Russia was going through particularly difficult times stirred Lenin's displeasure, even though his mentor, Marx, had been against marriage.

(4) The final Question of the Four Question Template consists of what obstacles the Marxism system must overcome to achieve its goals. Primarily, the system's focus is on the evil of capitalism. It also stands against fascism as well as all other WV systems, secular or religious.

At least, the Marxist WV did succeed in building a society and has changed enough to still survive in a world that needs something far better. It managed to even accumulate a few constructive accomplishments:

First, it promoted the universal brotherhood of mankind. Soviet Marx-Leninism was a true universal-brotherhood WV system because it taught the racial and ethnic unity and equality of all mankind (except capitalists).

Second, it was militant in being ambitious to spread its WV and way of thinking as a revolution throughout the world.

Third, Marxist Cuba has turned out to be the only nation on Earth that managed to deal with its AIDS patients by isolating them when it needed to.

Fourth, Marxist China has been effective in slowing its own population growth.

Fifth, East Asian Marxism has managed to promote the equality of the sexes within a patriarchal system.

Sixth, it developed the militant Party system.

Back in the earliest mainstream societies, male shamans provided leadership, but with the advent of the mother-goddess age, the concept of a priestess-hood took shape. Well into the monogamous-patriarchal age, the concept of the priesthood being effeminate continued, including into Christianity. Then, as Medieval Europeans barbarized Christianity, the Pope set up a masculine, disciplined political party system, the Guelph Party. The militant-monk-type tradition also developed. With the Reformation, secularized Europe began developing masculine-type secular-political parties, the first being in Fascist Spain, that while the Christian clergy system drifted back again into effeminacy. Another step was taken when Marx-Leninism arose and evolved the political party concept into a disciplined male-oriented clerical system. Finally, Mussolini and later Hitler adopted the party's militancy concept and succeeded in over-developing its masculine character.

Seventh, Marx-Leninism is progressive in being non-theistic, and doctrinally antagonistic to all belief in "ghosts," "gods" and "miracles." Mostly because of that, the whole Marxist system's nineteenth century non-"spirit"-based WV is marginally more science-compatible, more accurate and hence, more advanced than all the still surviving far-more-ancient "spirit"-based WV systems. The problem is that its many defects mean it is unlikely to survive long-term. But because of it being non-theistic, it has shown the world that the old near-monotheistic age is over.

Only a new, non-Marxist non-theistic WV system could possibly spread across the world and unite it. Marxism's many flaws make it unable to ever do that. Marx's contempt for "religions,"and his follower's belief he had invented a new science, kept them unaware that its WV system's function was to bond the people into an effective society. They had developed a non-"spirit" religion that so hated religions that its developers were unable to learn from and find out why the old systems, despite being "spirit"-based, still "worked."

Among the most basic intellectual-scientific flaws of the Marxist WV system is its economic imperative doctrine. Ideological systems, not economics, form societies and drive the changes they undergo. All earlier mainstream societies and civilizations except Islam arose with the idealism that then enabled communism to function, but never in an egalitarian form in the mainstream. Every society has to have government. Western civilization began with small communes during the Dark Ages and evolved feudal system governments as populations grew during the Feudal Age. The only "economic imperative" is that they then evolved into capitalism. The type of economic system a people have is the *result* of the condition of the WV belief system and society, not the *cause* of it.

Beside all the system's so-far mentioned defects, one of the strangest and most discreditable Marxist myths is "dialectical materialism" (DM). Some scholars are still trying to make some sense out of it. The original idea of dialectics was extracted from Hegel's ponderous, Appendix-word-trick #9, metaphysical double-talk. Marx, Engels and later, Mao Zedong, puffed it up into a grand, supposedly universal, "dialectical" principle, or process, or law or set of laws.

A rough idea of what DM means is "the process by which something (such as capitalism transforming into "Communism") slips from one paradigm into another or a way to look at such a change." In further explaining this "principle," proponents deal mostly with what to them are "contradictions." Both matter and living organisms are regarded as only transforming from one contradiction to another, the new one, each time, "negating" the older one. Also, everything is supposed to move from quantity to quality, and back to quantity again, back and forth. That means that history is supposed to move back and forth like a pendulum.

In trying to make DM concrete with examples, Engels and his supporters could only come up with banal and obvious "illustrations" which never seemed to clarify anything and which left most analysts frustrated, confused, and still wondering how DM might be usefully applied. It is supposed to prove that the so-called "struggle of the masses" introduces "a new element" into the laws of science, an element that supposedly changes the natural, normal destiny of mankind and provides a new "purpose," "possibility," or "paradigm," one that makes an egalitarian society possible because of changing "human nature" (our instincts)?

Marxist theorists can neither explain DM to each other nor agree upon what it is but they still have faith that it "works." It is just that they are not quite sure how. No wonder Albert Einstein, in June of 1940, wrote in reply to Professor Sidney Hook that he had read Engel's complete manuscript on DM which the professor had sent him and, in the most diplomatic language possible, stated he found it "ridiculous."

A version of DM interpreted by Mao Zedong is still a defining doctrine of the present Chinese Marxist WV and regime.

In brief, such fundamental flaws cannot be rectified, not even by Marxist China's adopting Western secular nationalistic and capitalistic doctrines. Marxism arose with the seeming intention of transforming the world. Instead, it thrives on capitalist-driven consumer materialism. It did manage to show that the Monotheistic Age had ended and that the Non-Theistic Age has arrived, but the Marxist WV is so riddled with faults as to be an offense against atheism.

Leading into the present

The mono-mate barbaric, Nazi WV-based society's war of conquest included an extermination campaign against the much-older racial-tribal type WV system of Judaism. After the Nazi defeat by the combined might of the secularized Christian WV-based society, a huge flood of destitute Judaic WV-believing-people sought refuge outside of Europe. The more affluent, best educated ones were allowed into the US and other industrialized nations. The rest were surreptitiously encouraged to move into Islam, to their "Holy Land" in Palestine. This they did, and since they would have to take it away from the Muslims, the US began extended powerful economic, military and diplomatic support to keep them there.

US support for Israel has persisted even as Israel continued to expand its borders. Indeed, it has no borders other than the extent of what it considers its "Promised Lands," and into which it is expanding at a slow stop and go pace, presently, of just one housing tract at a time, those being in its fortified colonies now known as "settlements." The Judaic WV based system sees its borders as only what faces the sea, and its government operates without a constitution.

Such a picture does not please the Islamic world. Muslims consider the forced-on-them Israeli state to be an offensive, humiliating blot on Islam. This is understandable when you consider their society's long and glorious history, and their having been one of the greatest civilizations on Earth. That helps to explain why they took up arms to defend their society from the invaders, and why their subsequent defeats strikingly compounded their humiliation. With Israel having the full military, economic and political might of the US behind it, they were forced to give up and accept their debasement and disgrace, to face the realization that their whole fourteen centuries of glorious civilization had been in effect, "dragged through the dirt."

They then mostly resigned themselves to their lowered status, although, not without deep, underlying and unending resentment. Men who have been profoundly humiliated do not tend to forget. Insult to an individual's society and its heritage is an insult to the individual. Even as Muslims adopt and adapt to the secular world, most of them doing it successfully, there usually remains that deeply repressed hurt, one that forms into a subtle, suppressed, and usually unrecognized hope for an eventual restitution and revenge. Millions of Muslims live in the US and other Western countries. They have suppressed that resentment and become patriotic and productive citizens. They will stay that way as long as they are not blamed and targeted for the actions of the small number of destructive fanatics at the extreme edge of their faith.

Islam is deeply divided among separate sects, but all resent US help for Israel. Important to keeping that deep animosity alive is the constant flow of Muslim news reports depicting, almost daily, the unending ways the Israeli government harasses, mistreats, even kills, Palestinians. Such news is seldom found in the West's TV and Internet news, newspapers, and news magazines.

In response, the US has periodically placated Islam with show-piece, grandly orchestrated, Israeli-Palestinian "peace initiatives,"ones which have always failed and have no substantial bases for ever succeeding.

Islam has managed to adapt much to Western secular ways, but that adaptation is becoming more difficult because Israel's expansion has always been only at Islam's territorial expense. Worse yet, they now face what looks suspiciously like a US war on Islam, one which appears to them to be on behalf of Israel, a seemingly endless war in which many tens of thousands of innocent Muslim civilians have already been killed and which has managed to set Muslims against Muslims.

Against all this, Islam has no international recourse. The only functional part of the UN is the Security Council and it is dominated by the five nations who hold veto power, one being an atheist China and the other four being the US and three other Christian-Western nations that generally support the US. Even the repressive monarchy of North Korea has the Chinese veto. Islam has neither a veto nor a reliable Security Council supporter.

The long struggle with Israel and the US has steadily eroded the strong instinctive inhibition Muslims, as well as all other people, have against suicide and the murdering of women and children.

Because the American people have become divided and filled with stress, and insecurity. They respond with a "war on terror." The better course could be to give "the right of return" to the Palestinians. They would then vote out the Israeli government and vote in a Palestinian one. Next, they would eagerly dismantle the Israeli-built nuclear arms stockpile so Iran could feel safe and get her economic sanctions lifted by ceasing to enrich uranium.

Muslims are well aware that Israel is led by Zionist militants who promote contempt of the *Goyim* (the "non-Jewish races"). They also know that Israeli Zionism is based on the Talmud and the Torah, and both emphasize and promote the "re-conquest" of the "Promised Land," land which their Yahweh was supposed to have promised them, and all of which lies within Islam.

Ancient texts do tend to be self-*in*consistent and tend to stand against whatever they also suggest or command, but what is stated in both the Talmud and the Torah (the Old Testament, Genesis 15:18-21 and Ex. 23-31) is contradicted nowhere. Their Yahweh is supposed to have promised them all the land between the Nile and the Euphrates Rivers. Some claim that only refers to the land of the ancient Judaic kingdoms, those that seem to have once existed there, but even they are thought to have encompassed parts of Egypt's Sinai, part of Arabia, Jordan, and Syria and all of Lebanon. The Zionists, however, interpret it more literally to encompass half of Egypt and Saudi Arabia, all of Lebanon, Jordan and Syria and the Western half of Iraq.

Muslims tried to defend their society from the alien Judaic intrusion, first with their military might. That failed because the US supported Israel. So, the Palestinians tried the somewhat more Gandhi-like tactic of the *Intifada*. It also failed. Then, concern and resentment built up and has worked to re-shape the Muslim WV in a more dangerous direction. Only in desperation did their militants begin to resort to the forbidden, to terrorism, that is, to the building of fear in the West, especially the US, by killing her civilians, both men, women, and children, even if they, the militants, have to die to do it. Muslims are basically human in the same way are all people. The prospect of Nirvana, Heaven, Paradise or whatever, no matter how it is described, has no ability to take away the desire to live, but enough humiliation and degradation can make any man willing to die to achieve revenge.

Problems with the world order

As mentioned before, the Western secular system adapted to fit a liberalized Christian WV in a way that enabled it to also adapt to the other liberalized faiths. As with all secular WV systems, Secular Humanism has a relatively confused, Four Question Template core. Being more accurate but doctrinally weak, it had to promote tolerance and humanism, not strict adherence to doctrine. When the US grew to be "the spiritual center" of Secular Humanism, it was free to divide and split into a number of single-issue secular cults. The capitalist doctrine split off "Von Mises Libertarians" as well as "Anarco-Capitalists" and public social welfare minded European "socialists." The ideal of Individualism and privacy, that is, the doctrinal hyper-inflating of the loner's ego, split off Ann Rand's cult of "Objectivism." During the last half of the past century, the "liberty-democracy-freedom-equality" doctrines split off a mix of aggressive "entitlement cults," such as those pushing for criminal rights, sexual freedom, vegetarianism, nudism, gay rights, etc. Still other such secular-cult "causes" arose in support of gun-ownership, as well as promoting unisex culture, animal welfare, the ending both capital punishment and atomic power. Considering all this, it hardly seems surprising that there even developed an anarchist "back to nature and the hunting-gathering age" movement called "anarcho-primitivism."

As in all the other civilizations, "women's liberation" was the first secular cult and the most sensitive indicator of a weakening society. Throughout the mainstream, each society eventually became too ideologically divided for men to work together as an efficient team, so their governing suffered. In response, the women, especially in the US, began to pick up on it in the 1800s. By the 1950s and 1960s, the growing social discord accelerated the women's movement. That meant a long, relative decline in the stature of the men. The society they had build was dividing and failing, women were pushing for equality in an instinctive effort to shore it back up. Upon once achieving "equality," however, society is still dividing and, hence, failing. So, and in order to keep trying, women eventually become "superior." In just such a way in prehistory, they replaced the hunting society by turning it into their own gathering-to-agriculture Fem-Fertility one.

Already, women constitute much of the military, women CEO's make more money than male CEOs, most university students are female, and the wife is the main provider in many more homes. The society was ceasing to belong to the Alphas, and by no longer "owning" it, they instinctively came to feel they had less responsibility for it, and therefore, less reason to seek "the greater good." Society had become more like a hunted prey they could use for their own benefit.

The various segments of society have been moving in opposite directions. The US profusion of discontent-caused and ever-more-extreme secular cults has tended to weaken the prestige of the whole Western secular system. In response, social activists tried to reduce the effects of the secular disunity by "educating the public" to the importance of being tolerant and humane. They also promoted the doctrine that each and every view had merit because each of us has "a right to his own opinion." The old saying that "in unity there is strength" was forgotten. Instead, the public was encouraged to "celebrate diversity" because "it enriched the culture."

Even if diversity did enrich the culture, the ideological divide between people still tended to turn political and religious discussion into unpleasant confrontations. Since that had to be avoided in order to preserve public harmony, social discourse took on such neutral, relatively banal subjects as cooking, sports, popular music, and restaurants. Neighbors took to deliberately avoiding contact with each other because knowing the other's beliefs could result in enmity. The media, in turn, shifted to platitudes and what had become "politically correct." The ideological disorder had broken down social intercourse between people on those subjects that were most important to the welfare of all. At the very time people felt isolated by their ideological division and in most need of close and secure social-personal contact.

Without consistent answers to the questions of the Four Question Template, people were corporate-influenced to see the "pursuit of happiness" the corporate retailer's way and began the collecting of "stuff." Being without any other liberalized-secular WV system's central goal, the materialism-focused public turned into "shoppers" and "consumers." Both husband and wife worked to support a material welfare that would be the envy of kings, but to what end? Their lives still seemed meaningless. If their "purpose" was not the illusory Christian "Kingdom of God," was the young individual to look forward to the whole rest of his life with no goal other than the accumulating of more wealth than his friends and neighbors? Was that all? Young and idealistic people wanted a better reason for living. A few resorted to the gurus of Nepal and Tibet, but most sought it in the social science academic consensus popularly known as "getting a liberal education."

However, finding the "meaning" in the "liberal arts" proved to be all but impossible. The foundation of the liberal educational program consisted of conflicting, economic, sociological, psychological, political, and other academic social theories. Students dutifully absorbed what was assigned to them but could not manage to sort out of it anything that could be passionately held. Their liberal education was merely the detailed academic rationale for the Secular Humanism they had been absorbing since they were infants. It only supported its same divided and really not quite adequate secular doctrines. Without the multi-divided and obsolete old religious doctrines, the academic consensus has been unable to supply a consistent, complete and fully viable world-view.

The role secular systems play is only to sustain the old systems by supplementing their most ancient doctrines. They only need to supply a few more accurate, more science-compatible, doctrines in order to help sustain the old WV system for a few more generations or centuries. Moreover, the reconciling of Western secular doctrines with Christianity had to be complicated and confused so that the Accord-caused compromising could remain unnoticed. The task was done successfully enough to preserve the Christian WV-base and, hence, its whole society and civilization.

Both the secular and the Christian WV systems can be expected to keep splintering. All the complex and different ways to believe came to cause the American people to feel stressed, "adrift," "rootless," and "left out." The ideological dividing had lost them the feeling they were still in the family-troop. Then, in the 1960-1970s, the pace of social disintegration picked up with protests against the long and unpopular war with North Vietnam. Crowds of young people manned with placards, demonstrated against the war by burning the American flag. Public opinion in the younger US generations had turned "against the establishment" with a feeling of "liberation."

They had taken the the secular ideal of "freedom" and interpreted it literally. To a sickening degree, their way of life fulfilled the freedom promise. It was total liberty and total freedom. Full freedom meant "anything goes." What could be freer than "free-love?" It was the "Hippy" era with young people "dropping out of society," letting their hair grow long, living in vans, and smoking, injecting and ingesting mind-altering drugs. Their bazaar new way of life spread among young adults throughout the Western world.

But was even that enough freedom? Could there ever be too much? Once you reach "the right amount" of freedom should more of it be disdained and cease to any longer be the goal, or even be prohibited? If not, what "rights" and "freedoms" were left that the Hippies had failed to achieve?

In the US, there followed the promoting of gay culture by staging deliberately vulgar gay-rights parades in San Francisco. Also, and animal-rightists were protesting the fencing of cows. Crowds were enthralled with charismatic Yogi "cosmic consciousness" meditators and by their "good vibrations." It became almost impossible to execute serial killers and to build atomic power plants. Environmental extremists were spiking forest trees that loggers were set to saw down, and feminists had become so militant that conservatives were lampooning them as "feminazis."

More mature people tended to feel their secular society had gone mad. People were being "stressed out" by social-problem-awareness and antagonistic activist demonstrations. They were so "turned off" by their disintegrating society that the very word "society" itself, came to evoke disdain. People were beginning to think that even the myths and miracles of the old faith, by contrast, were not so ridiculous and out-of-date after all. At least they seemed to embody a more solid, stable, moral and healthy society.

Even science and technology began to lose prestige. People took to resisting such new technology as disease inoculations, the irradiating of foods, cloning, stem cell research, and crop genetic engineering. Western society had become so weakly bonded that no one could any longer be trusted to honestly regulate its most dangerous technologies. Science came to be seen as a questionable asset that was conspiring to clone them, waste money on space platforms, implant spy-chips in them and sneak fluoride into their drinking water.

By 1970, the religious conservatives of mostly the older generations had begun a long struggle to regain control of public opinion. It helped that the Hippy's were coming to discover that the "total freedom" of their anarchist way of life and its lack of cleanliness were causing assorted strange and disgusting diseases and infections, also that their drugs were killing them. Besides, their "square" parents were not going to support them forever.

The over-doing of the freedom ideal faded and then came to an end. The whole Hippy era had become such an embarrassment that both the media and academia, with good reason, still mostly avoid it. The movement had effectively trashed the whole idea of "freedom." Yet, it was the prime secular ideal and needed to remain. As an ideal, it had to continue providing some unity in the US and the world. All the secular ideals had to be kept until they were replaced, either by religious regression or a whole new WV and way of thinking. People still needed to idealize "freedom" at the very time they were backing off and retreating from it.

Serious damage had been done, however. In the 1980s and 1990s, the breakdown of the secular WV system led to the rise of crime, narcotic addiction, suicide, and high divorce rates in the US. In order to "solve" the growing problems, the US academic community developed a list of political, economic, social psychological theories to explain it. The result was the building up of a credentialed government and business financed social-problem-"cure" superstructure, one dedicated to "educating the public" on the seriousness of each such social problem and an appeal for funds so the "war" on it could be "won." The US ended up with a social-pathology industry and a constantly enlarging social problem list, one that ultimately swelled to some forty separate social problems.

Not only was the stress level rising but the level of hostility as well, more so in the US where the people had been epigenetically programed for stress. Her vast empty lands had attracted colonists who natural-selected themselves out of their old countries by being the ones most sensitive to over-crowding. Once on the new continent, their generations got used to spreading out and traveling distances, first on the horse, then in automobiles. As America became rapidly developed, the use of the auto kept families spreading out into the vast spaces that remained, and the urbane, income-centered cities became densely populated at unheard of speeds. Travel and the long distances remained as families disbursed so members could move to and take advantage of economic opportunities in distant states. Finally, the urbane crowding and divided families began to break down more of the sense of well being. The wide personal distance people were used to was being crimped by all those "other people," those strangers. The old "our-hunting-gathering-group-is-too-large" feeling of being crowded struck with increasing impact. The stress-buildup was accelerating. The American people are more sensitive to over-crowding than any other people, even those who have lived many generations in such crowded lands as Java, Japan and China.

Western secularized society is unable to effectively deal with the crowding problem. The still lingering emphasis on the old-religion fem-fertility creator-god and his admonition to "be fruitful and multiply," has left the US with a spirit-based "sacredness of life" legacy, one that became confused with "thou shall not kill" (murder). This old heritage prevents modern civilization from dealing rationally with its global over-crowding problem. In the US Christian WV-led West, its religious regression-based position against birth control, abortions, and the death penalty became an increasingly unmovable barrier.

As social problems multiplied, much of the humanity that the people no longer sincerely felt towards each other became expressed as a favoring of animals. Society then witnessed the multiplying of "animal liberation" causes which were filled with vegetarians opposed to the use of leather and the wearing of furs. Their animosity towards society was focusing on animals needing to be "liberated," as having "human rights," and against their being used in medical research. If "to worship" means that something is to be considered more worthy than people, then the animal cultists worshiped animals. Sickening civilizations generally move back toward totemism.

People noticed that "freedom" and "rights" were enabling books to be published on how to evade taxes and assassinate people, that Nazi-like race hatred organizations could demonstrate, that pedophiles could move into your neighborhood, and that nudists had a right to parts of the beach.

The process of re-stabilizing of the old society has been piecemeal and difficult. In each subsequent decade, only slow change has occurred. The Hippy era and the still growing list of social problems had given the American people a disturbing and unwelcome insight into the weakened state of their society. Soon, that window of insight closed, but the social problems themselves remained. Only reference to them faded from public communication.

People also indulged themselves with the sensual. Beginning with the Hippy movement and with the subsequent help of Playboy Magazine, sexual pleasure became "liberated," and people achieved freedom from "outmoded Victorian standards." From then on, all the various means of communication filled with erotic triggers. The lives of normal men filled with sexual overtones. "Sexual freedom" became an ideal, one that many tried to live up to during the very time deadly, sexually-transmitted diseases were spreading. The very basis of modern society, the patriarchal monogamous marital system, was breaking down.

There was a feeling of estrangement and mistrust. People came to feel isolated, and lost the feeling of being protected by the group. They were being driven to find new ways to deal with the stress and the lack of closeness they were feeling. Whatever they found that helped them generally became an addiction because life otherwise seemed meaningless.

The break down of the family meant, in many homes, that no one was in charge. Without an authority, it no longer functioned like a family-troop and became dysfunctional. Children felt left out, adrift in a dangerous, chaotic-seeming world. Many families became single-parent ones, and men became "sensitive."

People acquired a subconscious, paranoid-like fear of saying something that might offend others. Insecurity generated fear that was exploited by the commercial media into war-fear, "severe" weather-fear, fear of being a "loser," fear of vaccines, crime-fear, and finally terrorism-fear.

The breaking down of society kept young men still favoring an assortment of anarchist-leaning life styles. Many adopt bad manners, unethical conduct, lost any sense of honor, defiantly dressed with appalling sloppiness, made promises daily that they never kept, engaged in trivial acts of vandalism, wore pants that sagged down to their knees and, for a while, followed a fad of having rings through their noses and tongues.

The continuing break down of the patriarchal-monogamous system made homosexuality increasingly visible. As explained earlier, the rationing-of-women role of patriarchal monogamy had, from the beginning, barred homosexuals from the marital system. As society weakened and monogamy unraveled, many bisexuals turned to a polygamous homosexual life style and society grew many times more vulnerable to AIDS and other venereal diseases.

"The End Of History?"

During the long years of the Cold War between the US and the Soviet Union, the social structure of the Bolshevik-Marxist system was also weakening, ending finally with the collapse of the Soviet government in 1991. Suddenly, it seemed in the West that the grand old secular ideal of a "world democracy" might actually be attainable, and there was an exuberant return of hope. Perhaps democracy really was, after all, "the ultimate goal of all mankind," indeed, the culmination of "more than a hundred thousand year plus striving of the whole human species!" It seemed that achieving that final goal would then bring about the end of the long human struggle and, thus, "the end of history." Author Francis Fukuyama even proclaimed that in his 1989 essay, "The End of History." Unlike other more cautious social theorists, he alone had carried our prime secular ideal to its logical conclusion.

But the end of history!? How absurd! Social theorists have long been geared to subconsciously shape and support Secular Humanist ideals as long as they could do so without being blatantly irrational, but the academic world was not prepared to defend the notion that history was about to end. Fukuyama, however, had backed it into a corner. The social theorist consensus had to either conclude that "democracy" was not "the ultimate objective of all human history" or deny his obvious logic. If it did not do one or the other, it inferred the academic community agreed with his ludicrous conclusion.

No one dared mention there was even a problem, but it took months of hesitation and confusion before the social theory consensus managed to escape from its dilemma. It was forced to resort to stratagem #14 in the Appendix, that is, to rebut it with incomprehensible double-talk. Then, it used word-trick #8 to "officially" declare Fukuyama's thesis disproved. Thus, it became the "general consensus" that Fukuyama's (eminently correct) logic had been proven wrong.

The "End of History" debacle was, thus, resolved in a way that avoided harm to the vital democracy ideal, and enabled it to continue serving its essential role in the secular system.

Nevertheless, the inherent problems that go with the Democracy ideal explain the negative US public attitude towards politicians and accounts for the peculiar wall of mistrust existing between the American people and their leaders. In the rancorous US Presidential elections, the public forces the presidential candidates into a grueling, expensive and self-defeating almost-two-year-long election campaign, one that includes the humiliating spectacle of being lined up on stage in a row before the TV cameras where they have to take turns praising themselves, making impossible promises, and denigrating each other.

Because elected officials have to cater to the conflicting emotions felt by their contentious public, even the most honest of them have been forced to manipulate the system to do whatever unpopular deeds needed to be done, all in a way that has also enabled them to be adequately compensated for the high financial and emotional cost involved in getting elected. The nation as well as the society comprise such an unwieldy, confused mass of people and so ideologically splintered into opposing factions that the political leaders in both the States and the Federal System find it difficult to feel the full Alpha sense of responsibility.

It even becomes easy to understand why such systems become corrupt. The corrupt politician is the Alpha hunter, the one who uses his Political Action Committee and lobbyists as his Beta-ladened, hunting-party team. He works with them to vanquish the unwieldy nation as his prey and to partake of it for the benefit of the only real group he owns and feels group-responsible for, that is, his family, his lodge and friends. This is the elected politician who feels the rush of power that comes from being part of the Washington scene. His election victory is felt less as a reward for gaining the power to run things responsibly, and more as the proud hunter standing beside his trophy.

The dividing of the people leads their government to become corrupt, but even a nation divided against itself still has to have government. It and its departments have to ultimately decide almost everything. People would not even want to, for example, vote for the right speed limit put on each roadway speed limit sign on each road in each town and city. To be effective, government has to have enough power and authority to be respected, to decide, and to be obeyed in order for society to function. As with "God," so it is with government. It can be loved only when it is also feared. As in Ancient Greece, democratic ideals ultimately undermine the very civilization those ideals at first help to unify.

The affluent class and its economic empire

The national oath claims the US to be ". . .one nation, indivisible . . ." and it is a grand ideal to have, but the nation has always been divided. One of its many ways is into its upper income, middle income and the laboring class. Each class has its own characteristics consisting of far more than the spread in income. It is not a caste system, but each economic group is, in important ways, distinctive, though saying so is considered "politically incorrect" and seldom done.

The more conservative US wealthy class believes that the (over)-commercialized society they built has brought about the wealth and incentive necessary to take back society from the Hippy way of life. They also believe that the lower-income classes are comparatively sloven, obese, callous, unreliable and tend to slaughter the language. Moreover, many of the poor seem to them to take unjust advantage of public welfare. Instead of finding work, the conservative affluent know that some "just sit around all day trying to figure out how to get more government entitlements." They are recognizing that "unemployment insurance" might become the public dole. Of course, this is not to say that corporations, at the same time, are not lobbying Congress for their own government subsidies, import tariffs, low-interest loans, cash infusions, and "pork barrel" entitlements.

The wealthy also remind us that "welfare mothers" and their born-out-of-wedlock children are often being government-supported to produce even more children, and that the "socialist safety net" for the poor, such as unemployment insurance, encourages sloth and cheating. In poor area schools which provide the free lunch program, most of the students tend to be the heaviest. The conservative class notices the breakdown of school discipline and that students harass the ones who study hard "for thinking they are better." They also harass their teachers. No one is in control.

To the conservative affluent class, the problem is that the laboring class has become a demanding body of unionized workers looking for more work privilege.

It is often said that "everyone should stand on his own," but who does? We are social animals and always depend on each other. Who but their upper class parents endow and finance the clutter of social science theory, arts, and intellectual-philosophical trivia of the "higher" education that brings them the best jobs? Who provides the contacts that enabled their children to end up with lucrative careers? People praise the hardy pioneers, but they were usually homesteading government land taken from the railroads and given to them. Government assistance is not just what makes people dependent and fail but what makes society run. Government help fails only when society fails. It fails only because a dividing ideological bond erodes the closeness people need in order to cooperate, care for, and help each other.

One of the many reasons the size of the underclass is growing is that it is being victimized by credential inflation. Wading through years of the liberal educational system's confused pedagogy has become so daunting and expensive that the system has had to bait it. Its denseness has had to be idealized and made to confer status to the graduate by providing him with "an open mind." It's self-inconsistency has also had to be shrouded with gold as "the only way to get a good job." By such means, the affluent class managed to make a "liberal education" become a tower of status, a limiting initiation rite for the "elite" into the corporate, judicial, political and financial world, a rite which they, the affluent class, have jealously guarded and maintained. They have all been through its grueling self-punishment and are determined to accept no one else who has not also endured it. The rest are relegated in status to that of the mere "multitude." None of our civilization's Confucian-like over-educated Mandarin management members would want to hire someone with "a closed mind" and "no status."

The classicist's endowment-controlled university system has over-bloated the whole educational and accreditation process until it no longer teaches the young to develop work skill needed to do specialty or professional jobs. There is a lack of apprenticeship courses and programs. The whole classist "big name" university system is taxpayer and endowment supported, but the best the young can do is look for a non-fraudulent corporate Internet program and seek out an on-the-job apprentice-ship training program. The relatively useless Liberal Arts courses even fail in teaching creative thinking. The "gold test" for creativity, the Torrance test, shows creativity in the US has been in decline since 1990.

The affluent class also feels that the reason the common people lean toward liberalism is that they are attracted by the false allure of socialism/communism. It is felt that they need to be turned back from "being attracted to the libertine ways of the 1960s, that is, by being reminded of those "God-given qualities that made America great." They see that as "guiding us back to Republican core values." To the affluent, there is no middle-ground, "you're either for us or against us." They feel they have solved the problem of not only what has gone wrong but also what to do about it.

They oppose support and assistance to the poor and feel that upper income tax rates should be reduced because, no matter how much wealth they garner, it is never enough. They figure that high income and corporate taxes result in "income redistribution," that it causes an unfair, disproportionate tax burden for those who, because of being cultured, better educated, and having top-rate executive or professional skills, should instead, be treated with respect and consideration. The corporate heads see themselves as justified in garnering, at stockholder expense, more than two hundred and fifty times as much compensation as received by the lowest paid worker. After all, they and their Board of Directors were the ones who promote and maintain, and are intent on protecting, the civilization that is enjoyed by all. The control of the US they held between 1880 and 1930 is what they think needs to be restored.

The liberal middle classes disagree. Most of them know there is a large middle ground between total *laissez faire* capitalism and socialism-Marxism. They see executive compensation being fair if it is no more than fifteen times that of the lowest paid worker. They complain about the Big Business class' unsavory practice of perk-and-campaign-fund bribing of their Congressmen to get them to pass loophole-laden-laws that legalize their dishonesty. But because of the secular ideal of race and class equality, liberals find it difficult to think, write, or speak in class-difference terms. Since "all people are equal," speaking of the business class seems undemocratic and more like "Communist" rhetoric. On this subject and in this way, liberals effectively muzzle themselves.

The affluent class hesitated to openly push only for such blatantly selfish achievements as the lowering of their income taxes. It became important for them to find an ideal that they could use to justify their actions. They needed an ideal around which they could rally and take back the control of government that the Great Depression had wrenched from them.

People are expert at rationalizing. When they need a new ideal, they generally find one and, as to be expected, a satisfactory ideal did turn up. They began to hear about a few economic doctrines taught by a rather obscure Austrian economist named Ludwig Von Mises (1881-1973). A claim was found among his writings that an ideal state of being can be reached by **unfettered** capitalism, that is, "free enterprise" business being without government regulations, providing most services of government, and commercially exploiting most of the nation's environmental, communal (commons) assets, such as its beaches, forests, water supply, mineral wealth, etc.

They took to calling their new Von Mises doctrine, "Libertarian," because, coming from the word "liberty," it seemed to ennoble them. It was a serviceable hidden-agenda-ideal for the affluent class to unite behind. The Von Mises doctrine provided all the justification they needed for whatever ruthless economic policies they might employ in order to gain control over "Big Government." It even idealized their efforts to increase their individual personal wealth. It was a Pied Piper way to lead the people back to "what made this country great." By such means they could control their secular society and ideologically reshape it so, they reasoned, prevent it from otherwise sliding back into the counter-culture liberal era if the 1960s, the one with its communist and socialist drug culture, free-love, and anti-establishment way of life.

The Von Mises theme was further elaborated by Ann Rand in her novel, "Atlas Shrugged." Together, the two works form the "sacred scriptures" of the affluent class. Together, they set the plan for how business is to save civilization.

Is it really possible for business to run all aspects of government? If it is possible, it certainly is not desirable any more than it is for government to run all business (Marxism). Corporations are government legislated legal entities. Aside from paying themselves well, executive duty is legally shaped to benefit the stockholders. So, with profits being the goal, it is the duty of management to see that, for example, the for-profit prison systems forgoes the expense of rehabilitating prisoners. For-profit hospitals are motivated to ignore Living Wills and pour elaborate and expensive care into the aged and dying to collect the most profit from Medicare. The garment industry finds it cheaper to destroy unsold clothing than ship them to poor countries. Fraudulent Universities spring up, advertise, and teach expensive programs and degrees that employers will not accept. Markets save money by throwing older food in dumpsters as the homeless go hungry. And when military services are taken over by private corporations, they pay more lobbyists to pressure Congress into financing more wars, especially in the Near East where each war makes the next one all the more necessary. More wars mean more earnings and dividends for the stockholders, more bonuses for top management, and more promotions for military officers.

By hiding the anti-democratic and anti-pacifist aspects of their agenda, the moneyed class has miraculously managed to enlist the support of a vast army of middle and lower economic class citizens, those who still nurse the fast-fading illusion of being like the rich or of becoming rich themselves some day. The affluent also enlisted vast numbers of the poor to their "cause" by appealing to their religiousness. "Miracles"and Bible-story-like-beliefs could became among the core "values" of the Republican Party.

The new-conservatives in the US then opened war on Big Government. Their most effective tactic has been for the larger corporations ("big business") with the most numerous and most generous lobbyists, to get Congress to reduce or end government regulations, even to simply "convert" or corrupt the very government regulators themselves. After all, big business has the money to do both. Of course, this is not to infer that government has not also grown "big" nor that it has not grown inefficient, but Big Business has also grown big and inefficient, such as in the Dilbert way (no wonder the Dilbert business-related cartoons have never brightened up the staid, old Wall Street Journal). Why else has Big Business so often lobbied for tariffs and subsidies as well as other unjustifiable advantages as low-interest loans? Yet, the new-conservatives see that as being efficient. It is an efficient, though parasitic way to enhance profits for their stockholders even though at the expense of the non-stock holding public. If there were no government left, corporations would just feed off each other that way.

In fact, they do. Weak ones are taken over by corporate conglomerates, and some are sucked dry and discarded like so much garbage.

The corporation is the real-world "god" of the New-Conservative rich. Those government designed legal phantom-entities are what the rich claim have Constitutional and God-given human rights and privileges. They see unfettered advertising to be their corporation's Constitutional "right of free speech." They like corporations to have the ability to sue anyone who would protest their policies by threatening to boycott them.

As the conservative Libertarian movement grew, it absorbed a religious-like militancy from the very fanaticism of the Marxist WV religion it opposed. So, it came to see the world as being divided into only "good" and "evil." In just that simplistic, militantly Bible-like way, the upper income conservative class came to figure that Christian, unfettered, free-enterprise economics was the "good" and liberal-Hippy-atheistic-Marxism/socialism was the "evil," including all the other WV systems except Judaism. What was taking shape was a Christian-moral-faith-based conservatism that had been intensified by the all-out Cold War struggle with Bolshevism and Maoist Marxism into a type of militant, regressive way-of-thinking that typically occurs late in every civilization.

The conservative Libertarian "core value" movement's crowning achievement was what shaped up to be a world economic government, one that sometimes promoted the world's corporate profits at the expense of the small businesses and working people of the world's less-developed nations. This "government" was set up by a series of three treaties or groups of treaties beginning as early as 1944 and which had been ratified by most nations. Its main purpose was to remove the protective tariff barriers of under-developed nations so their *commons* assets, such as their forests, ports, beaches, oil and gas as well as their other mineral wealth, could be accessed and commercialized by the large, international corporations. Much of that was accomplished in the form of needed International Monetary Fund World Bank emergency loans for those nations which were made helpless by some man made or natural disaster. Most such loans were arranged "for the people who had been made destitute by the calamity, those who had suffered the most" but little of which ever went to them. Such loans had "conditions" that often required the removal of tariffs protecting their small industries and corporatizing certain of the nation's commons. Wherever part of the commons was corporatized, the situation developed where millions of people could live in dire poverty while immense wealth was being pumped or mined right out from under them, sold abroad, and all the profit going to their rulers and the corporate world's stockholders located tens of thousands of miles away.

Thus it is possible to understand why some insurgencies have arisen. People organize to protest the extracting of their resources with all the proceeds going elsewhere. They are then beaten and shot at. So, they adopt whatever method is available in order to fight back. In the press, they are labeled "ethnic insurgencies" that eventually degenerate, for lack of a coherent WV, into drug running, rape motivated, predatory gangs.

The system also allows people all over the underdeveloped world to become hungry because big tracts of land are tended by immense machines that enable them to export the food at low prices. The farmers in the smaller countries, unable to compete, tend to go out of business. Without the all-important farm income, the impoverished people can hardly afford even the imported food. In some cases, such as Brazil, half of all agricultural land is owned by only one per cent of the population.

The Libertarian New-Conservative corporatizing movement has no official headquarters. Its way of thinking is promoted through non-profit "research" institutes, "think tanks" and "charitable foundations," those such as the Heritage Foundation and the Manhattan, Hoover, Hudson, American Enterprise and CATO Institutes. All are generously funded by wealthy individuals and major corporations. These interests all want to keep US troops garrisoned in over a hundred separate nations and stay in charge of the world economy. To keep control means control of the UN Security Council and that involves the implied willingness to use the impressive power of the US military. With the world's most high-tech military machine and its subsidiary, NATO, the US can continue its role of "making the world safe for Democracy" and "raising living standards in the under-developed world."

Both the "think tanks" and their government seek to promote their cause by providing financial help to a number of over-populated, basket-case beggar-state regimes. Much of the funds are used to pay academic consultants to set up research projects to study the problem and assess which areas need most help, what kind of help, and how that help should be provided. These "study projects" tend to continue however long it takes until the funds are used up.

When one considers how the affluent class handled its responsibilities, one might wonder if it is inherently wrong for the wealthy to rule society. Yet, those who rule should be affluent because civilization needs to provide wealth as a reward for those with the best skills, including business skills. Normally, in a united and healthy society, the people of a nation want their leaders to exhibit wealth. It is one way they can show them off to the rest of the world. They have pride in their leaders. It is just that leadership should never be hereditary-based or include legal privileges. It should include adhering to a separate, class based morally progressive ideology or code of honor to unite them and provide them with the insight and integrity to honestly and fairly monitor, as well as run, the economic and political system.

Where the US ruling class come from

The nature and makeup of America's affluent class helps to explain why it has failed its responsibilities. One reason is that it is partially filled with US Southern descendent's of the Civil War era aristocracy. They and well-off believers in the Midwest and the Southern Bible belt tend to regard the Bible as "the inerrant world of God." The Libertarian affluent and the vast multitude of "God feating" people together provide a solid US voting block that both the conservative upper income class and the "God fearers"can count on in the elections.

Most affluent business leaders from the more urbane states only go to church to be "accepted" and are mostly non-praying liberal Christians. They may even be non-theists themselves, but they think it is better for everyone to be more religious. They feel a self-righteous moral responsibility to be for Creationism and Intelligent Design, as well as against birth control and abortions, gay marriage, the death penalty, and against us being responsible for global warming. They see the Bible-belt partnership as a marriage-of-convenience, but one in which they believe, they the corporate elite, hold control.

Another of their traits is their almost never openly expressed racism. All people with dark skin tend to be resented, even if only subconsciously. They dislike the thought of becoming a white racial minority by 2050, and still see a white person as "a black" even if only one of his ancestors was dark.

Another trait of the rich is the real or professed appreciation for a museum-type modern or classic artistic culture and having a status-building "liberal education" certificate from some famous-name university. They want to feel "above the common man." They speak reverently of the "dedicated men in our military service" but feel it is alright for them to be expendable in order to serve their war objectives.

Finally, they like to think of themselves as patriots and regard the rest of the world as a threat to US sovereignty. They want everyone to own a gun and to be more patriotic. They like to encourage people to take the oath of allegiance, and view "God's blessings" as raining down on America. Even if they travel to foreign resorts, it is only to see native dances, wild animals, and take nature tours. They still view the rest of humanity with partially concealed indifference or even disdain. They see "God Bless America" as a fact rather than a request.

Within the New-Conservative movement, it is regarded as being "in bad taste" for members to discuss their varying race, class, religious/moral, patriotic and "good"/"evil" beliefs. They are all tightly held together by the Von Mises and Ann Rand militants so that they easily manage to play golf, hunt, and go on resort junkets with each other with minimal controversy or dissension.

By backing the Fundamentalist believers, the Libertarian Right claims "the moral high ground" even though those who are corporate department heads, tend to have their "good" compromised by their loop-hole-enabled tax evasion, off-shore bank accounts, creative accounting, lying by omission in the company reports, and inflating their executive pay with bonuses, stock options, and ending it with a "golden parachute." Cities subsidize the big corporate retail stores so they will buttress their large new shopping malls while there is no such subsidy for the small merchant shops that have to compete with them. The agro-corporations squeeze out even large, thousand acre-plus family-run farms. Big corporations manage all that by having their own corporate law departments prepare legislation that is loop hole-laden. They finance the election campaigns of Congressmen so they will pass laws that make it legal for their business interests to do what should be illegal and make illegal what should be legal. It is never called bribery because such government manipulating is their responsibility to the stockholders.

It is easy to find fault and place blame, but business, capital and corporations are not inherently corrupt. It is just that a disunited WV and way-of-thinking is unable to bond huge masses of people together well enough that they can feel the same small-group closeness they evolved in. They cannot possibly deal with "the others" with the same familiarity and understanding, to feel genuine concern for the multi-millions of people in their society. As stated before, we individually, are able to know, like, and recognize at most a few hundred other people. Our small group nature shows up in the way people can express so much compassion for a distressed individual shown on TV, even a dog, but very little more when they read about thousands of people in another part of the world who are hit by a natural disaster and in more distress. Compassion for large groups of people only exists to the extent it can be conditioned in us by a strong, united WV system.

It is possible, however, for people to hate large groups of other people.

For more than four thousand years, a WV belief system operating a capitalist economy has been the only system that can successfully handle the economic needs of such large conglomerates of people. The capitalist system's main weakness is that the decline of the WV ideological bond, its society, and its civilization corrupts the capitalists and makes the economic system increasingly rapacious and brutal.

The wave of regression

In response to the Hippy-era excesses, many morally conservative Americans in all economic classes became so concerned about the future that they turned away from the splintering secular-cult WV system back to their old religion's more stable moral standards. They were hanging on to the one thing that had at least worked in the past and could seemingly save society from total social-moral disintegration. Concerned middle and lower class working Americans were, accordingly, becoming less convincingly secular and less liberal in their mainline Christian beliefs. Many were moving to the Baptist, Evangelical and Pentecostal churches, those that preached "the inerrant world of God." In some, people pray with rattlesnakes, "speak in tongues," and "exorcise demons." By 2003, the mainline church parking lots were as near empty on Sundays as the "inerrant-word-of-God" ones were full.

The US had started to turn back and away from secular thinking in the early 1970s, but people have all along remained generally unaware they have lost faith in their secular ideals because they need to keep the impression their society is still "moving forward," not regressing. Religious revivals have occurred before in the US but not religious regression. Church attendance is declining nationwide, but less people believe in evolution and have less loyalty to Western secular-sponsored science. Many are taking up other "spiritual" ideologies such as the motley collection of god-is-nature, polytheistic, pseudo-druid, witchcraft and Wiccan cults. The proportion of those in the US who have their own individual-based belief in "spirits" has been growing. Regression occurs mainline WV bonded systems in response to a fast-pace dividing of its secular system.

Among the forces arrayed against Christian regression is the liberal academic community. It has not had enough influence to convince even half the people that we evolved from smaller primates, but undermines what little influence it does have by proposing ever more extreme, even absurd, secular system solutions to society's social problems. It has even seemed to it's activists that it is discriminatory for owners to reject tenants and job applicants who are unreliable. After all, "people are all equal and even unreliable people have rights."

Libertarian Big Business conservatives prefer to ignore that the partnership they share with the regressing Christian militants, gives the faithful influence on the drift of the whole civilization towards the cause of "Christ's Return." To the Christian militants, Jesus's return would follow a nuclear war Armageddon "End Times" and lead to a wondrous "God's Kingdom" here or in "Heaven." That tends to slightly reduce the motive of the conservative class to avoid such a conflict. All but the militantly faithful are well aware that such a war would cause nothing but destruction and the "God fearing" would be wrong again, but what difference would that make if we are all dead?

Social activists seek to solve society's national and world problems by means of a changing academic social theory consensus. One such effort has been to promote "multiculturalism" in the schools. That has meant focusing on the African heritage, the plight of Japanese-Americans interred during WW II, the way America's indigenous tribes were treated, and so on, all of which is, by inference, blamed on "the white man," hence, on Western civilization. Many American Iroquois tribesmen have even been issued valid "Iroquois nation" passports. In such ways, the secular-academic community has sought to be helpful in order to better justify itself, but even the general public has begun to wish they would stop. Instead of building world unity, their efforts mostly serve to weaken popular respect for Western society itself and hence, for the very secular doctrines and ideals it has stood for and which have been holding the religiously divided world together. It destroys what sense of belonging its citizens still have in it and the pride they once felt for it, for their secular-built world society and civilization. Little is left for the people to any longer feel responsible for or dedicated to.

Present trends in the US

The modern way of life is shaping the new generations to accommodate to their new, minimalist society. Its young men are growing up filled with praise, being overly protected, and with little prospect of achieving status in their now shattered and feminized society. They look at their "American-Dream" future and feel a gnawing emptiness. It seems like a purposeless life dedicated only to the spending of more than one's friends and neighbors. Besides, to get "the American Dream," they must go through a long, expensive, grueling, largely irrelevant university program. Without much ambition, self-discipline, or genuine curiosity, many end up as amateur artists, dancers, philosophers, actors, professional students, even Mount-Everest-climbing or big-wave-surfing "sports-nuts." Others just give up and live at home with their parents where they dissolve into their room-confined, computerized electronic world of virtual reality.

At the moment, openly gay culture in the military and other such secular "causes" are still dominant in public opinion, still "politically correct." The nation's conservatives do not want "a gay marching army," one they imagine as being like the San Francisco Gay Parades of the 1960s and 1970s. What they and the militancy want is presently balanced by the power of the gay activists. The regressive Libertarian-Christians regard the army as the center of our very survival as a society, not as a "social experiment."

Incremental shifts in public opinion now mean conservative crowds can be mobilized to demonstrate, as they have done in their "Tea Party," an ability that white liberals have been losing. To the religious right, going back to "Christian values" is the only way to preserve monogamy, retain a patriarchal-monogamous system, and prevent the collapse of society. They feel that doing so is necessary even if it is at the cost of the Constitution's secular goals and its doctrines, at the cost even of its science.

Both the Left and the Right are weakening society in their efforts to save it.

The secular ideology also promotes "equality." Of course, no two things are ever equal and everything is different, including gay and heterosexual cultures. The sexes are different, and there is also nothing equal about men and women even though neither is more important than the other.

Generations of women playing a greater role in society means generations of men playing a lesser role. Having less authority tends to make men weaker, less reliable and less masculine. It is a process of undermining the patriarchal-monogamous system and what makes such systems regress in order to survive.

The walls between us

One of the more bizarre results of the decline of our world is the building of fortified fences and walls. We are building walls across the globe to keep out unwanted refugees from places that are even more over-crowded. Beside the fortified fencing and walls between North and South Korea, Israel is weaving them throughout Palestine. There is the US funded one Egypt is building between it and Gaza. Walls exist between Saudi Arabia and Iraq as well as Saudi Arabia and Yemen. There is also one between South Africa and Zimbabwe. Between the US and Mexico there are six hundred miles of metal fencing and an eighty-five mile canal-moat. Up to thirteen hundred miles of electronic barrier are being planned. Another barrier is set to be built between Israel and Egypt. There is also the 2,500 mile barrier India is building around Bangladesh, and another one exists between Bangladesh and Burma. None of this is even intended to have any effect on reducing the Earth's over-crowding problem.

The corpulent crowd

Amazingly, another result of over-crowding is obesity. All over the world, people are accumulating fat. In the US and many other countries, it affects even the poor more than the rich, and over indulgence has not been the main cause. Biological researchers have observed that prolonged stress in experimental animals causes obesity, perhaps by reducing the hours of sleep which also leads to obesity. It can also be caused by an overload of neuro-and other toxins, such as ones caused from the way the food is processed. In addition, there is evidence that chemicals used in non-food industries contribute to obesity in infants, a handicap which they generally carry on through life. Finally, calorie-overloaded American cheap-food franchises, backed by corporate food and processing firms, have competed with each other in an increasingly successful marketing campaign to wean the world away from healthy food in favor of their high sugar and fat, nutrient depleted, fast-food drinks and meals. Add the lack of exercise and a fat-promoting, epigenetic-based virus that was recently discovered to cause weight gain, and we have a multitude of causes for the world's present obesity plague.

What the corporate agricultural and food processing industry does to our food is generally defended as necessary in order to feed the world's growing population. The only reason over crowded people of the world can still afford to eat is because so much of it is cooked or mixed with chemicals in order to keep down growing, handling and storage costs, but an effective, responsible world order would keep population numbers down so that people could still have healthy food.

Much of the blame for the costly US health care system is that the insurance, drug-making, and law corporations bleed it for profit, and the 2010 Health Care law cannot change that.

All civilizations ultimately lose the health war because the extravagance of civilization itself makes it, by nature, a profligacy. Progress enables human numbers to swell and the death rate to decline. So the dividing ideological system arouses the human, over-crowding stress response. The gradual build up of stress precipitates a decline in health. Deleterious epigenetic-microRNA changes mysteriously occur and cause rising cancer, diabetes, bipolar, autism, asthma, epilepsy, Parkinson's and obesity rates to rise. The stress reduces resistance to disease so that nations and societies are culled by virus and bacteria and end in plagues sometimes serious enough to drop population numbers. Our civilization has managed to map the human genome, but the epigenetic genome is many times more complicated and may not be usefully understood during the life time left to our present civilization. There is no Libertarian or magic technological cure for the health system without effective population control.

Terror

In September of 2001, four passenger planes were hijacked by militant Muslims primed to strike the US center of financial and military power. The plan was to retaliate for the Christian-secular WV-based US support for Israel. For some of the terrorists at least, knew they were going to die in the attack. Most of the World Trade Center was left a total ruin, and part of the Pentagon was heavily damaged, all at the cost of lives of more than three thousand innocent men and women.

In response to the terrorist attack, the rest of the world noticed that the American government then slighted the UN, started two wars with Islam, and threatened a third. The American people had become so fearful, frail, fragile that they were willing to call up their troops, tear away "freedom" and "rights," and indefinitely prison and torture war prisoners without trial, all so their government could allay their terror of terrorism. In their obsession with the 9/11 strike, they subsequently erected monuments and memorials, created ceremonies, an anniversary, even a new and patch worked flag. They also lavished wealth on the less-than-needy people who lost relatives in the attack.

The US government's first act was to pulverize the meager infrastructure of Afghanistan's few cities. The US managed to then take over from the tribes that supported her, set up a city-based government in the agricultural country, and chased Osama bin Laden into Afghanistan. The Muslim-regressive Taliban regime collapsed. The US installed regime was corrupt, and the US military took to destroying the nation's poppy crop. So, the Taliban regrouped and began to fight back. If the West did not want them to grow and process poppies, the West should not buy them.

Osama bin Laden, then went into hiding where he has remained as a god to stand for and draw together the most militant fringe of reactionary Islam.

President Bush, who had publicly claimed he was going to "rid the world of evil" then claimed that the secular regime in Iraq had nuclear and biological weapons. In order to protect the American people from them, he ordered an impressive "shock and awe" invasion of Iraq in order to replace the regime then running the country, all so the weapons of mass destruction (WMD) could be found and destroyed.

It turned out Iraq did *not* have any WMDs. The CIA had only been badgered by the Administration into claiming Iraq *might* have them.

Despite the Army request for at least 200,000 troops to take and hold both nations, the Administration set out to do it with 100,000 by first reducing it to ashes by bombing and artillery to compensate for the lack of troops. The subsequent effort to rebuild what the US had destroyed was bungled by too few occupying troops to keep order and by construction company corruption. A suicide bombing insurgency then developed.

So many seemingly unintended failures could have been surreptitiously intended because they benefited both the militant agenda of Fundamentalist Christian regression and the interests of the corporate backed military-industrial complex. A successful campaign followed by an effective occupation would adversely affect US Christian regression by boosting the secular cause of freedom, rights, and democracy. Its failure was a step in helping to trash those ideals by showing that all attempts to achieve democracy for other countries, such as Iraq and Afghanistan, fail even when her militarily *imposes* it on them. It also ends in extensive waste of US service mens' lives and the nation's material wealth. In addition, such effort tends to end up in corruption, terrorism, an indefinite occupation and leaving behind only weak governments. The policy benefited Libertarian-Christian militants by making even more unrealistic the 1990s grand ideal of "democratizing" the world. The less faith people have in their secular ideals, the more they are attracted to the ideals of the old religion. Also, the more the public discards its secular doctrines of tolerance and compassion, the more it becomes unmoved by tens of thousands of innocent Muslim civilians accidentally killed by the "war on terror." Conversely, the more innocent civilians killed by the war, the more Muslims interpret the Quran with hatred for the West, and feel less compassion for the innocent Western civilians killed by their terrorists.

The decline of the secular ideals and tolerance enables the religious right of the Christian, Muslim, and Judaic faiths to become more aggressive in fighting over territory and its natural resources. It also encourages the type of military climax the regressive militants think would bring about the arrival of "the Messiah," a basic belief in all three "Religions of the Book."

At this moment, the US has caused weak states to come into being in Iraq, Afghanistan, Pakistan, Mexico, and Jamaica. As time passes, more may well be added to the list. In Iraq, the divisive issue between the Shiite, Sunni and Kurd cults of Islam makes government and the allocation of her oil resources highly contentious. US troops in Iraq may have to remain there indefinitely. Moreover, the potential Israeli-US attack on Shiite Iran over the nuclear issue leaves the success of "democracy" anywhere in the region in doubt.

All that has happened because what is subconsciously wanted by the most militant groups tends to determine what happens. America's clumsy failures in Islam are really not a policy but a process. If the process slows down, the US public loses fear of terrorism. That motivates the militants of all three faiths to again stir up the social evolutionary swarm-theory type antagonistic-retaliatory alliance process again.

fifteen --- SOCIAL EVOLUTION

It is time to back off from all the detail "and look at the forest instead of the trees." The objective here is to sum up the natural selection process that accounts for the growth of the human cultural heritage, to explain, for example, what causes societies and civilizations to "rise and fall." As the reader may by now realize, the social evolutionary process is complex, but it is not beyond human understanding.

So far here we have examined twelve societies. Four or more other major societies existed, but as explained earlier, we did not examine the New World civilizations because they operated in a separate social evolutionary mainstream which was held back by an absence of draft animals and high quality grains. We have not studied the Tibetan, Sikh, and other societies because they never achieved mainstream status, and we omitted the mainstream civilization of Persia because it is so intimately connected to the civilization in Babylon and has not been needed to explain the social evolutionary process.

What we have seen is that each mainstream WV-bonded society arose, then matured, grew old, and except for Christendom, Islam, Marxist East Asia, and the Hindu Middle East, all have also already been replaced or "died." The life-cycle nature of societies has been noted for centuries, but it has been rejected by the social theory consensus. Using the term "civilization" in a natural cause and effect way that would show its future course would directly contradict the belief that "God" has a role in human affairs. It would also mean that our secular beliefs are transitory, impermanent, and that they are also in the process of slowly evolving or that they are losing the status of any longer being "self evident" and "inherent truths."

Instead, as we have seen, mainstream societies behave similarly to organisms in that they are subject to natural selection and have a life cycle. They even exhibit a crude genetic-like ability to carry on traits and, therefore, mechanistically "reproduce." Doctrinal bits of information are absorbed from older WV systems and are then genetically-like re-formed into new WV systems that bond people into newer societies. This is our social evolutionary process, one that resembles but is not identical to biological processes. All this and Part 2 show how and why civilizations do "rise" or develop and they do "fall," die.

Does that mean societies are a new or different form of life? Even if they are not biological organisms, it would seem that they are still some form of life. It is not the nature of non-living entities to experience natural selection, have a life cycle, and reproduce. Social organisms are not what we think of when we think of life, but it could be that what we regard as life needs to be broadened. In the distance of outer space, there may be far stranger forms than we have so far encountered here. In fact, even here on Earth there are forms that are strange enough, such as sea animals that get their energy from chlorophyll, deep sea bacteria and six feet long worms that do not use oxygen, and prions and viruses which are not cellular.

So, just what is life? In the 19th century, it was commonly believed that organic matter could never be synthetically produced because it had a "divine spark." Then scientists learned to produce organic matter and the "divine spark" was no longer needed. Now, biologists are close to generating new life in the laboratory.

Since there are multi-cellular organisms made up of cooperating individual cells, and since the multi-cellular ones form a new type organism that differs from the single cell type, it seems logical to assume that multi-cellular organisms can, in turn, become organized into super-organisms. In the case of human societies, they are based on the cell because of being based on the human individual who is a multi-celled organism. So, the supra-organism of society is indirectly cellular based.

Certainly, the relationship between human societies and multi-cellular organisms can be carried too far. There is no basis for seeing social organisms as breathing, city-sized "social animals," ones with cybernetic brains, electric transmission line nervous systems, multiform transportation blood-vascular systems, and a big problem with waste disposal. Societies are not made up of such material things but of cellular beings, people, and operate only as biological-like social entities or organisms. Like all other life, they are held together and driven by a complex repertory of social instincts which shape the ideology-motivation that holds societies together. All that is what gives societies "life."

But the main reason to recognize societies as super-organisms is that it is practical to do so. Using the life cycle, reproduction and natural selection nature of human society to replace the ancient assumption of it being a sort of theistic creation gives us a picture of ourselves that is so much more accurate that we can, for the first time, use it to predict our own destiny.

In more detail, the three criteria for classifying society as social organisms are as follows:

#1. *They experience natural selection.* Anthropologists and other social scientists seek the natural selection process that occurs in group behavior in terms of sexual selection, "altruism," and kinship. They also deal with "groups," not societies. In biology, geneticists seek an explanation of our social grouping in terms of genes and micro RNA molecules. Neither the social theorists nor the geneticists explain what the social organismic unit is, what causes it to rise and fall, to have a life cycle, or offer any insight into the future of mankind. Neither approach shows the natural selection process that is involved in and between human social organisms.

In order to be affected by natural selection, an organism has to have the ability to pass on to future generations what has been natural-selected. Of course, collectives of organisms such as social organisms do not have genes, but human WV-bonded societies do have a genetic-like cultural-social process which enables them to pass on natural selected changes to future generations. Human mainstream societies are bound together by WV systems that can endure for centuries because they provide relatively self-consistent answers to the Four Question Template. That enables them to form WVs that are closed systems of thinking, ones in which each point and each argument supports the rest. The result is a system of relatively self-consistent, rigid, immutable principles and precepts able to bond people into a social organism, one that is provided with the stable, predictable, coherency characteristic of genetically based life. Weak WV ideologies and their weak ability to bond people into societies are crowded out, while successful ones form successful societies that grow and spawn new WV ideologies. The new WV ideologies, in turn, undergo a natural selection process in which the less effective ones fail to gather adherents while the better ones are selected instead and end up forming new societies.

In the past, all the WV belief systems were "spirit"-based, but WV systems have always been irrational in hindsight. All that has been essential is that a society's Four-Question-Template-answers not only be relatively self-consistent but, as well, more "advanced," that is, to be less *in*accurate, than the WV ideological system it replaces. Being less inaccurate means able to use fewer deities, myths and "miracles" to explain the world. The result is a more cause-and-effect understanding which, in turn, enables better technology and, as a result, more population growth. The fittest society has also had to be one bonded by a WV that adapted best to new conditions with, usually, the least re-conditioning or modifying of human instinct.

In short, more advanced societies better adapted to human nature and need were the ones which spread the furthest and competed the most effectively. Always, social organisms that had grown old and decadent and were holding back human cultural-technical progress were eventually replaced. In such ways, WV systems compete and are subject to being selected out with the more effective ones growing the most, surviving the longest, and leaving the most culture, science and technology to be picked up and passed on as the seed forming the next mainstream WV. It is also where the most effective technology is found and where, over a long period of time, human population growth has been most pronounced.

Human social evolutionary natural selection occurs geographically. The "mainstream" is a type of "breeding ground" where only the fittest social organisms survive. Non-mainstream, primitive societies lose territory and experience a relative decline in population and numbers. To the dismay of anthropologists, they undergo a slow death upon contact with mainstream society, and on our increasingly crowded planet, such sub-societies are finding it ever more difficult to avoid contact with us. Soon, they will all be extinct. Only the fittest societies can acquire a "territory," that is, have national self-rule or acquire it but lose it, or be a parasitic one that is sponsored and protected by one or more successful ones.

The evolutionary survival of the fittest process of the social organism first began in its original breeding ground in Africa. It then moved to the Near East and Asia Minor. From there it spread East into Asia to encompass the whole Euro-Asian landmass. It then spread to the New World. Now, the whole world has become the breeding ground of mankind's mainstream social organisms.

The term, "breeding ground," refers to the breeding of societies, not individuals. Also, in that context, "population growth" refers only to technological growth that enables a long-term, *sustainable*, population increase. Now, however, population growth is continuing beyond the carrying capacity of the world's environment, the bonding power of its dividing WV systems, and their technological ability to adapt to the limiting of space and resources.

So, briefly, social organisms are bonded by WV ideological systems that substitute for a genetic basis. This has enabled natural selection to improve human culture and to support our growth in numbers. It is only necessary that each ideological or genetic system carries on the natural selected changes to subsequent generations.

#2. Societies reproduce. Societies reproduce by answering the Four Question Template questions with the society's secular-age-enabled advances in thinking. This is what led Jesus' disciples to reshape their Jewish god and his life and sayings into a successful new WV system, and what enabled Karl Marx, Mohammad and their disciples to evolve their own universal brotherhood barbarian-like but society-bonding mainstream WV systems. And it explains how the mass of Hindu doctrines arose out of the the animism/polytheism of prehistory. It is a natural selecting of the more advanced traits, doctrines, and understanding from older WV systems and from secular ideologies and the advances they make possible. Less "spirit"-based and more natural cause and effect thought is subconsciously re-assembled into the theology of a whole new Four-Question-answer-based WV system. It is a genetic-*like* transfer in that the new is shaped by the combining of the old in a process comparable to that of conception, bearing, and then giving birth. The result is a new WV belief system and the society it bonds. Old societies produce newer ones which are, in turn, able to provide a base for still more human intellectual-cultural growth in the mainstream and the ultimate bonding of people into an even larger body of people than the earlier societies.

#3. Societies have a life cycle. The life cycle of the social organism is the "pattern" societies have followed. Only life experiences this cycle. Many earlier scholars, such as Herbert Spencer, Arnold J. Toynbee, and Oswald Spengler noticed that societies experience a life cycle pattern. Historians have also noticed that intermediate cycles periodically occur in the monogamous-patriarchal social organisms. Progressive dynasties weaken and are replaced with new and more vigorous ones. All the twelve mainstream societies examined here have experienced the life cycle. In the mainstream now, only the Christian, Marxist, Muslim, and Hindu WV-based societies are left. The earlier WV ideological systems and their societies have all died.

The four remaining mainstream WV systems are all in the process of completing their cycle and ultimately doomed to die like the rest. All are dispensable. All life carries within it the seed of its own destruction. Death is so inherent in life that the noted philosopher, Arthur Schopenhauer

(1788-1860), regarded life as only postponed death. Our present system and way of life will finally come to an end. Even our secular system is dispensable and equally doomed. Indeed, such secular systems tend to have even shorter life spans. Later on here we will consider what type of society will follow, if one is to follow.

Briefly, then, societies and civilizations "rise" and "fall" because social organisms have a life cycle. In order to help the reader "see the forest instead of just trees," the whole rise and fall process is condensed below into a single, large, paragraph:

"Civilization is the technological, artistic and intellectual product of a mainstream patriarchal-monogamous type WV-bonded society. Society, in turn, is a social organism created by the ability of mainstream WV and ways-of-thinking to bond us into them. A mainstream WV and way-of-thinking is a language-based, relatively closed world-view (WV) and way-of-thinking built up from consistent answers to our origin, goal, means and obstacles-questions of the Four Question Template. Because such WV systems work to condition our primate, small-group social instincts, they bond people into larger-than-hunting-gathering-group "mainstream" societies, ones holding territory in the area of the world where the largest societies are competing for survival and to reproduce, hence, their "breeding ground." As their society-bonding WV ideologies age, they gradually become inconsistent with the knowledge being accumulated in the mainstream, such as from being exposed to other, more advanced, that is, less *in*accurate, WV-based secularized societies and the science they foster. The more advanced ideals only secularize the society and are not able to replace the old WV system. That liberates people from the rigid doctrines of the past and enables science and the arts to flourish. To reduce dissension between the old and the newer, secular beliefs and doctrines, a compromising accord subconsciously takes shape. Time, however, is harsh on the now dividing and increasingly more inconsistent, dual-belief system, thus weakening the social bond. Social problems proliferation, and the weakened society is invaded by barbarians who convert to its faith, and initiate reforms that enable it to recover. However, the still dividing WV base continues to build stress from generation to generation. The barbarians meld into the system as social pathology returns. It becomes serious enough to drive people back to the fundamentals of their core faith at the cost of either corrupting or abandoning the more advanced secular views. Society regresses and stagnates until a new more appealing and more scientific WV and way-of-thinking appears, one that is shaped from both the old and newer beliefs and is, if necessary, more consistent with human nature. People convert to it at the expense of the others so that it overcomes the competition of both the older belief systems and other newer would-be WVs because of being able to make a more practical-for-the-times restructuring of society. The new system spreads to a larger area encompassing more people and becomes successful to enable it to set up their own government on its own territory. The old society dies, and the cycle then repeats itself."

sixteen --- THE SOCIAL BIOLOGY OF OVER POPULATION

Beginning with the development of the patriarchal-monogamous WV system and civilization, the decline phase of human society became pronounced, also explainable. Being, as we are, semi-polygamous, not monogamous, primates, our patriarchal-monogamous WV based civilizations have all been inherently unstable. Each time their ideological unity broke down, the society's leadership lost the decisiveness and efficiency of a patriarchal, semi-barbaric system and moved toward sexual freedom, feminism, humanism and compassion, all of which finally became distorted to impractical levels and Society moved back in the direction of the egalitarian communes of Fem-Fertility, polytheistic, prehistoric times. It is this WV-division-caused, cyclical breakdown of the patriarch-monogamous system that we define here as "decline." Other signs of decline consist of less idealism in the arts, animal worship, and the re-emergence of an effeminate gay culture characteristic of fashion houses, gay bars and gay parades.

All these same signs have became more pronounced in the US during the last half century, but similar signs are also appearing now in the other four mainstream societies.

As explained earlier, the only reason the patriarchal-monogamous system originally developed was because human numbers had increased to unwieldy proportions. The new patriarch monogamous WV system necessarily evolved through natural selection of WV systems and is the only type that can handle the build up of stress from crowding. When in WV-division-caused decline, stress has always built up until the patriarchal system has been regenerated or replaced with a new one. Only then could civilization flourish again.

Also, shown earlier, was that when societies declined, they experienced ideological regression. That functioned to save the patriarchal-monogamous system, but it always came at increasing cost to further progress. That was a normal social evolutionary trade-off in order to slow or arrest the civilization's social decline.

Due to centuries of ideological splintering, Islam and Hinduism underwent their religious regression centuries ago, much as militant Christian-Libertarians in Christian-WV-based Western society are trying to do now, especially in the US. The extent of the regression of most current societies has necessarily come in direct proportion to the extent of the popular loss of faith in the Western secular system.

The advances of science and technology are also, proportionately, slowed to the extent regression occurs. For over three centuries, the "spirit" and "miracle" nature of the old Christian WV has been incompatible with and inhibiting to the advances of Western science and technology. To be sure, it is one thing to say regression has slowed down science and technology in another society, but very different to say it now affects our own. It is only natural for us to be subjectively impressed with our current rate of technological progress because we depend upon it, even for our survival.

But societies do decline, including our own; it is regressing, and we are already feeling the science-technological consequences. The last great period of Western science was between 1855 and 1935, with the discoveries of Charles Darwin, Albert Einstein and, between 1907 and 1935, by all the world's most brilliant scientists, of the relativity of knowledge and that there is no such thing in science as "Truth," something even most scientists are still unable to deal with.

The momentum of the scientific age and its technology has continued, but the tedious processing of the genome up to the epigenetic barrier, the theories of black holes and invisible matter, as well as the electronic gadgetry of the present age only comprise the technological wake of the Pure Science Age. Why is it that scientists have discovered that "there are stars older then the universe?"

Finally, the decline process can also be explainable as a social biological subject. As world population growth continues, social evolutionary forces are still at work changing and forcing the world's societies to evolve, even in a new-to-us direction. We are, after all, hardly the only animals who have to deal with population growth. Like them, we can also become "over-crowded." It helps to think of all life, including ours, as having an evolution-based "population-increase survival security goal," a mechanistic process by which populations "strive" to increase in number as if to achieve security against becoming extinct. Characteristic of living matter is that it either adjusts its growth in numbers to what its territory will support, or it increases its territory. If it can do neither, it generally suffers a population crash.

Some animals have an instinctive culling process that helps keep the birth rate under control. The smaller egg may be abandoned, or left to freeze. Slime mold organisms mass suicidally into stems that rise up so they can be attached to other animals. The weakest feathered offspring may be deliberately killed by the mother, one sibling may be allowed to kill another, or the sick or lame can be left behind in the migration.

We try to avoid those ways but we still put up with the Malthusian triad of war, famine and disease even though we have at our disposal non-Malthusian ways such as birth control, abortions, euthanasia, and capital punishment, all being applied too inadequately to slow the growth of world population. The implied plan our civilization follows is to control and limit our environmental impact and use our progressing technology to enable us to provide for our increasing numbers.

Is that realistic?

When group size increases beyond its normal number among other small group animals, the stress builds up until one of the dominant males leaves with a significant number of the group's members and forms another group. Both groups then compete for the same territory. Animals instinctively sense when their numbers have become more than what is optimal under the existing conditions and for that species. They feel "over-crowded" in the sense that stress builds up until their too-large group splits in two.

We also evolved an instinctive social nature as small group primates. We feel the same strain and tension other social animals feel when their groups have grown too large. Our numbers manage to grow so large only to the extent our WV ideological systems can unite us and enable us to progress scientifically, technologically. When the ideological unity breaks down and loses its ability to do that, we feel the stress, we feel "crowded." The amount of stress keeps increasing as the ideological system continues to divide and loses more of its bonding power. As the stress builds, people choose hunting-gathering size factions that become federated into systems that grow increasingly antagonistic to each other. These contentious alliances help to accelerate the social breakdown process.

In addition, animals feel increasing stress when their territory cannot be expanded at the rate their numbers are rising. The increase in stress tends to break down the animal's health so that the death rate rises and their numbers decline. In deer, the tension and stress can reach such levels that large numbers of them die of shock. In every case, it all happens because of an instinct-caused build-up of stress, not because the animals are starving to death or because they are so jammed together they cannot move.

With us, it is more complicated. Our understanding of the world and ourselves grows and with it the technology needed to exploit the territory we have as our population increases. However, as the population continues to grow and the needed amounts of easily available land, water and natural resources decline, pressure is put on the standard of living of everyone. For example, oil is still one of the cheapest sources of energy, but before the 2010 Gulf of Mexico oil rig collapse, oil companies were prepared to drill down through five miles of ocean, mud, salt, and rock, where the temperature exceeds 450 degrees and where the pressure is twenty thousand pounds per square inch. There are now plans to drill still deeper wells off Brazil, while other plans are to drill in the arctic, also, to mine the bottom of the ocean floor. We have to keep spending more energy to get more energy. Even with technology, it is impossible to keep getting more and more out of less and less. At some point, human living conditions have to collapse, making the stress less manageable.

Throughout most of our social history, misfits and troublemakers have been singled out, ganged up on, and killed, a process that has biologically evolved us, through natural-selection, to be "tamed" or "domesticated," and thus better able to endure the stress our large societies inflict on us. However, there is, of course, a limit to this endurance-ability.

Clearly then, the maximum number of people we can sustain on our planet, before sliding down the other side of the population cycle, has little to do with the amount of food we could produce or the space we could find for housing. It is determined by *the amount of stress we can endure.*

When group animals increase in numbers and cannot expand their area, they fight over it. Groups of baboons, meerkats, lemurs, and many other group animals wage war over territory. When locusts become crowded, they begin cannibalizing the others, forcing them to swarm. Chimpanzees have been known to hunt down and kill every member of another troop. Rats and mice experience a collapse in their behavior and gang up on each other. Also, if you try to touch a wild animal crowded into a cage where it cannot run and escape, it will bite your hand. What happens is that the over-crowding builds up stress to levels that are increasingly expressed as hostility and belligerence. In other words, there is a deterioration in behavior.

The survival of technology depends upon the failure of regression, but the survival of society depends upon the regression of both the old religion and the secular system. The growing population pressure on our space and resources makes us more dependent on technology. The general standard of living is doomed to fall as the population increases and technology lags.

But if the world's territory were unlimited, all this would be of less concern. The Earth is limited, but the universe itself is not. Unlike other biological organisms, we are fortunate enough to have the whole universe into which we can expand. We have before us its unlimited territory, all for us to take. We could expand out into it long enough to keep on evolving, even to lasting as long as the universe.

Our present WV systems, however, cause us to show little interest both in controlling our numbers and expanding out into space. Our space efforts pale in comparison to the ultimate need. Only when we seize the opportunity can we continue to expand in territory and, eventually, our numbers as well. Instead of being ideologically focused on doing that, we are content to assume we can just drift along toward such goals. The feeling is that we will build space colonies, ultimately, someday off in the distant future when we feel comfortable diverting funds to such a program, funds which we now would rather spend on the many little things we "need." Until then, outer space will stay where it is and we can use it for the entrepreneurs to build tourist rockets so the rich can play in it.

In order to break out of man's downward spiral, there will have to be a new WV system capable of replacing all those that now divert and divide us. In order to keep stress under control, the broken down ideological WV systems must ultimately be replaced. No ideological WV system has ever been eternal; all are expendable. When such a system becomes old, divided and no longer a consistent, closed and effective WV system, it fails to meet the challenges and the whole series of complex, social-biological factors come into play. All of them increase stress until people are ultimately *forced* to find a new and better ideology, one that can bring back the unity they and their society needs to survive. Only when it is almost too late, will people be under such stress that they will find and take up a new WV that would at that time turn out the be "the wave of the future."

What would such a new WV system be like? The next two chapters are an attempt to answer that question. Their intent is to develop a facsimile of what such a new ideology might have to be like to succeed.

seventeen --- PROBLEMS AND SOLUTIONS

In the past, all societies eventually declined until each was replaced with a new society bonded by a new and more advanced (more accurate) WV and way of thinking. Developing such a new WV system is an old process in which each new WV system always evolved out of need. Each drew from the successes of the past and from the best of the secular system that had been propping up the old one. Each was shaped from the natural selecting out of the more effective parts, ones with a less "spirit"-based understanding. In each case, people then began to recognize it as "the wave of the future."

The whole process need not now be left to the mechanistic or swarm theory social, evolutionary natural selection process. Instead, let us try to do it deliberately. Perhaps in this way we can come up with a WV facsimile close to what will ultimately have to take shape.

Establishing such a new WV system would only happen as the stress buildup forces a world-wide, grass-roots, spread of the system at the expense of all the other, and older, ideologies. Once it manages to acquire territory and become mainstream, we can logically assume it would proceed step by step to achieve its real world, non-"spiritual" objectives and goals. That, in turn, would give us the ability to more accurately predict our future.

The first step in preparing the facsimile is to draw up a list of modern and potential world problems and their solutions, ones which make sense only in light of social evolution, not "solutions" aimed at reforming the present system. Rather than think in terms of patching up either the world's old WV systems or the 17th century-based secular one, we need to think in terms of starting over. That means an unavoidable clash with the way our now fading ideals have conditioned us to think and believe. But for a new one to be better, it has to be different; otherwise there is no point in even looking for it.

We can begin with probably the biggest problem. There is no longer room in the mainstream for more than one society and civilization. We can survive the nuclear arms age only by developing a single WV system, one capable of replacing all the others and bonding us all into a single, one world-society, a sort of United States of the World, something that becomes possible only by a new WV replacing all the others. One can imagine that happening only because of the immense stress that lies ahead.

We can develop a reasonable facsimile of the core or theology of such a new, Non-Theist WV system by adapting the social evolution of human society to answering the questions of the Four Question Template. In order to shape it to a one-world-society-task, we should list the needs it must meet. Then, we need to fit the needs to solutions that answer the Four Question template. Once we have built the core of the facsimile this way, we are in a position to combine both social evolution theory and the facsimile to view a description of the system's complete, self-consistent, closed World View and way of thinking. We would have a WV that would be consistent with the data of all the social, biological, and natural sciences.

Once we have the whole facsimile before us, we know the real-world goals as well as the morality of the means it would seek to employ in order to achieve them. Because the new, real-world goals would be achievable, we can be reasonably sure it would use its means to achieve them. That means we would be able to predict the general path it would follow. For the first time, we would have the ability to develop a reasonably accurate prediction of the long term future.

In structuring the facsimile, much of the secular-age ideals and beliefs would need to be adapted to be a part of the core of the new WV system, even some of the useful doctrines of the older belief systems. What is non-"miracle," accurate, and useful in the old "spirit"-based WV systems would be retained; new WV systems always need to have ties to the past, to earlier ones. Only what might be called "spiritual-gibberish," would be excluded. That means there would be nothing left, cynics might say, but it is only from the old WV systems that we learned the importance of monogamy, family traditions, the concept of a moral code, some of the dream-like feelings of "spirit"-based beliefs and the importance of a disciplined, militant, and dedicated clergy or party. All that would need to be kept.

Proposed below is a list of needed solutions, ones that might shape a society able to effectively deal with present and anticipated problems. In so doing, the word "doctrine" will often come up. This refers to everything the belief system would have its followers believe and, hence, everything they would "know." This includes all the ideals, standards, teachings, knowledge, beliefs and, of course, "truths" currently in general use. All of them are doctrines, and none of the facsimile doctrines would involve "spirits" or "miracles." All would be based on an objective interpretation of the social and natural science data. There are thirteen "needs" in the list:

(1) The first need is for all the new WV system's doctrines to be compatible with scientific, natural cause and effect. Since a doctrine must be rigid, clear, uncontested in order for the WV system to endure, we need a doctrine to the effect that "the answer to how we and the rest of the universe arose and operates" needs to always be more accurate because of always being the scientific consensus. Such a doctrine would need to be uncompromised and inflexible, even eternal, existing as the solid, central pillar of society's ideological support. For the first time, society would be intellectually and technologically uninhibited even during its "theocratic" or pre-secular age.

(2) The second need of the new WV system would be to establish a viable one-world political system, a need that has been poorly served by every WV belief system to this date. The need is for a world government and a lessening of the total sovereignty of each individual state. The transfer of loyalty that occurred in the US from the States to a national government is an adequate model for a similar transfer from nations to a world government. For a new WV and way of thinking to be successful, it must spread across the globe, topple old-religion-based governments, and ideologically binding the people and their governments into an enduring world government, one that focuses on the long term.

World government would need to be based on a flexible political ideal, one that would enable the various nations to operate together harmoniously even with their diverse political needs and old-system-based cultures. As shown earlier, no type of government is superior to all the others. The new, word-wide political system would need to be open to nations freely choosing which form of constitutional government its citizens thought could best govern them.

Those nations split by cultural, lingual and political diversity would need the checks-and-balances of a parliamentary republic. In other nations where the people mostly convert to the new science-based WV system, the cumbersome multi-party checks and balances of representative, parliamentary government would be needlessly inefficient. The people would form a single-party, theocratic (pre-secular) government, one that would be unified enough to represent the will of the people's single point of view and be centralized enough to represent it efficiently. No government needs the gigantic, ponderous, corrupt and inefficient bureaucracy which modern western governments force their taxpayers to support.

A new world society would need an aligning of the two political systems into a single but dual-constitutional system with representatives from each state collectively forming world government wherever it is to be located. Such a dual-constitutional system could consist of a charter with two distinct constitutions and a provision for regular plebiscites to decide which constitution the people would want to live under.

(3) The third need would be for flexibility in economic matters and, hence, to be compatible with both capitalism and communal institutions. As the experience with guild communes in Europe and the Kibbutz communes in Israel have shown, communal institutions can operate well in a capitalist economy. People would need to be free to establish communes, collectives or cooperatives if they wanted to.

The whole structure of the corporate entity needs to be modified in order to end it as an amoral and conscience-less enterprise dedicated only to management and stockholder gain. Instead, it can and should be turned into a noble entity with the goal equally of employee welfare, preserving the environment, providing constructive products and services to society and, as well, a fair return to its investors and managers. Corporations without such goals would need to have no moral or legal right to exist.

In some nations, a revolution would be needed, not against any single class but against the corrupt oligarchy which had been holding power. Such a revolution would not be based on class hatred but, as mentioned earlier, the need to reduce extremes of wealth between classes. No civilization can exist without classes. There always has to be those with more money and status. It is just that the class advantage of status needs to always be from its constructive contribution to society. An honorable upper-income class would involve itself in constructive economic, political, and cultural leadership. And, upward mobility would need to be federally encouraged and denied to no individual or class.

(4) The fourth need would be anti-racism. Without the doctrine of the equality of the races, an honest world government would be impossible. There are differences between the races but there is no difference in their ability to build civilization, and nothing else about race is important. To fully establish this anti-racist principle, the gradual but natural mixing of

all races, tribes, and ethnic groups would need to be encouraged. We are all just one race, the human race.

The school system of every country needs a set international educational standard that provides a history not of its nation but of its own former-religion-based whole social organism or civilization. There should be no focus on local histories of groups, tribes or nations.

(5) The fifth need is for society to environmentally protect our planet for the long term so it can function as an enduring space platform for the launching of colonies out into the rest of the solar system, and later on, into the rest of the universe. We need to control the use of chemicals that accumulate in us and the rest of the environment. As well, we would need to recycle everything, control our numbers, and monitor our Earth so it can serve serve us indefinitely. The Earth would need to be regareded as our homeland and serve as a model and example of how we are to take care of other planets other than this one.

(6) The sixth need of the new society is for it to be guided by a uniform and unified Party, not a political party but the nation-run Party of members dedicated to the goals and means of the new WV and way-of-thinking. This would be a governing Party. No patriarchal-monogamous civilization-type society can operate without a party-clergy-like system and none ever has. Islam even had to develop one because it was ruled out in its scriptures.

(7) The new society's Party organization would need to keep its role in the open. All Party books and records need to be freely open to all.

(8) In order to introduce competition and sustain its own integrity, the Party would need to have a dual-party system. In order to be both competitive and monolithic, it would need to have two separate "wings." One wing would be investigative and focus on the long term needs of society at the cost, wherever necessary, of near term welfare. Part of its emphasis would be focused on Party unity and guiding society toward barbarian-like militancy and practicality by managing the regulatory agencies, the military, and the justice systems.

The other wing of the Party, the service wing, would need to be made up of men and women who dedicate their lives to serving the more immediate needs of people. It would, for example, run charities. This wing would need to have no direct political power, but since it would fill most of the governments' service bureaucracies, it would have important, indirect power.

At some high level of the dual organization, the two wings would need to unite into one. Just below that, the top individual of the Service wing would need to function as a caring and loving leader. At the supreme peak of the pyramid of Party policy power would be the other leader and head of the Party. Since his focus would be on the long-term future of world society, he would function as the "Direct, Authorized Representative of the Social Organism" (DARSO). He would carry the ultimate responsibility of the whole society on his shoulders, not the immediate welfare of any single individual or segment of the society. He would need to provide leadership in times of crisis, those times when important changes would be needed which would bear on the society's long term development and survival.

The DARSO would be able to be removed from power by a majority of the nine-body International Supreme Court. To avoid him building into a "personality cult," all government would be prohibited from the production, distribution, and posting of pictures or statues of him. He would not perform routine ceremonial functions nor would he ever give political speeches. He would rarely have cause to speak, and when he does, it would be taken seriously. The whole objective of the changes are to give power to the government but to divide it so that if one part becomes corrupt, the other parts have the ability to change who is in charge so the process of cleaning it up can begin.

(9) The ninth need of the new society is that it be *militant*. It needs to be bonded by a militant universal brotherhood type of WV system, one that is aggressive and forceful because over-humanistic, decadent civilizations respond well to barbaric rejuvenation. The new society would need to be able to do whatever is necessary to solve long-term-type world problems.

(10) The tenth need is for the world to focus on and fund the space program. The Program would need to be centrally coordinated but developed regionally with various parts of the world contributing their expertise and resources to the whole project.

(11) The eleventh need is for preserving world competition in a one-world society. Since all is relative, we need to have contrasts so we can make judgments and find values. There needs to be competition and contrasts. The new one-world society has to deliberately base itself on dualistic institutions so it can have the competition on which natural selection takes place. Especially important would be competition between the world's separate mainstream cultures, such as the Christian, Muslim, Marx-Orient, and Hindu cultural heritages. The way to preserve natural selection competition in the new society without compromising its unity of belief would be, in addition to the four main cultural entities: (a) the

bifurcating of the Party into separate "wings," (b) the dual constitutional system, (c) the two economic systems, and (d) a dual citizenship system which divides those who accept the new WV from those who do not.

(12) The twelfth and last need is for the worldwide growth in human population to be slowed and brought to an end, even allowed to drop. Since we have learned to ration women only one to a man, we can learn to ration children only one to a family. Within a world in which millions suffer malnutrition because they are crowding the environment, society has the obligation to see that infants and children who are seriously impaired do not survive to be a burden to themselves, their parents and society. The only really humane thing to do is for society to take on the responsibility of relieving the strain and hardship of both victim and family. Having a child would be an honor and a privilege, and those with that privilege deserve to have their one child be normal enough to ultimately become a contributing member of society rather than a burden to it and to its parents.

(13) The thirteenth need is to protect the long term survival of the human race from threats such as the following:

a. RADIATION-BASED BOMBS, SHELLS AND MISSILES. At this time of writing there are from five to fifteen thousand nuclear missiles and bombs (not counting Israel's), many of which are hair triggered to be set off and in the hands of governments which are growing increasingly inefficient, irresponsible and, in some cases, already even run by religiously regressive regimes.

b. PLAGUE. Ebola, AIDS, flu or any other major new plagues can ravage us, our livestock, and/or the genetically-same-large-crop agricultural system. Also bio-terrorism and the malicious development of a non-biological nano-virus could become a major threat.

c. CLIMATE CHANGE. Climate change from the impact of a large comet or meteor or the explosion of one of the world's volcanic calderas can cause years of disastrous cooling, or we could have continuous destructive effects from Earth's currently rising temperature.

d. OUTER SPACE THREAT. There is a remote chance human life on Earth would be destroyed by a half-mile wide comet, a black hole or a burst of gamma radiation.

e. ALIEN LIFE THREAT. There is an even remoter possibility there might actually be another form of life out in the universe that is near enough to be a threat to us.

Until now, almost nothing effective has been done to protect the long term survival of the human race from such threats because the bulk of the world's old mainstream ideological systems are not scripturally focused on our long-term survival. They are not even concerned over our short-term survival.

To deal with such long-term threats, the new WV and way of thinking needs to be shaped to last as long as it takes to permanently ensure our survival.

eighteen --- A LIKENESS OF THE NEXT WV SYSTEM

We can now use the thirteen "needs" to help answer the questions of the Four Question Template. The result should provide us with a reasonable facsimile of what the core of the next mainstream WV system would need to resemble.

The first question is "<u>What is our origin?</u>" As suggested earlier, our origin and that of the universe would need to be "whatever the increasingly more accurate scientific consensus says it is." Such a rule would need to be regarded as unalterable. It would be rigidly held and unchanging, giving the scientific freedom needed for the continued increase in the accuracy of what we believe and the continued growth in technology. This would not change.

The second question is "<u>What is our goal?</u>" T need to be achieved for the survival and welfare of everyone. Its practical goals would be realizable and honed to solve specific problems. Below are eight realistic goals that a facsimile of a future society would logically provide as answers:

(1) *The establishment of world government.* Once we achieve a true, whole-WV and way of thinking, human need and want would evolve us toward world government naturally and inevitably.

(2) *The building of a better, newer, worldwide civilization.* Building a new society with a new WV and way of thinking would end our present troubled, old civilization and begin a new and better one.

(3) *The expansion out into space.* We need to build up an atmosphere similar to Earth's on another planet or moon in our solar system, or whatever is necessary to set up self-supporting colonies out beyond our own planet. Many planets within our galaxy, ones similar to ours, are being discovered all the time now.

(4) *An enduring, undivided society.* To achieve our goals, we need a single, new society based upon a WV and way of thinking, doctrinally adjusted to last at least as long as it takes to colonize our own solar system. To insure the society lasts that long, its WV and way of thinking needs to be protected and kept unified.

(5) *Take control over our own population growth and conserve our Earth's resources.* Mankind cannot keep getting more out of less. It is time for us to take charge of our own destiny and think responsibly about the relationship we have between our numbers and resources.

(6) *The perpetuation of science.* Society needs to continue achieving a more accurate understanding of ourselves and our universe. That means ending with a non-"spirit," non-"miracle" WV age way-of-thinking.

(7) *Provide equal opportunity for everyone.* Society is not obligated to make people equal but all who are fit to survive do deserve a chance to compete with each other equally. All have the right to equal justice, to be schooled, and to fairly compete for jobs.

(8) *The elimination of racial prejudice and the goal of the merging of the races.* It is important to continue blurring racial distinctions.

The third question is "<u>how do we achieve our goals?</u>" As evolved social animals, we are instinctively moral with a strong sense of justice and normally do the right thing. We only need moral standards to guide our legal system to help us more efficiently cooperate to achieve the society's goals.

We can start with the old Ten Commandments which are, by now, far from adequate. They do not, for example, forbid believers from kidnapping, enslaving, raping, stalking, gambling, taking bribes, defiling the dead or torturing prisoners. They also do not forbid the use in warfare of depleted uranium or cluster bombs and mines, ones that maim and kill decades after the war ends. The fact that they did not have them then only proves the Decalogue's obsolescence.

It is possible, however, to correct and update some of the Decalogue's moral-standard "commandments" to make them applicable to modern times. Then, we can add a whole additional Second Decalogue to deal with the important moral standards the older Ten failed to address. The combined total, below, would bring us to nineteen moral standards plus three that could be applied only to national governments because of being enforcible by world government:

The moral standard in the Decalogue against sacrilege can be usefully adapted to one against disrespect for those who have been elected or appointed to high government positions in society. In addition, it can be upgraded from being against blasphemy, to be against insults to the society's whole WV and way of thinking. It would be immoral, for example, to use profanity filled with sexual or toilet invective.

The second of the Decalogue's moral standards is against stealing. It needs no comment except that it should also include fraud, buying or receiving stolen or suspected-of-being-stolen property and cheating in general.

The third is "Thou shall not kill." Sometimes it is necessary to kill, but it is immoral to "murder." Every person who is not destructive to society has a right to live. However, sometimes, innocent acts cause the accidental killing of another person, or enemy troops are killed in battle. Also, individuals sometimes have to kill in self-defense. Even though the Bible says that "thou shall not kill," in the real world, killing has all along been not only acceptable but sometimes even commendable. Killing is a moral wrong when it is done intentionally, for self-gain, and/or with reckless disregard for others. Then, it is "murder."

The fourth is against showing disrespect for one's parents and the elderly, one that needs no modification. Older people should be treated with respect. Society suffers when all emphasis is on youth and when the parents and elderly are treated with disrespect, neglect, or indifference.

The fifth is the one about "coveting." Most of the world no longer has to deal with "coveting your neighbor's cow or "manservant" (slave), but we do allow coveting (envy), greed and gluttony to shape the West's over indulgent, materialistic life-style. Living solely for material gain and sensual pleasures is crude, demeaning, and immoral.

The sixth would be aimed at promiscuity, adultery, pornography, and incest. Its purpose would be to protect the patriarchal-monogamous nature of the system, protect our genetic heritage, and limit the spread of venereal disease. Also, such firm sexual-relations standards are basic to the 5,000-year successful patriarchal-monogamous WV system. Such standards restrain society from regressing back in the direction of the primitive, free-love, women-controlled, and no longer viable communal system of prehistory.

The seventh would be against the taking and giving of bribes. The responsibility held by people in high government office would be to the long-term betterment of society.

The eighth would be against assault. It would need to include rape, torturing, forcible detention (kidnap), repeated harassing, hurling intimidating threats to the relatively defenseless and stalking.

The ninth would be against lying. Lying is immoral when it is done at the expense of another person or of society. People need to be bound to their word.

The tenth moral standard would be against the taking of intoxicants (including mind-distorting drugs such as cocaine, heroin and the many designer drugs), aphrodisiacs, stimulants and/or euphoria inducing drugs. Neither do people or society need to consume the high-alcohol-content beverages, tobacco, chat, and marijuana. To be normal is to be natural and live moderately. Should they also be illegal? It is up to society to decide.

The eleventh would be against the fraudulent use of language to obscure clarity. Since we are not to lie to each other, we are equally obligated to write and speak honestly to each other without word-trickery.

The twelfth involves bodily modesty. It is best for human sexual matters to be only private. Covering the body serves not only to protect it from the elements, but also to reduce its sexual nature in public. Men should not be subjected to the constant distraction and erotic stimulation so characteristic of the West's modern, secular, sex-mad, sex-in-advertising, Bonobo-like culture.

The hiding of women's sexuality in public should not, however, come at the expense of the individual. Women should not have to burden themselves with shrouds that destroy all originality in dress and obstruct access to sunlight, eating, seeing and even fresh air. The feminine contribution to the visible world is vital and is needed to lend balance to public life. A world in which all public affairs are conducted devoid of any signs of women is a drab, mean, and grubby one. The masculine world is a half world and needs to be visibly and constantly contrasted with the feminine in order for it to be whole. The masculine purpose of a society demands a culture that protects the feminine, not eliminates it.

The thirteenth involves good citizenship. We should all conserve energy, comply with the need to be a reliable witness, be on time, give to charity, help apprehend suspects, and be informed when voting in elections. We should, as well, try to prevent a crime or injury, help in case of accident or natural disaster, warn others of threats, report crimes, and be thrifty enough to be debt-free.

The fourteenth is being kind to other animals. A next-society doctrine would be that we should never be cruel to them, but we should also not worship them. We should not hesitate to use, hunt (when abundant and for human consumption), confine, domesticate or kill them to provide for our own needs. Since we are by nature meat-eating animals, it is incumbent upon us to follow our nature by controlling animal population numbers through balanced human hunting/culling. At the same time, society needs to rationally restrain the loss of species.

The fifteenth would be against gambling.

The sixteenth would be a moral need to respect your own body enough to take proper care of it. There should be the self-discipline to keep clean and avoid excessive weight gain. The individual needs to take care of the body so it can take care of him or her.

The seventeenth would be the protecting of our environment from auditory, visual, odorous, chemical and physical pollution. Besides not contaminating our air, earth, oceans, lakes and streams, this would include protection from the overload of promotional verbiage, graffiti, spam, and hacker piracy, all of which pollute our sources of communication and learning.

The eighteenth would be against promoting or inciting race hatred. There is only one race, the human race, and we would all be one people.

The nineteenth moral standard would reject all forms of slavery. Exodus 21:20-21 and Leviticus, 25:50 of the Old Testament, teaches people that "God" gave "His People" the privilege of having slaves. No one has such a "privilege." Also included would be the selling of children or the forcing of women into prostitution. No one would have the right to kidnap, buy, or dominate another human being.

In addition to the above nineteen moral standard for the individual, there should be three more that would be applicable only to government. The new society would have world government, so it would finally be possible to enforce a code of international conduct in and between its separate states. Governments should adhere to many of the nineteen moral standards as well.

The twentieth, is a government rule against the torturing of prisoners. Prisons should provide the inmates with only austere, Spartan conditions and with strict discipline even though rehabilitation programs should be available and basic health care provided. It is immoral for government to deprive prisoners of needed sleep, prevent them from exercising and getting some sunlight. It is also immoral for government to expose prisoners to loud noise or humiliating them either as physical-mental punishment for the original crime or in order to get information. All such coercive efforts are "torture." Permission to use such tactics on special enemies of the state would need to be enacted by special legislation passed by world government only for that single case.

The twenty-first, a second governmental moral standard would be against the manufacturing, distributing, buying, selling or sewing of any type of mine or other ordinance which commonly explodes and kills civilians after the fighting is over. This applies to those on land, water, or in space, except in defense of the human race itself.

And the twenty-second and third governmental moral standard would be against the manufacture, sale, possession and use of weapons of mass death and destruction except, possibly, by world government in defense of humanity.

So, in answer to the third question of the Four Question Template, "how do we achieve our goals?," we have the above nineteen to twenty-two moral standards designed to help people live and work together in better harmony and the more efficient function of society.

Believers would be free to eat without doctrinal meddling, including beef, shellfish, and pork. There would need to be no taboos against abortion, cloning, executions, suicide, marital divorce, remarriage, developing safe nuclear power, being homosexual. These might even be considered a near "Decalogue of Rights."

The above list of moral standards would give a proposed WV system all the ability it needs to do whatever necessary to achieve all the goals essential to the survival of human civilization. That means that over-humanistic considerations would not limit its power to be as forceful and aggressive, even barbaric, as would be needed to effectively, efficiently, achieve them. What is important for our survival is to succeed, not to find fault and excuses. The Christian Bible says "the meek and sorrowful shall inherit the Earth," and indeed, they have; but a new society would take it away from them.

The fourth and last question of the Four Question Template is: "What obstacle stands in the way of achieving our goals?"

Past societies set up "evil gods" as scapegoats to explain their society's failings even though their objectives were all only pie-in-the-sky. All the old societies had the "blame" doctrine because people preferred to blame scapegoats instead of themselves, their clerics, or their beliefs. But when a mistake is made, it is more effective to place blame where it belongs so we more readily learn from our mistakes and avoid repeating them.

The real-world obstacles which the new society would target would be the possible rise of mono-mate barbaric religious cults, corporate-promoted materialism, the survival of Marx-Leninist-socialist thinking, terrorism, over-humanism, and superstition. The new society would wage "war" on all types of ignorance that blocks or slows human progress. Its most prominent weapon against all beliefs that tend to drag on science would be an effective, scientific determinist-based educational system, one antagonistic to all regressive psychic and spirit fads. A duty of the Party would be to help focus public efforts against obstacles to the survival of society. In this world, we are not helpless to understand and to change things. We are not helpless as long as we are not ignorant.

To some people, the Four Question Template should include a fifth question dealing with death. The academic social theory consensus considers the so-called "mystery of death" to be one of the basic components of religion. It may have been to the individual, but not to society. In a new society, many will at first miss the illusion of "life after death," but the old "spirit"-based WV systems never provided the support to the dying and bereaved that they promised. The old Hindu WV religious system promised those who were righteous an end to reincarnation and, hence, "an end to suffering." In other words, for the righteous, it promised nothing more than an end to existence, yet it was able to create a society that built one of the world's greatest civilizations. The promise of escaping from death has never even been needed in the mainstream. Despite the belief in an "after life" common to most "spirit"-based WV systems, people have always, feared death. The after-death-oxymora never fully convinces anyone.

In such ways, all the questions of the Four Question Template can be answered in a new Non-Theistic Age WV way, one that is consistent with the patriarchal-monogamous and universal-brotherhood WV formula. All can be proposed as the core of a WV system able to bring us fully into the Non-Theistic Age. When we are finally ready to colonize other parts of our solar system, we will not need the help of "spirits" to bravely face the mysteries and dangers ahead. To meet the challenge we only need to stand united together.

PART 4 ---- "PROPHESY"

nineteen--- HOW EVENTS MAY UNWIND

The objective now is to, as accurately as possible, draw a picture of what is in store for the world between now and when we move successfully out of the Monotheistic into the Non-Theistic Age. Considering what information we have so far, the effects of the decline should become more obvious and troubling during the years and decades to come and at an accelerating rate. We are not going to deal with futuristic forecasts of "amazing technological wonders to come." We will instead, concentrate on what will happen to people, the world's people, the world affairs of the human race.

First, looking back, religious regression typically set in and served to sustain a splintered World View-based civilization during its decline. Normally, the regression sustained the society until the old WV was extensively modified or replaced by a new one. In the past, the WV-regression process came at the cost of slowing and then ending the growth of science and technology. Each time it would return in the next dynastic recovery or by the replacement of the old WV by a new one.

The modern world is also showing some signs of regression, but unlike with those of the past, some of the typical changes are not happening and the others are occurring only minimally. We are not in a typical decline. Instead, we are experiencing something that has occurred only twice before in the social evolution of the human race.

The first time such a decline occurred was six to eight thousand years ago with the mainstream transition from animism to polytheism. Since that was in prehistory, we know too little about it for it to be of help in understanding the details of the process. However, we do have considerable detail about the second such time, e.g., the mainstream transition from polytheism to monotheism.

Once the Romans had established their empire, they depended partially on the Hellenic Age, secular ideology, its so called "culture," to spread and help unite it, but by the time of Jesus, the Hellenic secular WV system had split into a number of secular cults, or what are now termed "philosophies," ones such as Sophism, Hedonism, Skepticism, Neo-Platonism, Epicureanism, Stoicism, Eclecticism, etc. The list had been growing from about 500 B.C. on and, in combination, they had broken down the Empire's secular WV system's semblance of unity. The ultimate result was growing discontent and stress. The coinage was constantly being debased and violent mobs had to be appeased with bread and entertainment in the Colosseum in order to keep them from rioting. By the time of Jesus, social problems and stress had built up enough that the leaders of the older faiths were making vociferous efforts to attract people back to their old polytheisms in hopes of stabilizing their again-sinking societies. That is, Egypt, Babylon, and Greece all resumed the same ideological regression they had been undergoing before they became part of the Roman-Hellenic Empire.

People were not, however, regressing in enough numbers to stop the social, moral disintegration. Many people were hoping to find something better than the old faiths. Even among the polytheists, a central, all-powerful god had generally been lording over the other gods. The dual-god Persian WV system had welded together an empire that Rome, unlike Greece earlier, had been unable to conquer, and monotheism had been a concept of the elite for over a thousand years. By Roman times it had enough popular appeal to become the advanced idea of the age, the "wave of the future."

What appealed to many was the deity of Judaism, as touched on in chapter 11. The old faith was not fault-free or even needed to be. The Judaics had evolved as a mono-mate barbaric WV tribal-racist system, one which called its god, *Yahweh*. Their beliefs had isolated them from the other and still polytheistic Hebrew tribes, but the isolation tightened the bond among them and fostered both a contentiousness with Rome and a fanatical loyalty to each other, to their belief system, and to their tribal history. They had also skillfully streamlined, and put into their heritage, the Babylonian origin-of-the-world myths and added, all down in writing, what was, for those times, a magnificently distilled and refined ten-item moral code.

Therefore, there were good reasons for others in the Empire to admire them. People could not and did not want to become "Jews," but the need for a Judaic-like WV had nevertheless taken root, and as often happens in human social evolution, when there is a need, an ideological solution evolves. People began to convert in mass to the Judic-modified Jesus WV system and, by the thousands, the old gods began falling in their graves. The Jesus Apostles had managed to turn the Judaic system's more useful doctrines into a universal WV system, one that, for those times, had immense appeal.

Now, we are in the third such transition era, one similar to that of the Roman Empire. Again, a secular civilization, ours, is struggling to keep together its empire or "World Community of Nations." Again, a science age has reduced the belief in "miracles" and "gods," now to none at all. We are in the process of changing again. This time the change is from the Monotheistic to the Non-Theistic Age.

Even with its racist, tribal nature, Judaism was in some ways advanced enough to pave the way into a new era. Similarly, the very existence now of the also faulty Marxist-WV-based society proves that a non-theistic WV is able to bond a mainstream society. Marxism might not survive, but it would not be because it is atheistic. It had enabled Non-Theism to become the new "Wave of the Future."

As it was two thousand years ago, people are not now returning to their obsolescent old "spirit"-based monotheisms in the numbers needed to stabilize any of the four WV-based societies, and social-moral deterioration has resumed in each. The Christian, Islamic, Hindu and Marxist societies can be expected to continue experiencing stress-build-up until world conditions become so desperate that, as in Roman times, people will be forced to move out of the Old Age into the New One.

Since World War II, the US has been the very center of the Western secular society and its civilization. All over the world, people of other WV faiths have been aware of America's secular ways and, because they represented her prosperity and immense military power, they respected her and her ideals, e.g., awe + fear = respect. So, they also respected her view of women, politics, and "rights." They respected them not because they were "inherent truths" but because people subliminally presumed they were the cause of America's prosperity and power. That made her ideals desirable, something one should want. Eagerly, then, they adopted them and, similarly, combined them with their own old "spirit"-based WV systems.

But as with the Roman Empire's Hellenic secular system, the US secular system has also splintered into a host of rigidly held secular cults, ones such as vegetarian, nudism, environmentalism, individualism, pacifism, animal rights, and anti-capital-punishment believers. The list includes big business Libertarian secular cultism which seeks to replace government with corporate businesses. All these ideologies are are often held religiously. Among the more extreme, anarchistic, militant and fanatical offshoots is the "Sovereign Citizens" who hope to tear down the central government and restore a "pre-US Constitution utopia." Others include the radical Animal Liberation and Earth Liberation Fronts. Their way to save the Earth is to "return to nature," that is, to return to a hunting-gathering-like age depopulation. There are also, over a hundred racist, Neo-Nazi "Skinhead" groups with a fast growing total of more than ten thousand members who advocate overthrowing the government and re-forming it into re-segregated parts.

Most of the above ideologies are, in varying degrees, anarchistic. As their groups proliferate, people turn against the one organization essential to the development and sustaining of civilization; they turn against government. Their ideals of Liberty and freedom are too easily interpreted to mean liberty and freedom *from* government, to be anti-government. Indeed, the secular ideal of " liberty," by its very nature, lends itself to anarchist causes. People have long been mouthing the very ideals that are causing the chaos they must now struggle with daily.

Yet, the secular anarchisms mentioned above are not the most powerful anarchisms in the modern world. All anarchism are not secular. One of the two most powerful of all is Marxism, its goal being to replace government with an idealistic and impossible communal, egalitarian system. The other is militant Christianity in the US. Its very origin and appeal was based on its promise to replace government with an imaginary "Kingdom of God." Now, with world conditions returning to a Roman Empire type pathological condition, returning with it is the Christian goal of a rivers-of-blood-Armageddon to be followed by the myth of His-Return. Not only do its militants back up the power of the anarchistic anti-government Libertarian Right but their cause also spawns hundreds of US government-hating Christian-based militias in the South and Midwest.

The growth of anarchism occurs because the unity of the secular and old-religion WV systems has been shattered. People cannot understand the cause or solution to their growing unease, so they blame "the establishment" or "the system," the only tangible part of which, to them, is government. They blame it instead of the ideological discord that causes their government's incompetence. In the US, anarchist sentiment is aided by Congress being the mere face of corporate lobbyists hired by the affluent, and militant, Libertarian-driven business class. Even though most Americans still hang on to the gross illusion that they just need to vote out the present politicians in order to bring in good government, the more corrupt the Libertarians make the government by using their lavish advertising revenue to make the media focus on the faults of "Big Government" and away from those of "Big Business."

The general inability of much of the world to effectively regress means that there is nothing to stop the gradual WV division-caused social-problem behavioral breakdown of the whole civilization. The spread of anarchism contributes to behavioral deterioration not just within the four societies but also between their governments and societies as a whole. That is, there is a growing behavioral deterioration underway in international world affairs.

In the old polytheistic Hindu and in the Marxist Chinese WV-based societies, the growth of their urbane middle class and the build up of their superstructure has inclined their citizens to think they are building the "post-United States world." It is a tempting thought, but they, along with Islam and Brazil, are all still part of the aging American secular world order and have all built their hopes on the US model, on the corporation, the automobile, consumerism, credit cards, food engineering, and labor-saving lack of exercise and franchise food eating obesity. They all have the same profligacy and corruption. Some tourist meccas in Islamic Turkey, are even adopting gay bars and nudist hotels as one of the standards for becoming more Western.

So, as America must finally stumble and fall, the would-be nations must also do so. They are making the same mistakes and ending up with the same shortages, pollution, crime, social problems and environmental degradation. They all have severely fractured WV systems, too many people, and not enough water, mineral, land and energy resources. They are extracting and cutting down what resources they have left. Most of their cities are jammed inside with bumper-to-bumper traffic and surrounded outside by slums. Their atmospheres are seasonally orange-gray from pollution.

The Marxist society is the only one so far that has not yet shown any signs of ideological regression, but due to the so far Progeric pace of the Marxist WV system's life cycle, their own regression attempt should begin soon. Even the vast spread of their Xinhau news network all over the world in direct competition with the AP and other western news services assures her no success. She has the only WV system built on self-destructive class and economic doctrines, the only one with instability built deep into its WV. The very business class it has been encouraging is, by doctrine, forced to feel that by earning its wealth, it has done something wrong, even unsavory. Instead of expecting the business class to live up to high moral standards, its Marxist doctrines expect them to make obscene profits while at the same time doing so in a malevolent way at heavy cost to the workers. Their Marxist WV also expects the working people to hate their employers and to rise up and over-throw them.

It would only take an over-heated economy for Marxist China to experience one of the periodic super-crashes typical of the capitalist economic system, and nowhere else would such an economic collapse bring about such massive social disorder. An attempt by the Party to use its control of the unions to improve worker pay and benefits would, proportionately, kill the export growth and slow infrastructural improvements. China is too crowded and short of resources to support anything like what the US middle class achieved and called, "the American dream," the one that, there, is fading fast. The end of growth in the Chinese Marxist system would bring about a monumental crisis and cause the Marxist Party to try to regress back to a disastrous city-based form of communism reminiscent of the rural-based one of Mao Zedong.

Already, the people of Marxist Chinese society are suffering from such intense disparity between rural and urban incomes that the suicide rate for young men working in the factories is accelerating. On six different occasions in mid-2010, men who were enraged by the system took knives or hatchets to schools and stabbed or hacked to death as many small children and adults as they could. Such information was then censored from the news.

For the last forty years, the US Democratic Party has been imperceptibly pulled in an ever less radical more conservative direction by the growing intensity of the more militant Conservatives. But full religious regression in the rest of Christendom is not happening even though the rest of the West is moving toward a racist, anti-immigrant conservatism, one that is, so far, without the US religious, Libertarian, and anti-social welfare emphasis.

Islam already has some states that have regressed, and the "war on terror" would easily enlarge their number. Regression is going on in the US, and in much of Northern India (along with a Maoist Marxism insurgency along the Eastern part of India), but Western secularism seems to be keeping regression to a minimum so far in all four of the world's mainstream societies.

The Retaliatory Tripartite Alliance

Nevertheless, the number of Americans regressing back to old Christianity may well become enough to make the US an exception to the slow and uncertain pace of regression underway in the rest of the Western world. The key to total reactionary Christian-Libertarian control lies with its three-way retaliatory alliance with Israeli and Islamic militancy. Their tripartite retaliatory relationship is the most potent means the militants of all three faiths have to achieve further regression, and destroy the world's secular civilization. It succeeds by periodically generating new recruits to the militancy of each.

Especially vital to the Retaliatory Alliance is the Israeli-US relationship. Israel's non-mainstream, Zionist, mono-mate barbarian WV system is openly secular but has a long-term multi-party hidden agenda of reclaiming the "Promised Land." Its agenda also includes replacing the two mosques on the Temple Mount. The ultimate removal of the mosques has long been planned so that Israel can rebuild its Temple there, the home where the Judaic militants avow their Yahweh resides. Their synagogues are only meeting houses where their hand scrolled copies of the Torah are kept. Two thousand years ago, the Romans tore down their Temple in Jerusalem, leaving Yahweh without a house. All throughout the two thousand years since, they have flocked to what is left of the Temple's foundation to lament their misery to Yahweh and their failure to rebuild his Temple for him. From the Zionist Israeli WV way-of-thinking, achieving the goal and regaining all their "Promised Lands" could lead to the arrival of their (Judaic) Messiah and bring about a "New Age" under Yahweh in which his old tribal moral laws are imposed on the rest of the world. Everything their secular government does is subtly shaped by their militants to serve those two ends.

The continued presence of Judaic Israel deep in Islam is vital to the Christian Right, and is now the main reason the US can be expected to keep supporting Israel. Also, it helps that there are more Judaic tribalists in the US than there are even in Israel.

While America's unrelenting support is essential, the Israeli Zionists still need to keep their more liberal public stirred up and feeling backed into a corner by the Muslim threat. It helps keep the liberals among them emotionally united with the Judaic Right in a belligerently defensive, hence, retaliatory way. Already, Israel herself has almost reached the final stage of regression, the stage in which the Zionist militants gain the ability to crush internal dissent.

Most young Muslim men still seek a better and more secular way of being Muslim, but as anti-Muslim sentiment grows in the Judaic-Hindu and Christian West, more young Muslim men find it difficult to feel and be Western. More would come to satisfy their still subliminal resentment with the vicious, revenge-based jihadist ideal that only to them could seem wondrous, awe inspiring.

There has also been a Retaliatory Alliance process between the US and East Asian Marxism. In it, militant North Korea is used by its partner, Marxist China, as a retaliatory alliance nuisance and threat to the non-Marxist world. The US government, for decades, periodically went through the motions of dealing with the repressive state's effort to build an arsenal of long range nuclear missiles, but each time the US attempted to end the North's nuclear ambition, America ended up paying some sort of concessionary tribute to the barbarians. Also, each time, the Chinese Marxist WV system gained status because of the West's persistent failure to end their stooge-state's provocations.

The buildup of stress

The rapid, multi-caused decline is also aggravated by the need of each nation and society for natural resources that must increasingly come from, or at the expense of, the other societies. The Earth's resources grow less accessible and need ever more energy and technology to extract, while at the same time, world population continues to grow with the crest not expected before 2050. Over-crowding contributes to the rising stress levels and the general, if irregular, decline in living standards among workers and rural farmers. At the same time, in the urban centers, the secular business class continues to become wealthier, more extravagant, and the wealth concentrating into ever fewer corporate monopolies.

As mentioned earlier, we are social animals whose moral behavior is founded on our social instinct repertoire. When crowding forces tension and stress to build up in our groups and society, the general outcome is a breakdown in moral behavior, a process of behavioral deterioration. Other group animals also feel increasing stress as their numbers mount. Their stress builds up until the group breaks up into smaller groups. With us, the continued ideological dividing weakens the bond further, adding to the instinctively felt sense that the group (society) has become too large. Its members can no longer feel they live in the tight, ideological-bonded, communal hunter-gathering size group in which they had evolved to feel the most secure. Their ideological systems forbid them to think of "the people" as being excessive or themselves as being over-populated, but their physiological response to the others, the buildup of stress, is still the same with us as with all other over-sized groups of social animals.

Whether it is too many people or too many of something else, whatever is in over-abundance loses value. This is as true with us as it is with everything else. The intuitive value which the individual attributes to "the others" declines as their numbers rise and "crowding" takes place. The individual feels more stress.

Each individual tries to maintain at least a surface acceptance of the "other people," no matter how difficult it becomes. Each individual has to bear the insult of rude drivers in increasingly crowded city traffic. The streets and highways are jammed with those "other people." They get in the way and slow the individual down. He becomes impatient with them, and resents the slow driver ahead, or the one behind who tailgates. He wishes "the others" would go away.

As the social bond divides while population numbers increase, stress levels must increases proportionately. It then becomes possible for an individual to even perceive "the others" as having no value at all, to have *zero* value. Beyond that, levels of stress can climb to where people in general subconsciously sense that "the others" have *negative* value. That is, they wish they were dead. The sense of being over-crowded builds up stress and ensures a just-under-the-surface feeling of hostility, resentment, and even hate. So, it is possible to explain much of what is now occurring. Such as the growing instances of "road rage," anarchism and terrorism.

During the latter part of the Roman Empire, indications are that people were as tense as they are now, but unlike now, there were no nuclear arms to make it worse. The poor of the Roman Empire first converted to Christianity because they wanted to believe the Jesus-rumored promise to save them, and leave those "too rich to pass through the eye of a needle" to an End-Times destruction of the whole world, the one the people had grown to hate. The Armageddon concept of rivers of blood flowing from "the others," appealed to them and helps explain why the myth of "His Return" is still growing in significance in much of the US.

Theoretically, there is no limit to the amount of stress that can build up. The over-crowded-caused tension and hostility could build world-wide to where masses of people would have an underlying desire for everyone to be dead. This helps to explain the degeneration of the secular environmental awareness into the hostile anarchistic extremes of the back-to-nature eco-terrorist, animal liberation and the other "people-die-off" movements.

In short, stress builds up and ultimately, the nation's secular and religious division has grown to where the US government has become virtually deadlocked. Inexorably, the longer this goes on, the more people subliminally wish for a powerful leader to come forward and take over complete control. In just this way, every Age of Democracy ultimately destroys itself. Either religious regression supplies that for a while or, if not too late, people will be forced to adopt a WV consistent with the arrival of the Non-Theistic Age. If that is what it will take to reverse the dooming course, that is what the people will do in order to survive.

If not, when will it all come together to bring us a doomsday crisis? Normally, the long term social evolutionary trend is limited to centuries. Now, however, we have for-the-first time the over-presence of nuclear warheads, the approach of the rare and climactic end of the monotheistic age plus the biological-based over-population crisis and the resulting explosive build up of stress. All these together, indicate we are now moving into the end times crisis at an accelerating rate, one that needs to be measured in years or, hopefully, decades, not centuries.

Bearing up under all the stress, oppression, and fear are those US generations that had no unsupervised play and wasted too much time with electronic gadgetry. Ones who had been taught to be genderless, praised for everything they attempted to do, and grown up with underdeveloped immune systems from their too antiseptic home environment. They had become fat from lack of exercise and had growing health problems from eating overly processed, enzyme deficient, foods. What they had learned at home and in school was to defy any authority that tried to limit their "freedom of expression," and had been taught they would always get a good grade if they "made an effort." Some learned "fuzzy math" and had been taught to read "by the whole word" so they were unable to comprehend the exact meaning of any written concept. Often, they end up with over-blown expectations that prove to be beyond attainment because they cannot possibly buy enough to fill the emptiness in their lives. In trying to escape society's growing stress and personal tension, emails, face-book and their other software gadgetry enables them to balloon their personal space into infinity in order to have at least a virtual-world social-life.

In order to alleviate the stress, social activists use the academic social theory consensus to promote the "liberty" and "equality" ideals to extremes which tend to destroy the very democratic way of life the people no longer as intently aspire to achieve. Be reminded of the humiliating September 2010 spectacle of most of the heads of the American government having to cajole a single Pentecostal preacher into not burning up copies of the Quran, a non event of no significance until it was taken up by the media and spread all over the world. It is the same regarding the building of an Islamic center two blocks from the 9/11 "ground zero," another non-issue. This is the sort of thing that could alienate the vast Muslim populations of South East Asia's Indonesia, South Philippines and Malaysia, moving even them from the secular world into Muslim anti-Western militancy. It is difficult to respect a government that is so destructively controlled by an advertising-commercial-driven media that considers only its advertisers and the profits obtained from them, a media which has no control over itself or even the ability to criticize itself.

The US news media and entertainment industries are undermining her ideals in other ways, as well. They export unsavory glimpses of her many deplorable social problems, her environmental and infrastructural break-down disasters, and her antagonistic political polarization.

Fear is one of the most potent manifestations of the rising stress level, especially fear of terrorism. Every year in the US, over thirty thousand people are killed because they got into their car, but terrorism is what fills them with fear. No one really believes we will win the war on terror. Women are instinctively sensitive to the Alpha-male government's inability to protect them. They sense that their alpha team, their patriarchal, male leadership, is incapable of protecting its "family-group," that is, its nation and society. Men, in turn, sense the woman's fear, but feel their helplessness and their inability to end it. The men are failing their most basic, millions-of-years-old role of protecting their females and offspring. The men sense their failure and feel a collective loss of self-worth, and loss of status. Their very manhood comes into doubt.

In nature, as mentioned earlier, the female in such a family-troop seeks to leave the group with her offspring to find security in a better led group, but in modern society, women have nowhere to go. In desperation, they take the initiative and, under the guise of "equality," they gradually take over society as if they could, in that way, hope to restore their sense of security.

In response, men become more belligerent when dealing with "the enemy." Each terrorist attack or attempted attack brings out a male show of anger and puts more pressure on the leadership to retaliate and/or, further persecute Muslim citizens. Muslims living the Western way of life are forced to feel they and their faith are not American and are being singled out and persecuted.

It was in response to both the internal and external terrorist threat, that the US government set up the Department of Homeland Security. It also grossly multiplied the size of the spy (intelligence) bureaucracy. Everywhere, people are videoed, their cell phones located, and their conversations recorded. As the war against terrorism continues in the years to come, Americans would keep their same Constitution, Liberty Bell, Statue of Liberty and Bill of Rights, but end up with a much transformed, very different, system.

When the stress-built hostility in people cannot be kept under control, there are a number of ways it can be expressed, and all of them are presently showing up all over the globe. A young man may just suddenly want to end his tension-filled, purposeless life in a way that he can get back at the society he blames. He may control his feelings long enough to find what to him is a plausible ideal that would "ennoble" his hostility. He wants to kill enough people that he can feel he has revenged himself for all that he has had to endure and which he feels "the others" have brought down on him. Only then would he be ready to end his own life, and to leave it as his *final gesture*.

America has an intense addiction to narcotics and other such illegal drugs. Also, she has an over-abundance of automatic firearms. This is all drug-supplying and gun-smuggling gangs in other countries need to deal with to take over towns, cities, provinces, states and sometimes even sovereign nations.

No such problems, however, would deter the US from "its world leadership responsibilities." Policies which are openly referred to as "America-first" and "enlightened self-interest" are thought of as being part of her self-appointed responsibility. The US Libertarian-Christian three way antagonistic alliance process with Israel and Islam will invariably provide enough Muslim retaliation to justify the US effort to keep alive the "save the world from terrorism" campaign. It will do so even as her national power seems to become less inspiring and more oppressive to the rest of the world.

So the troublesome crumbling of American secular ideals would not soon diminish the intent or ability of the Libertarian-Christian conservatives and the US military-industrial complex to maintain the control they now have over the world. With about a million and a half US men and women in uniform and her troops garrisoned in almost one hundred and thirty nations, other people in the West would continue to ask themselves "how small a contingent do we have to send the US so she can still call it a *coalition*?"

America would need to continue turning her embassies into giant, reinforced concrete fortresses guarded by armed troops, moats, and razor-wire-topped barriers. The time when America's leaders would be honored with ticker-tape parades would be only a far distant memory. They would continue to sneak in and out of countries to avoid bombs and being shot at. Argentina's Eva Peron managed a motorcade tour of Europe decades ago with nothing more than a few tomatoes thrown at her.

Fatigue and the lagging foreign support can only cause the US to feel forced into a corner. But with nowhere else to go, she can only turn around and fight. The whole civilization works only as long as America stays powerful enough to still have plausible ideals, and as long as her technological war machine remains unsurpassed. Her leaders know that if she finally loses her will and power, the respect the world had for her would collapse and be replaced with contempt. Her financial empire would crash, and Western society's well crafted civilization would crumble into oblivion. Expect a world of immense stress, hardship and disorder before that occurs.

The cost to the US of maintaining such a potent war machine and supporting the affluence of the well-off business elite plus the growing cost of supporting the poor must all eventually lead to hyper-inflation. When people grow weary of it, they would clamor for price and wage controls. The government would then impose them, then rationing. The decline of the global free trade system and the reinstating of tariffs would accelerate. While price controls are hardly among the "core values" of Von Mises and the New-Conservative Libertarian religious-right ideologues, such "principles" are expendable when the whole price/wage control program could be run by corporations. Especially appealing would be the wage control part. Controls would keep wages from rising, but not prices. There would also be shortages and an ebbing and then flowing black market which would enable the rich and unscrupulous to buy everything they want tax-free.

The world's several hundred Al Qaeda operatives, and the many thousands of others of the scattered militant Muslim army, would hardly be able to believe their own combined ability. Bin Laden could be long since dead and buried. There is nothing he needs to do but sit up there as a god to keep his followers motivated and moving. There is so much fear ebbing and then flowing in the US that it serves to embolden them. It causes other young men to be attracted to their cause. It adds to all their confidence, and gives them a much longed-for sense of power. In time, they will ask themselves, "is it possible we can induce, threaten, and scare this whole increasingly resented and ever so fragile civilization into actually destroying itself with its own weapons of mass death and destruction?"

The American people would give up hope that they could elect to Congress representatives who could ever deal effectively with the economy, or be effective against terrorism. Their hopes would be dashed so many times that no justification would be left for having any. Political promises to maintain roads, bridges, and levies, or drill for more oil off shore, would go unfulfilled. Cost-effective fuel-efficient cars and needed new nuclear and alternative power plants would have failed to be built. Poorly maintained bridges would still end up collapsing, levies breaking, roads filling with potholes, and the energy shortage even worse. People would cease thinking about the future and, instead, look back and fill with nostalgia. Their focus would be more on antique auctions, the "cool" music of "the good old days," and idealizing the life of the Amish and ancient Celts.

The exploration and colonizing of the solar system would become a forgotten dream. The annual anniversary media blitz about the first moon walk would continue to be shown as "America's *greatest moment*," all because NASA scuttled the shuttle and has had too little funds to do much of anything since.

The American grand plan to bring "the American way of life" to the rest of the world would be thought of not only as unachievable, but increasingly, not even desirable. The "global economy" would be seen as profiting the extravagant class by importing, and using up the very resources and laying waste the environment that the growing populations need the most. Their young men would have been watching as the "great economic growth engine" raced madly by, and then disappear in a cloud of smoke. Left behind and without status, they would come to be without goals and ideals to replace those they had lost. They would come to realize that the West had been mostly only teaching the poor how to make luxuries for the rich.

The relentless wars, wariness and worry in America would build a pool of resentment that would be focused not just on government but, as well, at the rest of the world. After all, that would be where the media would show crowds burning the American flag. With that and the increasing resistance in the UN, which so many Americans despise anyway, the corporate-system-backed media would inflame the people's already blatant xenophobia enough to make the people feel that the rest of the world should "get what it deserves."

Eventually, the Internet would be loaded with so many scams and hacker attacks that it would break down permanently and all on it would be lost forever. Race and "ethnic" riots would become common and with increasingly deadly police and army responses. Global Warming-caused natural disasters, would mean mass starvation. A virulent new pandemic could further collapse human population numbers, but it would still leave the world as badly divided.

All over the world, great cities would become crowded and hemmed in by slums controlled by drug and extortion gangs. The insane, the mentally and physically disabled, and the unemployed homeless would be left alone to roam, beg, suffer, and die in the streets. It was nice to be humane, but only as long as those who control government could, would or even know how to afford it. People would be driven into a death-wish-like state. Nothing would seem to help, they would sense no positive solution other than to end it all, not by killing themselves but that conditions had become so miserable and the outlook so dismal that they would feel it was better for everyone if we just got it all over with now.

The world-wide path to reach such abysmal times would be shaped by the seemingly endless population pressure and the small but militant minority of die-hard Christians, Muslims, Judaics, and Marxists. They and the secular Environmental back-to-nature extremists, would all be swarm-theory-behavior-shaped by a subconscious intent to drive all "the two-many others" to oblivion. All this would be while the secular majority would be blaming government and science-technology instead of their chaotic ideological division, the Libertarian corporate advertiser's-controlled media, the military-industrial complex and the relentless population growth.

No longer having leadership that people can look up to, or anything to look forward to, people everywhere would fill with so much hostility, resentment, and despair that they would long to see the crashing down end of not just the whole civilization, but possibly the end of humanity as well. No alternative would seem to be in sight.

That is, all would lose hope except those of the faithful who await "the return of the Savior." To them, we have to be destroyed to be "saved." Their myth of millenarianism is basic, not just to Protestant Fundamentalism but also to militant believers of the Muslim and Judaic faiths, the belief that rivers of blood must precede it. Without a new and viable WV alternative ideological system, the End Times would quickly approach. It would not only be the one they have for so long anticipated, but as well, that the regressive Millennialists would unknowingly help bring about because of being the basic component of the Antagonistic Alliance. Thinking only of their Great Illusion, they could not realize that the climactic Armageddon their Libertarian-led military had been so long moving them towards, would *not* end up producing a "Savior," and would *not* be followed by a "Kingdom of God." The Earth's animals would *not* then all live in peace and harmony, and nature would *not* be restored. The whole of their ancient, "End Times" doctrines were from the beginning and are now, nothing more than an over-population-caused wish to destroy "the others" so they, themselves, could then "stand atop the ashes."

The non-theistic public would be stressed the most. Being in chronic disorder, it could do nothing to slow the trend. Unaware of where it would all end, being united by no WV and hence lacking a common goal, they would stand helpless and afraid because they would be the only ones who would know that there would be no "Savior." We are also shaping Internet virus into a means of destroying the power systems that bring water, electricity and light to the developed world, thus, ultimately having yet another way of collapsing our civilization.

There is at present no resource able to provide the insight and integrity needed to responsibly lead the world out of its downward spiral. The affluent class has shamefully neglected its responsibility to the future of mankind and allowed the world to become over-populated, its resources over-exploited, parts of the environment polluted, myriads of useful-to-us species lost and nuclear armed nations to proliferate.

As the atomic debacle comes into full view, Israeli Zionists would expect the arrival of the Judaic "Messiah," the control of the world by Yahweh, and the imposition of his old tribal law. But Global Earth would not be turned into a Judaic kingdom under Israelite sharia, even imposed by Yahweh, or anyone else. It would lead, instead, to events even worse.

Indeed, does old Yahweh really have such a plan? By then, might he not, instead, disapprove of the worldwide mess his Zionist-mesmerized "Chosen People" have helped make? After all, the cause of militant Judaism has not had an encouraging historical record. With individuals, only criminals and the mentally disturbed claim they are always being persecuted, their disorder and crimes merely seen, by them, always, as acting in their own justified self-defense. The Zionists tend to operate in a calamity-causing way because they have always been divided into contending factions. To unite, they have learned to stir up trouble with the rest of the world so they are then forced to group up with their backs to each other and defend themselves. Thus, their crusade has invariably drawn out the wrath of civilizations, as with that of Egypt, Mesopotamia, Imperial Rome, and certainly that of Islam.

So, for the machinations of the Zionists to drive masses of Muslim young men into terrorist organizations that undermine our civilization would not be out of character. The US has allied itself with a mere few fanatically Zionist *million* believers of the mono-mate barbaric Judaic WV system in a morally bankrupt global struggle against a relatively newer and, hence religiously more advanced, and largely secularized, universal-brotherhood mainstream Islamic society of some *1.3 billion* followers.

That is no way to run the world.

The suicidal nature of the age would come into full view, but by then, the people would come to be ever less concerned about it. The ominous multiplying of pressures would end the fear of a nuclear war, a war that would by then come to seem inevitable, even welcomed as "the easy way out." After all, the nuclear missiles are already there "just sitting around." They can destroy "the enemy," whoever it might be by, without loss of their own lives. Collateral damage is only to be expected. Random terrorist nuclear explosions would have already been occurring. Nuclear arms that once helped save our civilization would just as easily end it, just as easily because people would not want to save it. People made miserable and without hope want only escape.

So, sometime in this decade or in those to come, the hand above the nuclear missile button would begin to tremble, and the Atomic Clock would approach midnight. If no new WV system has by then begun the process of transforming the world into a new, one world civilization, the Clock would finally strike twelve.

We can imagine the grim, final and massive exchange of nuclear fire power and the ensuing world-wide crash in human numbers. There would then indeed be the much-longed-for "End Times," the one so eagerly awaited for thousands of years by billions of fanatical believers of the world's old "spirit"-based WV systems. The Muslim *Yawm al-Qiyamah* day of judgment and the "missing (Mahdi) leader" or "the Hidden (Shiite) Imam," the Mayan Quetzalcoatl (and midnight 12/21/2012), the Hindu coming of Vishnu, the Avatar, the Hopi Blue Star (UFO) Kochina, the Next Buddha ("Maitreya"), the cosmic regeneration and reuniting with Mazda, the Messiah of Judaism, and a returning Jesus would all be seen looming through the mists.

But it would all be mere illusion. Instead of a vast panorama of awesome specters marching to our rescue, there would be nothing except sulfurous smoke, radiation, and the few surviving members of the then depleted human race. Even they would all be divided still by the same old religions, each still claiming to have "the Truth" and "the Light," but in a world that had suddenly and dramatically turned dark. The faithful would have all been wrong again. No Anti-Christ would have arisen from the ground "speaking like dragons," and "those who do not love God would not have had their candle sticks torn away from them" (Rev 2:4-5). The stars would not have fallen from the Heavens, the people would not have become more righteous, and there would be no Peace on Earth, just devastation. Huge areas of the globe would be left uninhabitable.

In short, no god would have saved us. All it would take would be a few of the world's remaining thousands of nuclear bombs.

About these End Times we have much to ponder. Even the not-so sober can recognize a certain justice fated to human affairs. The worst of the noxious desolation would be centered in that Gehenna dump that has for so long been ludicrously mislabeled "The Holy Land."

The end of the century would see a shrunken world of destitute survivors living in grinding, unending, poverty. Civilization would only be a sort of Camelot-like legend being passed on in crude verse by the world's becoming-illiterate-again masses. It would be a world of poor people looking longingly back to the "good old secular days," but divided up into little feudal states, each run by a brutal gang of unemployed and idle but still well armed troops. Not even the little-known teotwawki survivalists and the New Mexico bunker-bound would still be around.

The economic destruction caused by inflation, would end all in a barter economy, and the world, even with much of the people killed off would not mean more resources for those who are left. The decline and end of new science and technology, along with the general over exploiting and trashing of the environment, would combine to prevent any improvement.

Conditions in the Muslim world would be even worse. Islam would have failed to become "great" again. Kurgan-like and lawless, it would fill with spies and assassins. Vicious warlords who ruled it would have no regard for human life and would think everyone (else) should kill and die for them in the service of Allah. Even idealistic youths would no longer blow themselves up to kill infidels. Those who had done so would be remembered with pity for being such fools. Instead of destroying the US and Christianity, Muslim terrorism would have served only to help resurrect and animate the still living corpse of old Christendom, helping it to preside over the disintegration of the world's last civilization. Islam's regressive relationship with terrorism would mean the faith's final denigration and shame, and her dessicated heartland turned into a thermonuclear, chemical and bio-toxic cemetery-wasteland.

Is there anything some leader could do to prevent such world-wide calamity, something that still might be done even now? We are where we are today not because of leaders but because of what people believe. Leaders, economic systems, "accident" or "luck" do not determine human destiny, only natural cause and effect. Our world is like a stage, and its people act out their parts by reading from their old, worn, tattered so called "sacred" scrolls and made-from-parchment scripts. As they do so, they act like drunks who think their spouted nonsense is ever so absolute, so awesome. By allowing themselves to drift away from all the science they have the potential to learn, they now at least, seem content to slowly sink like rats and mice into their own, separate version of the behavioral sink.

Human civilization would have been only a single long and slow rise followed by a single, spectacular fall. Without a new path to follow, we would face the worst: we would have experienced social evolution in reverse.

This, then, is a possible future end-time scenario, one *that we are going to avoid.*

twenty   --- THE ALTERNATIVE

The objective now is to take the facsimile of a possible new WV developed in chapters seventeen and eighteen and integrate it into the decline process. When conditions become dire enough to turn masses of people throughout the world into making such a drastic but necessary change in their world view, they will do so. They would turn to whatever WV system would be needed so they could end the decline. And only when they do, would they be able to form a genuine world society, one able to begin building the next civilization. That would all be possible because such a new system would have only achievable goals, not illusionary, "miracle" ones.

This is the way real social evolutionary science works; it is useful to us---in this case, mostly because it enables us to peer into the future. We even have the means to reasonably describe the whole course of the next society and its civilization because it would strive to accomplish its real world goals, and do so by the approximate moral means established by the WV system itself. We gain the ability to look into the decades, centuries, even the millennium or more to come. That is what we will attempt in this chapter.

The build up of stress, and the increasingly dismal world conditions, would lead a desperate public to be open to drastic change. By that time, the full scope of the impending catastrophe would be coming into view. Or, the new WV might not arrive and spread in time. The catastrophe may have already occurred. It took more than three hundred years for Christians to end the polytheistic and bring in the monotheistic age. Conversion takes time even when communication takes only milliseconds. People can be slow to grasp what is going on and would need time to become familiar with the new way-of-thinking. They would need more time to envy the bond and sense of brotherhood its members come to feel.

More time would be needed to watch it spread long enough for people to gain confidence in its ultimate success. It is not easy for the individual to change his WV and-way-of-thinking, even when world conditions become desperate.

Yet, one can be deceived by appearances. The innate intelligence, adaptability, and survival drive of the human species should not be underestimated. The social evolutionary process has proved efficient until now. The old religious beliefs are not as deeply held as the faithful lead themselves to believe. When reading their scriptures, they have to shift into a hypnotic state in which they believe illusions and suspend their own moral judgment. They know they need to accept the old beliefs on faith because they know the "miracles" and doctrines are irrational, unscientific. People do not walk on water or part the Red Sea, and those who convince themselves that death would be followed by "Heaven," "Paradise," or "nirvana" still want to live. They evolved with an instinct to live, and most people would change beliefs if they had to in order to survive. The faithful do their daily rituals and prayers in order to keep reminding themselves what they *want* to believe, *should* believe and are *supposed* to believe, all of which they work on in order to preserve the security and fellowship provided by the others. Following its rituals, observing its holidays, and going to church all serve to fortify beliefs which, in our more advanced age, would otherwise be dismissed. Accepting them becomes such a difficult and arduous burden as to take a heavy psychological toll. Counseling is a common service needed by Christian Fundamentalists sects. Parishioners and preachers alike wonder why they are so unhappy when they should be ecstatic. Even just to treat their preachers requires some thirty "therapy centers" scattered across the US. Also, their counseling is based on the science of psychology, not on Christian doctrine.

Even so, people might continue to resist change until it is too late. If the change-over to the new WV comes after the end of a weapons of mass destruction debacle, even the faithful would see for themselves that no one came to "save" them. The new society would have the monumental task of rebuilding civilization. How long that would take would depend upon how much of the human cultural heritage could be saved and not have to be discovered all over again.

We will first take the liberty of dividing the next one to two thousand-years into three sections. The First Period would start when a new science-based WV begins to spread and last until those who believe the new WV can set up its own government in at least one nation. Then, the new society would be established within the beginning of its territory and become mainstream. In the Second Period, the new society would spread until it encompasses the whole globe. These two periods would, in turn, lead to the Third, the period covering the rest of the civilization's anticipated one to two-thousand-year life cycle.

The First Period

Without a viable-ideologically united and thus a fully functioning society in our now divided world, conditions would deteriorate as described previously. Ultimately, tension would become so severe that normal people everywhere would be looking for something or anyone, who could take over, make the hard choices, and then have the power to carry them out at whatever cost. To them, that would be the "new wave," that is, the type of leadership-rule able to arise and be effective only when people have a single, advanced and united WV.

In the forefront would be intellectual individuals who would take up a new more scientific WV and way-of-thinking. They would have the ability to grasp its basics and explain it to others. There could be book clubs. When the new WV was simplified into its basics and, hence, its most effective form, it would be taken up by activists who would spread it with dedication and enthusiasm to responsible people everywhere.

Even those who were once the most faith-filled would recognize the extent to which their "spirit" or "economic-imperative"-based societies had failed, and in this scientific age, how inane the doctrines that had been going into everyone's ears and coming out of their mouths. Most of the believers of the old religions would then abandon their fruitless self-convincing efforts. The desperate need for a powerful, convincing, and self-consistent system of thinking able to "turn the world around" would be satisfied. The common fellowship needed to keep believing in "miracle" and "spirit"-based doctrines would melt away. People would rise up from their kneeling and cease resisting the very science and technology the world needs to survive. They would welcome and convert to the new WV system and bring the anything-for-profit age to an end.

People would join not only against the "spirit"-based systems but, as well, against the rich and greedy Libertarians who had used the "spirituality" of the ignorant to manipulate us all for their own profit and at the expense of everyone else.

But they would resist. From the very beginning, there would be fierce and oppressive opposition, not just from the Libertarians but, as well, from the world's other many parasitic, and generally destructive special interests that now control us all. The WV system's new moral climate alone would be an overwhelming threat to the tobacco industry, the whole political lobbying industry, the distilleries, gambling syndicates, pornographers and drug cartels. In direct opposition to the new WV would also be scores of assorted and regressive religious cults, the many assorted anarchistic and extremist single-issue secular cults, and thousands of other fanatical causes. Also in direct opposition would be the gun-lobby and the whole military-industrial complex.

Nevertheless, such formidable opposition cannot stop people from changing their beliefs if their very survival is at stake. Besides, persecution and oppression serve to test the endurance and strength of the new WV system and of its ability to unite, ennoble and motivate those who take up its banner. Honorable people would be effectively organized, regardless of the risk to their own personal safety. The very struggle itself would be essential in separating the leaders from the opportunists. Later on, those who first took up "the new wave" and spread its word would be among those who began to build the next civilization. Some alive now may well be among them.

The new WV system would be judged largely by the methods it employs. Even in an era of corruption and public relations corporate manipulation, the new WV system's moral standards would not deteriorate. When Religious-Right governments imprison and execute new believers, however, a state of war would exist, and the new system would no longer be bound by the old system's loophole-ladened legal system. It would be guided only by its own moral standards. There would martyrs but not ones carrying bombs into restaurants, trains, and planes. They would not kidnap innocent civilians for ransom, or spread poisons, atomic radiation, or dangerous biological agents.

The over a half century exposure of well over a third of the human race to Marxist atheism would lead to a top-down conversion in one or more Marxist states. Moving from the troubling Marx-Leninist WV philosophy to a new science-based one would be relatively simple. Where the old "spirit"-based WV systems are the oldest and weakest would also be where an early change-over could be expected, such as Indonesia, Singapore, and India. Also, those harboring the second oldest surviving WV mythology in Taiwan, Korea, Thailand, Cambodia and possibly Japan would be more open to adopting the new science-based WV. The people of sub-Sahara Africa would find it an ideal way to build unity between their tribal factions, and do so with the power and discipline such a task there would demand.

During the decades and generations to come, people all over the world would abandon their old mythological WV systems. They would not, however, abandon their own, great but separate cultural-historical heritages. This would be as it should.

The first nation to be taken over and kept under control by followers of the new WV could be honored as the eventual locale of world government. That would end the First Period.

The Second Period

The Second Period would be the time for everyone to either join or be left behind. The switch over to the new society would accelerate the ending of the one hundred thousand year belief in "spirits." The old religions would survive only as superstitions and held onto only by those who were the most ignorant.

If the first nation to convert turns out to be one of the larger, more powerful ones, a temporary reversal would be unlikely. World government headquarters would be set up there as more nations then convert as well. We can imagine, then that The Party would make arrangements to select the first DARSO from the ranks of those who had fought most actively for the cause. In the more secular-democratic nations and in others where a large segment of the population converts, the old system's leadership could even remain in office if they had been honest and capable in their role and were, in sworn testimony, willing to dedicate themselves to the new society's goals and standards.

Many in leadership positions in other countries would watch closely to observe how fair and efficient the transition would be. Extensive reforms would be needed, and the world would watch to see them implemented. The faster, more forceful and more efficient the reform process, the sooner other countries would follow.

As the switch-over to the new system occurs, we can imagine the new WV bonded nations forming an alliance, one that would seek to avoid war with any of the still surviving other WV-based systems.

The last nation to convert would carry a stigma that might last possibly a century. It might even be a much needed refuge for Gypsies, Jehovah's Witnesses, Scientologists, racist Zionists, US anarchist militias, fanatical environmental-animal liberationists and other secular extremist fanatics of all kinds.

Long before the end of the century, the world would, for the very first time, become a single society. Across the globe, people would celebrate the end of the atomic, chemical and biological war threat. Mankind would learn what it is to feel safe.

The Third Period

Even the Third Period would not usher in an idealistic, carefree age. Unless the population had been drastically reduced by radiation, biological terrorism or other causes, stringent birth control policies would have to be, logically, adopted and there would be major shortages of energy, grain and fresh water. The West nations would still be addicted to narcotics, and some in such a pathological condition as to be ungovernable. Drug cartels would be running others. In each country, the Party would have to forcefully impose drastic reforms and unmercifully destroy the gang rackets. Governments would have to be culled of their multiplying and duplicating bureaus, emptied of its agricultural and corporate subsidies, and stripped of wasteful government programs.

If the new system follows with the facsimile's dual constitutional feature, nations would conform to a plebiscite, and international law would be monitored and enforced by world government. Any government that failed to represent the will of the people would be put in the hands of those who would represent it. To enforce its will, an international military service would be developed under direct world government control. Politicians and businessmen everywhere who had betrayed their responsibility would be brought to justice and those who were guilty would be executed. The new society would have the authority to impose harsh reforms because that would be, by then, what the old system's disorder and decline had shaped its desperate people to want.

The establishing of world unity would give people everywhere a sense of world-wide community well-being. Stress levels would plunge. People would be able to savor the sense of belonging, even in their new billions of people society, because their common WV would bring them together enough that they would feel once again to be members of the tight-knit family-troops they were evolved to live in. They would feel a "oneness" that no society has managed to provide in many centuries. Despite the privations, there would exist a widely felt euphoria.

Other than the declining and depleted ranks of the criminals, racists, pedophiles, cultists, anarchists, scam artists and others, life would be purposeful and secure. People would no longer have to see their "great leaders" ride in Pope-mobiles or in convoys of bulletproof limousines filled with bodyguards. When going on junkets to other countries, their leaders would not have to sneak in and out unnoticed for their own protection. For the first time in their lives, people would have control over the direction their society was moving, a society that would react as a unit with a central governing core cuing constructive expectation, not empty promises, moral platitudes, and commercial offers.

Society would even begin to behave in an organismic-like way, as though it had become a living entity. It would recover from near-death and, for the first time, know what it needed, wanted, and was intently determined and prepared to achieve.

In other words, the world would begin to recover, and a new civilization would begin to take shape. As it is with the cultural evolutionary process, mankind would have looked at its choices and have chosen the right "path." The unified, unsecularized (theocratic) age of the new and world wide society would have begun. World government would be in operation, and territorial disputes would begin to be settled.

The multi-type marriage system described earlier would logicallybe adopted, and new holidays would evolve, such as one commemorating the liberation. Internationally, the system's Party would obtain operating funds from Party investments, donations, tithes and/or taxes. The tax havens would be shut down and piracy would be forcefully, if need be even brutishly, eliminated. It would be world government for a well-governed world.

In the new society, people would be born free, but not born rich. Changes would be made to give the poor an equal chance.

Even so, the next civilization would have some inequality of wealth, just not based upon hereditary privilege. Any successful new society would have to have more educated people of honor, professional people and experts in their important fields, who would have to adhere to its nineteen moral prerogatives and live by the highest standard of personal integrity and courage. They would show nobility of character not by behaving arrogantly but, be expected to exhibit good manners and a sincere and friendly concern for others, especially people of other races, ethnicities, and economic classes.

Agricultural reform of the corporate commercial farms would have to take place in some nations. The people involved might even set up cooperative or agricultural communes, but only spontaneously and voluntarily. The revolution would not be against any given class. Honest financial, professional and business experts would need to continue making business profits and be well paid to serve society with their expertise.

In each nation in which the old government had to be overthrown, the new system would unrelentingly seek out and bring to justice all those who had been responsible for the old system's kleptocratic nature and its failure to organize rural public education, medical care, and build infrastructure. They would be held responsible for allowing corrupt and brutal police and/or military administration of the rural areas. Such people would be hunted down, brought to justice, convicted, and executed, with their loot confiscated. Banking systems would be forced to close out all their secret bank accounts and increase reserves. Labor unions would be monitored as closely as business in order to ensure both operate in a way that serves the long term interests of society.

Everyone suffers from a lack of justice. Sexual predators would be sterilized or executed. If there would still be too many people, the first to go would be those criminals who should not be returned to society and therefore, need not be housed in prisons at public expense. Imprisoned criminals still have the instinctive will to live, but even old and debilitated pets are humanely "executed." It is not for their welfare that prisoners are now being housed in cells for the rest of their lives. It is being done only so the prim can satisfy their vane pride in being the most overly "love-conquers-all" compassionate.

All people are not equal, but all would be equal before the law. In order to ensure that it is, the new society could be based upon the concept of "the hypothetical veil of ignorance" advanced by John Rawls in "A Theory of Justice" (1971). The most fairness can only be achieved when the system does not know (hence, the "veil of ignorance") anything else about the person to be judged other than what he or she is accused of. Also, the ponderous legal and court system would be simplified. The prime need is to end the favoritism now extended to white-collar criminals and the wealthy. The principle would stand that one's importance to society would entitle no one to be above the law.

Later, as conditions improve, the focus would shift to the immense space challenges that lie ahead. People would face the stark realization that our new home, the one we would eventually spread out into is a bleak expanse of extreme cold and heat, blackness and fire, airlessness and filled with radiation. Within that space are planets, some of which are molten or frozen rigid, with some atmosphered with ozone or carbon dioxide, others ladened with lakes of sulfuric acid. We would face the most all encompassing challenge we humans have ever dealt with before. We would need to make parts of it livable. The shrinking little curve of our Earth would have to cease being our border as we prepare to become a larger part of the rest of the universe. Its vastness extending out endlessly from us is ours to claim. Our task is to take control of it. The space program would need to be expanded and pure science be generously funded.

Logically, manufactured parts would be made interchangeable worldwide. Strict environmental reforms would be instituted, ones which would focus on long term needs. The present rate of depletion of resources and environmental deterioration would be brought under control. Waste of any kind would be avoided, conservation would become the way of life, and everything would be recycled. People would no longer freely deplete their underground water reserves, allow their topsoil to wash and blow away, cut down rather than cull their forests, or permit their land to be over grazed. Plastics that did not need to be long lasting would be made biodegradable. Laws affecting the environment and other international concerns would have to be passed and stringently enforced. All this would not be for the sake of "Mother Nature" but for the long-term benefit of mankind.

If the dual-nature Party system of the facsimile is adopted, its service wing would play a Peace Core-like role. It would be natural to expect it to provide a whole spectrum of services characteristic of a healthy society. The homeless would be taken in, not left to wander the streets or seek refuge in the libraries. The new society would be ashamed to so abandon its poor and helpless.

Even within what had formerly been the Western corporate "democracies," the Party might set up and staff information and help centers. These would meet such needs as day care, half-way-houses for runaway children, intervention for physically abused wives, addiction-therapy groups, and many other such services.

As stress levels fall, health needs would decline and people would feel they had became part of the close-knit community of their new family-troop-like, world-wide, society. Their health would be a society-responsibility that would not be ignored. Health care would mainly focus on providing needed health services for the general population, not for deformed fetuses, the profoundly impaired, the criminal, the obese, those in dangerous sports or those who want plastic surgery. It would not provide life support for the brain dead or to prop up the catastrophic health care of the aged and terminally ill. The new system would not "treated people-to-death." We all, do, after all, have to die. The new system would avoid the crowding out of basic health service to the general population by medical luxury and waste, a process of over-humanistic self-destruction.

Because of letting people become soft, obese, and stressed-out, civilization can be a profligacy that leaves a generational-trail of epigenetic deterioration in general health. Genetic misfits would logically be prevented from burdening their families and society. Society's long-term interests would come first and gone would be the dark ages of war, disease and starvation which have, in the past, had to restore the epigenetic health of regional populations.

The global economy

What economic reforms could be established might be as follows: such as setting up a single, gold-based currency and reformed by an international body of leading economists. They could reform commercial law so it was geared to directing capital into sound, long-term, energy-saving, environment-protecting projects, and infrastructural improving investments. Logically, also, the new system would not permit business to manipulate the media and, hence, control public opinion, all in order to stop the merchandising of immorality. No business would be government subsidized. Advertising would be regulated and could be taxed. The Party would keep watch and control over the military-industrial complex, and the manufacture of military hardware would be reduced.

The nature and functions of corporations would probably be changed. They would not be chartered to have the "rights" that free individuals have. The entire financial liability burden of retribution and restitution would cease resting entirely on the stockholders instead of those in charge and responsible.

More agricultural land would be made available by closing down old cemeteries. Cremation or a "green burial" would await the end of one's life. Marriage rites would probably be a Party and government ceremony followed by the family's reception.

With the final placement of the Party into a position of control throughout the world, it would then be able to arbitrate issues in a manner free from special interest influence. It would be in a position to make long term plans and decisions in dealing with significant problems. All such change would come about because of changes in goals similar to those listed earlier. Since the whole world would be focused on achieving them, public opinion would be concentrated on them as light is in a laser. When people all seek the same realizable goals, and agree on the means to achieve them, life takes on *purpose* and they work harmoniously with each other to fervently, effectively and efficiently achieve them. In the process, they succeed in accomplishing the betterment of both themselves, each other, and society.

With world government in place, national sovereignty would, of course, diminish in the same way state powers declined under the ideological unifying force of the American Constitution. Nationalism would no longer inspire such territorial aggressiveness as it does now.

The new society, however, would face a challenge the world has never faced before: there would be no other society to compete with. A similar situation occurred on Easter Island and its isolation helped doom it. Even just describing life forms is essentially only comparing one to another. More importantly, we as small group primates, exist best and most normally with at least some enmity between groups, such as exists between nations, sports teams, government bureaus and corporations. Here, some of the provisions of the facsimile would be important in preserve some healthy competition and promote natural selection without destroying the world's WV unity. It envisions the separate Islamic, Oriental, Hindu and Western "cultural centers" each providing cultural, scientific, social and technological competition with the others. Also, dualistic innovations established in the facsimile would help, such as the Party itself being divided into two wings, the duel capitalistic and communal economic systems, and the dual constitutional system.

The old and opposing religions would be in growing disfavor even as their mighty churches, mosques, and temples would remain and become social and cultural centers for their former believers. Most people would continue to cherish them as part of their ancient cultural heritages, including their history, holidays, language, art and customs; but no other WV system would exercise any power or have any "rights." The multi-cultural world would survive, but the old "spirit"-based WV system would exist only as furtive superstitions. Their believers might be helped to come into the twenty-first century by being heavily taxed.

Any new such system of World Government would have to also make and enforce the sometimes needed territorial adjustments and in a way that would be fair and in the best long term interests of the whole society.

Humanity would enter an age where people would again honor their commitments and do whatever they had promised to do. It would be a world where it would not be necessary to keep upgrading one's security system, and where a night nurse could walk home from work without fear of robbery or rape. People would once again feel confidence in their leaders, respect for their government and devotion to society.

It would be the time for real science and technology. No longer would technology be based only on exploiting and developing the great scientific discoveries of the 19th and early 20th centuries. An age of new and creative scientific ideas, thought, and theory would open up, creating a new base upon which explosive technological growth would follow.

The theocratic ages of the past achieved great construction projects such as the magnificent Gothic cathedrals of Europe, the fine mosques of Islam, and the great temples of India, China and Indochina. So also would the next civilization. Nothing built in the past could equal the triumph of constructing viable colonies out in our solar system, a project reminiscent of the building of the Great Wall of China, and of the Polynesian and Micronesian exploration and colonizing of the entire Pacific Ocean.

As society forges ahead in the coming centuries, people would realize they are part of the first society ever built to actually be achieving its goals and, hence, the only society to ever function according to plan. The new society would be measurably and continuously accomplishing its goals and objectives, something that would be a totally new experience for the human race.

For the first time, civilization would begin its great creative-intellectual golden era during its long pre-secular, "theocratic" age, the age of an undivided-WV. There would be an effervescence of the arts, such as literature, poetry, sculpture, music, the graphic arts as well as of architecture. The cultural Golden Age would sweep across from continent to continent in great, majestic waves. People would want the arts to be beautiful again because only that would express their new idealism.

Ultimately, mankind would begin to spread colonies throughout space, the planets and moons of our Solar System. We are looking at a future of the human race that would ultimately include the scattering of mankind out into the rest of the universe with a human species life span of tens to hundreds of thousands of years or more. We can imagine voyages of space exploration and colonizing of planets and moons of hundreds of light years distant. Ahead would be mankind's most majestic achievement of all ages.

Even as we move out into space, the Earth would remain as our enduring home. Logically, it would function as the intimate center of the universe, and as such would always be treated with our personal care and respect, even with reverence. It would become our perpetual "mother"-planet, our "sacred nexus to the heavens." As such, we would then, at least, care for it as if it were our own very precious gem-like miniature model of how we would manage wherever else we are in our universe.

The drift to a subsequent system

Later on, a time would come when there would be someone who would most fully understands where we had come from and how we were to best go on to do the rest. He will lay out a new plan for us, a plan for the conquest and colonizing of the universe beyond our solar system. It would be his plan that would eventually replace the WV facsimile referred to here.

But first, conditions would have to change enough that people would need his plan. Even societies, as with all life, are finite. In a perfect world-view and way of thinking structured to prevent decline, all seeds of eventual decline would be excluded. In this world, however, nothing is perfect and all social organisms have a life cycle. No matter how well the path is laid out, many of the hazards ahead cannot be anticipated and prepared for ahead of time. Immense changes and new technologies are to come. Strange and now unimaginable aids, new rules, obstacles and goals would be needed. New ideals would have to be taken to heart, ones which would be in conflict with some of those we would have had long been following. They would secularize society, and we would set up the accord, break free of long-held customs and standards, then ultimately fall into decline. When the people accomplish their common goals, or have to give up on some of them, they would then focus away from the goals and the common good. They would become self-indulgent. They would become obsessed with material gain, with the sensual, and awesome social problems would appear, those same wretched memes which plague the modern world. All things come to an eventual end, even WV belief systems, their societies, and their civilizations. All are expendable; nothing lasts forever. Our new society would also grow old and have to be replaced.

This concludes our explanation for the rise and fall of civilizations, of social evolution, an explanation of the "whole human story," and a picture of two possible and contrasting paths ahead for mankind. We can now, perhaps, rest assured at least, that the human race can survive. It can build the Earth as a protected platform from which we can begin an age of unlimited exploration, colonization and the conquest of the universe, not all to be accomplished with one plan but with one plan after another and each on to the next.

THE END

GLOSSARY:

These words are used in the text only as defined below, each used only with that one definition. Multi-meaning omnibus words are avoided. The purpose of restricting word usage to single-meaning definitions is to reduce confusion and rationalizing so that the terms can be applied more objectively.

ACCORD: a swarm-theory process involving the rationalized, unrecognized, compromise, and subsequent easing of tension occurring between believers of an old WV ("religion") and the co-believers of a newer ("secular") system of doctrines, a process in which there is a subconscious wish to make both beliefs seem compatible. The Western Accord is the one that ended the Age of Enlightenment.

ACCURACY: a comparative quality dealing with the relativity of all knowledge. No knowledge is absolute, final, or "perfect." Hence, there is no such thing in science as "truth." A theory cannot even be "truer," or "more true." It can only be *more accurate.*

ANTAGONISTIC-RETALIATORY ALLIANCE: an unspoken, swarm-theory "partnership" between militant-religious antagonists of two or more mainstream WV-based societies in which, by attacking the other in retaliating for being attacked, each always justifies the other's retaliating in return. The process can be a vicious circle because it serves to draw ever more of its own people away from their secular ("profane") beliefs to more old-religion militancy. By drawing in and making both WV systems more militant, the process tends to feed upon itself.

BARBARISM: Any male dominated WV system that fosters aggressiveness and practicalness in response to the male territorial and hunting instincts.

BEHAVIORAL SINK or pit: the behavioral collapse characteristic of the "population control mechanism" in some mammals, including man. It is triggered by the sense of being crowded, a sense that, in man, is engendered by the splintering, dividing and hence weakening of the society's ideological bond. In the past, the "sink" has been avoided in man because of religious regression and, barring that, conversion to a more advanced and united WV system.

CAPITALISM: an economic system based on the implied ideal that the individual can trade, save and invest to his own best advantage but only while doing so in a way that best serves all. The system works only within a careful network of regulations. When the business class looses its moral willingness to follow that legal framework, that is, when it controls the legislative process and changes business law to its own advantage at the expense of the rest of society, then the system becomes corrupt and exploitive.

CIVILIZATION: a mainstream, hierarchically-organized, urban society based on a patriarchal-monogamous WV system and exhibiting a more advanced and creative artistic, technological and intellectual culture.

COMMUNES and COMMUNISM: The relatively egalitarian social and economic system that commonly existed in mainstream prehistoric times, one in which property is held in common and people live and work collectively. In the last 5,000 years, many communal, egalitarian groups have existed, but no communal society has been egalitarian, all have had to have government. Agriculture brought a large population increase and, with it, such social chaos that, every since, the sovereignty of the people has had to be replaced by the hierarchy of government.

CONDITIONING: the process by which a society's bonding WV belief system shapes and focuses the way the instinctive social nature of its citizens is expressed.

CULT: Any non-mainstream ideology, including secular single-issue activist causes or denominations.

CULTURE: the art and science of a society. The word is never used here as a substitute for "religion" or "society."

CULTURAL EVOLUTION: A misleading term for *social* evolution.

DARSO: "direct authorized representative of the social organism," a possible title for a future world leader, one who represented the barbaric willingness of the system to lead for the long term.

DEMOCRACY: an egalitarian political system in which the people are sovereign. Democracy still functions in communes but not in nations.

DEMOCRATIC DOGMA: the central political goal and "means" doctrine of Secular Humanism. Its doctrine is that all government is tyrannical unless it is run by elected representatives whose rule ideally consists of discerning what, on balance, the public wants, and then enacting it. In reality, the "leaders" manipulate public opinion in order to do what they think is best for their country and/or themselves. The "democracies" existing in modern times are multi-party, constitutional hierarchies ruled by announced advocates of democracy.

DETERMINISM: the non-theistic principle that all change is the result of natural (not "spirit") cause and effect, and that there is no such thing as a "miracle."

DOCTRINE: All beliefs that are worded in a way intended to be socially constructive, whether or not the beliefs constitute a WV society-bonding belief system.

DOGMA: All doctrines that the user of the term does not approve of.

EPIGENETIC: the phenomena of health and mental defects passed on in affluent-age-families from one generation to the next and which have in the past had to be ultimately weeded out by brutal "hard times." The mechanism does not involve genetic change but rather that of the peripheral part of the genome, including the microRNAs, which triggers the genes.

EVOLUTION: genetic change wrought by natural selection in living organisms.

FAMILY: the most basic dominance-centered group with enough relatedness and instinctive-based bonds of intimacy to exist as a single commune. In the anthropoid apes, families exist as (1) semi-monogamous families (the gibbon), (2) harem families (the gorilla) and (3) modified-harem families (chimpanzee). Mankind is instinctively #3, but crowding necessitated the social-evolution of government and the patriarchal-monogamous WV system.

FAMILY-TROOP: The basic, instinctive primate modified-harem social-family unit long existing in the form of small, dominant-male-run hunting-gathering groups. Only language and the development of "spirit"-based WV and way-of-thinking belief system managed to extend the human family-troop size and, thus, form "societies."

FASCISM: Any more barbaric type of secular modification of a society's WV system.

FOUR QUESTION TEMPLATE: the core of four questions which every mainstream WV belief system must provide answer for in order to bond people into a society: "what is our origin, our goal(s), the means (morals), and what obstacles stand in our way?"

GLOBAL COMMUNITY: the weak ideological world unity made possible by the Accord between the world's old faiths and Secular Humanism.

GOVERNMENT: a patriarchal monogamous WV hierarchal system essential to the survival of any mass of people larger than town-size.

HUMANISM: The state of being humane, that is, of being tolerant and sensitively sympathetic to the interests and welfare of other people and, even, of all living matter. Among people who are ideologically divided, humanism helps minimize friction between the factions to the very same degree it limits the ability of society to function in a practical, united, forceful, and successful, way.

IDEOLOGY: often used here as a synonym for WORLD VIEW, (WV) and a cohesive collection of secular doctrines.

INDIVIDUALISM: a Secular Humanist myth-ideal in which the individual is regarded as distinct and independent from society and to have "free-will."

INSTINCT: evolution-shaped potential motivation which is innate. It is expressed only in the way it is learned to be expressed, a process called "conditioning."

JUDAISM, (and JUDAIC): a non-mainstream WV system with its own, self-enforced doctrine that its membership is determined not by what a person believes but by what the *mother* thought her clan was or the father's last name. This text does not define any WV system according to Judaic doctrines(!) and, hence, does not use the word "Jew." Regardless of Judaic doctrine, everyone who believes in Judaism is a Judaic, and anyone borne by a member of the Judaic clan is not Judaic or "Jew" if he or she does not believe in Judaism. Judaism's seclusive and "Chosen People" doctrines make it a racist clan as well as a religion.

KNOWLEDGE: what humanity believes that is more accurate than what it used to believe.

KURGAN: people bonded together by a racist, polygynous, territorially aggressive, male-god WV and way-of-thinking originally based on nomadic herding technology.

MAINSTREAM SOCIETY: those societies that participate in the main social evolutionary process, a process which moved its "society breeding ground" from Africa to the Near East and then to the whole Euro-Asian land mass and finally, now, Secular Humanism has extended it to the whole planet.

MARXISM: a mainstream, marginally barbaric WV system and society based on the philosophy of Karl Marx as modified by, especially, Lenin and Mao Zedong.

MONO-MATE, BARBARIC WV SYSTEM: a relatively less primitive and less aggressive but more successful form of barbarian WV system, one which adopted monogamy but still retains the Kurgan doctrine of racial superiority.

MORAL SYSTEM: a way the third question of the Four Question Template is answered and the means by which the people of a mainstream society cooperate to achieve the collective goals of their WV system, in other words, their means to their ends.

MYTH: important beliefs that have been superseded by more accurate beliefs and which are no longer adequately defended by an entrenched clergy. Also, see "superstition." Myths are a part of an ideology that shapes the way people are to think.

NATION: a secular political unit in a society which is made possible in a patriarchal monogamous WV-based society and the establishing of an organized governmental hierarchy. Tribes are not "nations," and "kingdoms" are non-secular ones.

NON-THEISTS: all people whose beliefs or non-belief regarding "spirits" and "miracles" are compatible with science, in other words, a position that no deity exists that answers prayer or in any way alters natural cause and effect. Deism and pan-deism, as well as agnosticism and atheism, are all Non-Theisms.

PROGRESS: all more accurate science and technological change that enables sustainable human population growth and expansion of a mainstream society's territory.

"PURPOSE:" the term used in a "spirit"-based WV system for its goals.

RATIONALIZE: the subconscious, self-serving, self-deception process normally attributed to the brain-stem. The academic rationalizing that was essential to the building of our world civilization consisted of many stratagems, many of which are found in the Appendix.

RELIGIOUS REGRESSION: The eventual society-decline return to control in a society of its originating, founding WV belief system. This has normally served the function of stabilizing the society and preventing further "behavioral sink" social pathology. But to just that degree it succeeds, it loses its ability to develop or even use technology.

RELIGION: a term used here only for a specific type of world-view system, one that is "spirit"-based. The term "Word-View and way of thinking," or simply "WV," is mostly used for all such mainstream WV systems.

SCIENCE: the best methods currently in use to deal with what we believe is natural cause and effect. Because of being the best methodology developed so far, modern science has built up the most accurate theory so far of ourselves and the universe.

SECULAR BELIEFS: any popular ideal and belief system, which, by being more advanced (accurate) are inconsistent with the older and originating core belief system of a society. For the sake of the unity of society, secular beliefs and the older WV system have to be made to at least appear consistent with each other by means of an accord.

SECULAR HUMANISM: the secular theology of Christian, Western civilization. Its doctrines include "rights," the democratic dogma, being humane, the capitalist economic system, individualism, and science. The Western social-theory-consensus has shaped it all into an ideology that has managed to adapt to liberalized Christianity, then liberalized versions of all the other WV systems, in order to loosely bind all their societies into a global community of nations.

SOCIAL EVOLUTION: the non-biological, evolutionary, natural selection process of social organisms (mainstream WV system bonded masses of people) which accounts for the total growth of the human cultural heritage during the last approximately 40,000 years.

SOCIAL ORGANISM: See "society."

SOCIALISM: a social, economic, political ideology in which the people, through labor councils and/or egalitarian government, own and democratically run the economy. The intent is that public welfare provide for everyone to need. In the real world, socialist states function capitalistically and are all governed by a parliamentary system dominated by public welfare emphasizing socialist idealogues.

SOCIAL PROBLEMS: the rising crime rate, increase in suicide, drug addiction, corruption, graffiti, vandalism and more than thirty other such problems that arise when run-away, ideological division weakens a society. People feel the same stress and tension that occurs in other animal groups when their numbers exceed what is instinctive to that species and when those numbers press on the limits of their territory.

SOCIETY: the maximum mainstream-size group we all subconsciously use a common world-view (WV) and way-of-thinking mainstream belief system to bind ourselves into. Societies substitute for the hunting-gathering troop in which we evolved to function. Societies are social, not biological organisms and are a super-organism life form.

SUPERSTITION: all older and hence even less accurate mythology based beliefs that are no longer defended by a clergy.

SURVIVAL-SECURITY FACTOR: the tendency of individual living entities to have more offspring than the two who produce them.

SUBCONSCIOUSLY: rationalized brain-stem thinking that is not consciously recognized.

SWARM (theory) INTELLIGENCE (in humans): the way such living matter as swarms, mobs, groups and societies, operate for the survival of all by the individual just doing what he or she is socially and instinctively programmed to do in the group by his or her nature and environment, not by his or her own intellectual understanding of either his own nature or the social evolutionary process operating with his social group or society.

TERRITORIAL SENSE: the more male, instinctive, sense of his territory and spatial skills. The female more intensely senses her group as her home while the male more intensely senses it in the form of his group's territory.

THEOCRATIC AGE: The first age of every mainstream society which begins when bonded by a unified WV and its single party, and lasts until the WV divides and adopts secular doctrines.

THEOLOGY: the core of a mainstream WV and way-of-thinking belief system which consists of its answers to the Four Question Template. The theological core of four answers, when consistent, enables the structuring of a mainstream society's whole WV and way of thinking. This applies to all societies including non-"spirit"-based ones.

THEORY: the interpretation of data that generates the presently most accurate explanation for something. All science is theory because all of science is capable, ultimately, of being made more accurate.

TORTURE: Any treatment a prisoner has good reason to believe is more dangerous or painful than what is normally experienced each day and which is inflicted as punishment or to extract information.

TRUTH: an ancient religious word similar to "holy," "sacred," "spirit," etc. which is still used for whatever the speaker/writer wants the other person(s) to believe. Its use implies the existence of absolute knowledge instead of just relative accuracy. It is more thoroughly explained in item 12 of the APPENDIX.

WV: (WORLD-VIEW AND WAY-OF-THINKING): a type of ideology based upon a theology or core of belief that answers the questions of the Four Question Template. It provides an ability to bind large masses of people together effectively enough for them to occupy a territory and to create a mainstream society. Christianity is a "spirit"-based mainstream WV and East Asian Marxism is a non-"spirit"-based one.

APPENDIX

Listed below are twenty-one stratagems that social theorists have had to employ during the last century and a half in order to establish and maintain the Accord between science and the old "spirit"-based WV systems. The use of these stratagems has enabled the social theory consensus to bypass social evolution and enabled society theory to seem compatible with liberal versions of the world's old "spirit" based WV systems and provide the leadership needed to establish the "Global Community of Nations" and the "Global Economy."

#1. The "switching-of-meanings" stratagem. This involves the use of key words in other ways than the way they were first used or defined in the same text. It is universally but incorrectly assumed that the meaning intended for a key word can be determined by the context in which it is used. More often, the context does not provide even a clue as to which of a word's meanings the author intended.

#2. The inventing of new terminologies. The feeling is that the fracturing of our understanding of the world into little shards can always accommodate one more science splinter. Sometimes such a new science is split off and provided with a glossary of invented terms, each of which is only defined in terms of the other ones in order to facilitate rationalizing.

#3. Consistent refusal to agree on word meanings. An example is the word, "subconscious," which Sigmund Freud used for one of his mystical concepts. Later, when Freud's pseudo-science was abandoned, so also was the word even though no word can better represent the subconscious, non-conscious part of the mind. Another good example is the term, "fascism," a term which can be usefully used for a particular type of regressed, social-political system often observed in world history. Word-use agreements among social scientists would help avoid rationalizing enabled by confusion and help distinguish the same stages in one society to another.

#4. The use of descriptive definitions in preference to functional ones. Definitions are supposed to be useful to us. To be useful, definitions need to identify items and show the purpose or function they serve us. For example, pork is not "sliced pig" but rather "pig meat and parts prepared to be eaten by humans." When scholars define "religion" as "a belief in God or gods," they are only describing old "spirit" based ones and, thus, wrongly inferring (rationalizing) religions or WV systems serves no evolutionary function.

#5. The use of omnibus-words. These words represent numerous concepts that are often incompatible or inconsistent with each other. Using such conglomerate words results in confusion that can, in turn, hide rationalizing. Different concepts logically require separate words with separate meaning. "Culture" is an example of an omnibus or conglomerate word. In 1952, Alfred Kroeber noted that the word was being used by social theorists in one hundred and sixty-five different ways.

#6. The use of "weak verbs." Some social theorists have a penchant for stringing together long clauses connected by weak verbs. Some such words and clauses are "exemplifies," "suggests," "can be identified as," "are made intelligible," "indicates," "may be viewed as," "affects," and even "its identification means some interesting questions arise." The use of weak verbs enables some to write long sentences that say little or nothing. They tend to be used timorously as to avoid stating anything controversial, all of which explains their hidden agenda. They would rather write nothing new or important than chance saying something which could be interpreted as offending either religious or secular beliefs. The use of this stratagem can give the impression of objectivity to work that is not objective.

#7. Using substitute words for key concepts. Synonyms do not have the exact same meaning, so using them can be used subconsciously to mislead. An example is the way, *instinct* is avoided in social theory because it seems too "ape-man-like." The words "genes" and "hard-wired" are used instead, words which help avoid disturbing the Christian sensitivities of their more devout associates. It also avoids offending their Harvard Marxist colleagues, ones who won't acknowledge our instinctive base because they think we can all be molded to fit into the egalitarian communal society they imagine and idealize.

#8. Using official but inapplicable words and wording, specifically, the repeated use of official but false terms and descriptions. Official but inappropriate words are often used to gain advantage, such as "The People's Republic of China" and the "South China Sea."

#9. The use of double-talk. Double-talk is a skill used widely in many fields, including social theory. It is sometimes used to make writing seem "impressive" while hiding self-inconsistencies within its complicated and confusing verbiage. The academic need for this subterfuge is so overwhelming that those who do not use it and, instead, write with journalistic clarity, are treated condescendingly by colleagues for "catering to the layman." Students learn it from their professors and from academic texts and journals. Later, they do not realize they are using it to do "politically correct" research and write reports and papers that appear profound but lack meaning, relevance, and substance.

#10. The use of "trendy" expressions, affectations, jingoisms, and buzzwords. Social theorists have fashions in words like women have in clothes. At the present time, the fashion words of social science theory continue to be "contingencies," "cognitive," and "paradigms." Some academic buzzwords represent valid concepts, but their over-use clues us that they are being used to associate the user with the "timely" and, thus, help to make rationalized conclusions more acceptable.

#11. Diverting focus from the important to the trivial. Social theorists have to seek an understanding of our social world in ways that are not in blatant conflict with our secular and religious ideals. When that appears to be impossible, they are forced to then focus on the irrelevant. Most become experts at being precise on subjects that are unimportant and imprecise about ones that are. That explains why there is a tendency to pile up data that is useful only for endless quibbling over picayune academic issues. It is also of note that a 420 page book was published in the last ten years just to deal with the "right" way to handle reference citations.

Another form of it is when scholars elaborately over-document the obvious. Still others just rehash what others have written. Some even resort to nonsense subjects, such as "the sociology of the body," in order to sequester space which they can then fill up with words.

#12. The use of "propaganda words." These are words that are deceptively flattering or subtly critical while appearing to be merely descriptive. One example of a propaganda term is "Libertarian" being so easily associated with "liberty."

One of the most important propaganda-words of all is the word, "truth." As a concept instead of the word, it is widely use in the academic and scientific world. To fully clarify how it is used as a stratagem, we need to interrupt here and deal with it at some length.

People have an abiding love for the "truth" word because it is so useful for inflating the value of what they want others to believe. Epistemologists have said that no one has ever been able to clearly explain what is meant when the word is used. Can anything we use it for even remotely represent an ultimate, eternal, and absolute reality? Since we are finite beings, we cannot completely understand or be infinitely exact about anything. Unfortunately even so, this old-religion word, or one if its synonyms, is consistently used even in science.

The old "spirit"-based WV system's relatively static, rigid and closed set of beliefs keeps their believers used to thinking of knowledge as also being static and unchanging, to be, in other words, "truths." A few other such old-religion words are "sin," "holy," "divine," "sacred," "sacrament" and "evil."

Their use of such old-religion rigid-world terms explains why scientists still describe our universe in terms of static, rigid "laws," "principles," and "facts," even in being "exact," as in the so-called "exact sciences." It is impossible for scientists, or anyone else, to ever achieve any final, absolute anything. But most of those who are aware of this, claim the old "truth" concept must remain because our young college and university students would become discouraged and lose the "spirit of science" if they were taught the non-reality of "truth." The real reason is that scientists do not dare to undermine the Accord by confronting their essentially rigid old-religion way of thinking.

What "scientific" is, and all it is, is the improving of the accuracy of what we believe. It would be impossible to build a new civilization that is not bonded by a WV that recognizes that. All we can do, and need to achieve, ever, is the improving of the accuracy of what we believe.

It is useful, however, to call what we all think is obvious as "true." Also, everything we define is truly what we define it as. We cannot walk through brick walls (unless the mortar has disintegrated enough), and we cannot drink molten lead (at least, without dying). Moreover, it is *true* that we can never achieve infinite accuracy in anything, anywhere, anytime.

Most of what we understand is based on theories we call "laws" which are only mathematical formulations and appear to be "truth" only because math can be elegant and useful. Although the "laws of nature" are not "the truth," they are, nevertheless, practical because of being more accurate than the rules or generalizations we replaced them with.

The scientific method is largely how to measure and observe better. When, finally, someone notices that one of the old "laws of nature" is no longer satisfactory, a scientist somewhere then comes up with a newer theory or a way to supplement and improve the older one. "The law of the conservation of energy," for example, required the mythical concept of "potential energy." Even though no "potential energy" has ever been located or measured in anything, it had to be postulated in order for the math and the "law" to work. Then, Albert Einstein developed his Theory of Relativity and "potential energy" was not needed in astrophysics. Even so, Einstein had not found "the ultimate Truth." In time, even his main theory will also have to be improved upon, or replaced. Then we will be able to deal better with the discovery that some stars are supposed to be older than the universe. It might even enable us to find "dark matter" or explain why the photon turns out to be smaller than is presently consistent with quantum physics.

If we use "truth" in the usual propaganda-word way, we think of science as "acquiring truth." If so, then each new "truth" which replaces an older "truth" must be *more* "true." This means there have to be "degrees of truth." But how can that be? And if there are, then all our present beliefs are just "more true" than what we believed before. Carrying that forward, it seems to follow that someday we will achieve "the last degree of truth," or, in other words, "absolute knowledge." After that ideal state, we would never, then, have any further use for either science or religion! As "ultimate beings" with infinite wisdom and the ultimate knowledge of our then perfectly and completely understood universe, wouldn't we all think and behave exactly the same?

The illusory nature of scientific "truth" was discovered back in the 1920s and 1930s. Among the first to discover it was the philosopher of History, Benedetto Croce and the linguist, Ludwig Wittgenstein. In 1921, they explained that history and language cannot picture reality. In 1925, Alfred North Whitehead discovered it in philosophy and mathematics. In 1927, Werner Heisenberg discovered it in physics, and in 1929, Karl Mannheim in sociology. Finally, historians, Carl Becker, R. Collingwood and Charles A. Beard found it out between 1931 and 1935. All this was facilitated by Albert Einstein's 1905 discovery of the relative nature of everything.

It marked the end of Greek Logic that had ruled for thousands of years. For example, we hear that "of two contradictory statements, one at least is false." Really? Take two statements: "the sun is round, and the sun is not round." If indeed the sun is slightly pear shaped, are either or both statements "right?" Or is one more "wrong" than the other? The only way to resolve that is to see it as dealing, instead, with "accuracy" and has nothing to do with "true" or "false," "right" or "wrong."

The reaction to all that in the 1930s was worse than the problem, and resulted in universal, intellectual indigestion. Most scientists were not as brilliant and able to properly absorb the full import and implications of the new concept. Some notable academics resorted to mysticism and concluded that there must be different realities in the world. In Europe, some resorted to "deconstruction," "post-modernism," and the claim to "multiple truths." By then, the social theory consensus had accommodated to liberal Christian thought enough that they kept the truth concept but accommodated to the early past-century advances by using synonyms for it, such as "fact," "knowledge," and "law" (such as "laws of nature"), not more accurate or theory.

#13. Concept shattering. Social theorists consider even such words as "instinct" and "religion" to be troublesome because using them too easily opens the way to controversy and possibly coming to anti-religious conclusions. So, they use other words instead. This leads to a proliferation of substitute words. Instead of using the word, "instinct," for example, evolutionary psychology has come up with "hard wired," innate or genetic behavior and "functionally specialized computational devices." For "religion," social theorists have writen about "prime symbols," "form-worlds of great myth," "over-simplified diagrammatic formula," "socio-cultural phenomena," and "mythical configurations." So many words for a single concept serve only to confuse the concept's meaning and enable it to be more easily manipulated.

#14. The proliferating-of-clauses. This consists of writing such long and complex sentences that they *cannot be clearly diagrammed*. That means they are all but incomprehensible and their paragraph-long sentences are largely self-inconsistent, all of which helps to explain their meaninglessness. Clause-proliferated writing enables the author to make a point that he only pretended to prove but is seldom criticized because of its academic sophistication.

#15. Timidity in dealing with what is "politically sensitive." Subjects that people are hypersensitive about are not "political" but ideological. Women, homosexuals, the environment, animals and the like all deserve fair treatment, but such needs have all been turned into extremist ideological "causes" organized to prevent reasonable, balanced discussion.

#16. Inferring the weight of authority. This involve long, select bibliographies listing authorities comprising mere associates who happen to share the same or a similar view. The purpose can be less to give credit then to impress. Sometimes it takes up more pages than the content itself. In some cases, the author has generally only rehashed what others had written and said very little if anything new himself.

#17. Pseudo-objective word-usages. These rhetoric devices enable scholars to write and speak subjectively while appearing to be objective. In one form, certain adverbs are avoided such as, for example, "even," "still," "enough" and "just." That gives the appearance of making scholarly writing seem to be more formal, objective and scholarly while, at the same time, actually ignoring significant relationships.

Another form of pseudo-objective word-use is the constant focus of anthropologists on showing that humans and Neanderthals mated, how close they were to us, and how "un-caveman-like" they were, all in an effort to impress by seeming to be objective. The effort by some social theorists that life, including human life, has no "purpose" or goal is another ploy to appear objective. Our "purpose" or goal is what we together in our WV systems say it is.

#18. Writing abstractions instead of dealing with the concrete. Some social theorists indulge themselves by building abstract superstructures of thought without including illustrative examples. Without concrete examples, others are never sure whether or not what they are thinking is being communicated. It could be mere subterfuge even while giving the impression of being more erudite.

#19. Failing to explicitly connect ideas or concepts in order to be able to claim, or deny, a praised or criticized connection, whichever response is most convenient.

#20. The framing manipulation. This is a rarely used academic trick in which every issue is framed in a form loaded in a positive way in its favor. This forces the opposing theory into a deny-only mode.

#21. Irrelevant fussing and pomposity. Some scholars are known for presenting their research conclusions as unanimous while encasing them in a cloud of qualifying disclaimers that, in effect, belie what they had actually set out to show, all of which diverts the reader from their rationalizing. Others are infamous for repeatedly qualifying every assertion and going in for elaborate distinctions. They may even tell the reader what they do not mean or what they do not intend to show, and ask questions which they never actually answer.

Some social theorists also exhibit timidity by preceding their statements with such evasive phrases as "it is also evident that . . ." or "it is noteworthy that . . ." or "it can be recognized that. . . ." These muted disclaimers become a sort of ritual—such as preceding every statement with "God willing" or "Allah be praised." Such academic fussing is reminiscent of the way French Chefs fuss with food.

BIBLIOGRAPHY

The bibliographical material *not* included below is: (1) the various social theory consensus references from which the APPENDIX list was gleaned, (2) most website references (3) some of the pre-1985 references lost when transferring from the typewriter to the computer, and (4) my direct, personal investigation and observations made in Europe, the Americas, Indonesia, Malaysia and Singapore, some of the thirty-five nations I lived or traveled in.

The some three hundred bibliographical references below fall into either of the following two categories: (1) the works of thinkers who have helped in the development of social evolution theory and (2) works by historians, animal (especially primate) behaviorists, archaeologists, philologists, linguists, psychologists, anthropologists and others who provided data.

Abbasi, S. M. Madni, transl., Riyadh-Us-Saleheen, Kitab Bhavan, New Delhi, 1984, Preface, page 1X, 10-15.

Abu-Saud, Mahmoud, Concept of Islam, American Trust Publications, Indianapolis, 1983, page 7, 28-29, 61, 84.

Adams, Robert, The Evolutionary Process in Early Civilizations, in The Evolution of Man, Sold Tax, editor, University of Chicago Press, 1960, Vol II, page 161-165.

Adler, Alfred, Understanding Human Nature, Greenberg Publishing, NY, 1927, page 69, 90.

Akenson, Donald H., "God's Children," 1992, p 322.

Albrecht, Katherine, and Liz Mcintyre, The Spychips Threat, Thomas Nelson Inc., 2006

Alinei, Mario, The Paleolithic Continuity Theory on Indo-European Origins, 4.2.

Alla, Thomas B., editor, Animal Behavior, National Geographic Society publication, 1972, page 401.

Allman, William F., The Stone Age Present, Simon & Shuster, 1994, pages 202-208, 222-244. Also, a report by him on the work of Irwin Bernstein in "The Evolution of Aggression," U.S. News & World Report, May 11, 1992, pg 58.

Andreski, Stanislav, The Origins of War, page 132 of The Natural History of Aggression, edited by J. D. Carthy and F. J. Ebling, Academic Press, London and NY, 1964.

Andrews, Anthony P., First Cities, St. Remy Press, Smithsonian Books, Washington B.C., 1995, pages 24, 32, 46-50, 79-97.

Appel, Willa, Cults in America, Holt, Rinehard and Winston, NY, 1983.

Ardrey, Robert, The Territorial Imperative, Atheneum, NY, 1966, pages 87-9, 102, 351-2; The Social Contract, 1970, page 24-5, 228-229, 255, 261, 288-9; and The Hunting Hypothesis, 1976, pages 32, 41, 57-9, 110-112, 161.

Asla, Reza, No god but God, The Origins, Evolution and Future of Islam, Random House, 2005,

Bahn, Paul G. and Jean Vertut, Images of the Ice Age, Facts on File, NY, 1988, page 187-188.

Baigent, Michael, Richard Leigh, and Henry Lincoln, The Messianic Legacy, Corgi Books, 1987, page 106-109, 178, 185-192, 202.

Bakker, Cornelis B. and Marianne Bakker-Rabdau, No Trespassing! explorations in Human Territoriality, Chandler & Sharp Publishing, Inc., San Francisco, pages 30-31.

Barthel, Manfred, What the Bible Really Says, Wings Books, NY, 1980, pages 64-65.

Basham, A. L. editor, A Cultural History of India, Oxford University Press, 1975, pg. 26-29, 129, 458.

Bechert, Heinz, The Historical Buddha: His Teaching as a Way to Redemption, l. Buddhist Perspectives, in Christianity and the World Religions, Doubleday & Co. Inc., NY, 1986, pages 291-303.

Beck, Martin A., Atlas of Mesopotamia, 1962, pages 13-16

Beek, Gus W. van, "Prolegomenon," in James A. Montgomery's 1935 work "Arabia and the Bible, re-issued in 1969 by KTAV Publishing House, edited by Harry M. Orlinsky, page XXII-XXVII.

Begley, Sharon, "Early Exposure to Common Chemicals May Be Programming Kids to be Fat," Newsweek, Sept. 21, 2009, pg 57-62.

Bender, David L., editor, Science and Religion, Greenhaven Press, St. Paul, 1988, page 183.

Benedict, Ruth, Patterns of Culture, Penguin Books, Inc. NY, 1934, page 42-44

Bloodworth, Dennis, The Chinese Looking Glass, Farrar, Straus & Giroux, N.Y., 1967, Page 117, 173.

Bock, Kenneth, Human Nature and History, Columbia University Press, 1980, page 103.

Bower, Bruce, "True Believes," Skeptical Inquirer, Summer 1991, page 98-401

Braudel, Fernand, The Perspective of the World, Vol III, Harper and Row, NY, 1979, pages 84-8, and 93.

Brenner, Robert, "The Agrarian Roots of European Capitalism," for the Agrarian Class Structure and Economic Development In Pre-Industrial Europe Symposium, 1982. pages 21, 28-29.

Briffault, Robert, The Mothers, Vol 1, Johnson Reprint Corp. NY, 1969, page 471.

Brown, Lester R., "Could Food Shortages Bring Down Civilization?" Scientific American, May 2009, pp 50-57.

Bucaille, Maurice, The Bible, The Quran and Science, North American Trust Publication, Indianapolis, 1979, pages 118-9.

Bullough, Vern L and Bonnie, The Subordinate Sex, University of Illinois Press, 1973, pages 77, 87, 95-7.

Burnham, James, The Machiavellians, Gateway, 1943, pages 133-146.

Butterworth, E. A., Some Traces of the Pre-Olympian World, De Gruyter, NY & Berlin, 1966.

Calder, Nigel, The Human Conspiracy, British Broadcasting Company, London, 1976, pp 19, 23-32, 59, 411.

Calhoun, J. B., "Population Density and Social Pathology," Scientific American, February 1962.

Cambell, Joseph, Myths to Live By, Bantam Books, 1973, page 34-35, 178-179; with Bill Moyers, The Power of Myth, Doubleday, NY, 1988, pages 9, 55, 102-3, 227, and 1991 version, pages 15, 212-215 and 228.

Carleton, Gregory, Sexual Revolution in Bolshevik Russia, University of Pittsburgh Press, 2005, p 51.

Carrington, L., A Short History of the Chinese People, Goodrich, 1959, page 43-45, 148-152.

Carroll, Michael P., The Cult of the Virgin Mary, Princeton University Press, 1986, pp 20, 21, 38, 90-99.

Carter, George, Man and the Land, Holt, Rinehart and Winston, NY, 1964, page 56, 196, 436.

Cartmill, Matt, "The Gift of Gab," Discover, November 1998, pages 56-64

Cassirer, Ernst, An Essay on Man, Yale University Press, 1944, page 214-215, 1956 ed: pages 108-114, 167, and The Myth of the State, 1946, Yale University Press, (pages 210-216 in the 1955 Doublday Anchor edition.)

Casson, Lionel, "Biting the Bullet in Ancient Rome," Horizon, Winter, 1976, pages 18-21

Chamberlain, Jonathan, Chinese Gods, Pelanduk Publications, Malaysia, 1987.

Chambers, James, The Devil's Horsemen, Atheneum, NY, 1985, pages 80-95.

Chao, Kang, Man and Land in Chinese History, Standford University Press, 1986, Part 2.

Charmichael, Joel, The Birth of Christianity, Reality and Myth, Dorset Press, NY, 1989, pages 5-23, 35-46, 52-83, 88, 125, 132, 144-148, 152, 175.

Childe, V. Gordon, The Dawn of European Civilization, Alfred Knopf, NY 1958, sixth edition, page 119

Choi, Charles Q. "Humans Still Evolving as Our Brains Shrink," Live Science, Nov 13, 2009, http://www.livescience.com/history/091113-origins-evolving.html

Chuvin, Pierre, A Chronicle of the Last Pagans, Harvard, 1990.

Ciochin, Russell L., "Jungle Monuments of Angkor," Natural History Magazine, January 1990, page 53.

Clark, J. G. D., Radiocarbon dating and the expansion of farming from the Near East over Europe, Proceedings of the Prehistoric Society, 1965, page 21.

Clarke, Robin, "The Expanding Deserts," in Ecology 2000, edited by Sir Edmund Hillary, Beauford Books Inc., 1984, Part 4.

Cloud, John, "Why Genes aren't Destiny," Time, Jan.18, 2010, pp 49-57.

Cohen, Daniel, "Lost Cities and Forgotten Tribes" edited by Richard F. Dempewolff, Hearst Books, NY, 1974, page 25-9.

Cohen, Mark N. PhD., Health and the Rise of Civilization, Yale University Press, 1989.

Colander, David, Why Aren't Economists as Important as Garbagemen?, M. E. Sharpe, Inc., 1991, pages 7, 35-36, 41, 63, 74-5, 84.

Comber, Leon, Chinese Ancestor Worship in Malaysia, Malay Heritage Books, Singapore, 1954, page 1, 162-7.

Corning, Peter A., The Synergism Hypothesis, McGraw-Hill, 1989, page 286.

Comte, Auguste, The Positive Philosophy, in The Philosophers of Science, Random House, NY, 1947, page 234; Comte, Auguste, A General View of Positivism, 1856, Part 1, "Its General Character."

Conway, Flo and Jim Siegelman, Holy Terror, Dell Publishing, NY, 1984, Preface to the Delta Edition .

Cottrell, Leonard, The Horizon Book of Lost Worlds, Doubleday & Co., NY, 1962, page 102

Coulanges, Fustel, The Ancient City, Boston, 1874, pages 10-3 and 164-7.

Cowgill, George L., The Collapse of Ancient States and Civilizations, University of Arizona Press, Tuscon, 1988, page 247.

Crone, Patricia, and Michael Cook, Hagarism, Cambridge University Press, 1977, pages 42, 102, 107-112

Daly, Mary, The Church of the Second Sex, Harper & Row, N.Y., 1968, Part 7.

Danino,   Michael, 3500 Year Old Stone & Tamil Nadu politics, 2006,

http://varnam.org/blog/archives/2006/05/3500_year_old_stone_and_tamil.php

Daraul, Arkon, A History of Secret Societies, Simon & Schuster Pocket Books, NY, 1962, pages 37 and 43, 219, 298-300.

Darrah, John, The Real Camelot, 1981, Thomas & Hudson, page 28

Davidson, Basil, African Kingdoms, Time Inc., 1966, pages 35-38.

Davis, William Stearns, A Day in Old Rome, Biblo and Tannen, NY, pages 1-2, 100.

Deal, Terrence and Allan Kennedy, Corporate Cultures, Addison-Wesley Publishing Co., 1982, pages 10, 15, 85, 94-98.

De Camp, Sprague, Angkor--Jungle City of the Dead, in Lost Cities and Forgotten Tribes, edited by Richard F. Dempewolff, produced by Science Digest, Hearst Books, 1974, page 181-2.

Dempewolff, Richard F., Lost Cities and Forgotten Tribes, Hearst Books, NY, 1974, pages 25-29, 65.

De Montellano, Bernard Ortiz, Magic Melanin, Skeptical Inquirer, Winter 1992, page 162.

De Rosa, Peter, The Vicars of Christ, Crown Publishing, 1988, page 92-94, 112-3, 215-221.

Diamond, Deborah, "Aristotle's Ethos in the Modern Western World," Mensa Bulletin, April 1990, page 23.

Diamond, Jared, The Third Chimpanzee, Harper Collins Perennial, 1992, 200, 260-273.

Diop, Cheikh Anta, Civilization or Barbarism, Lawrence Hill Books, 1991.

Durant, Will, The Age of Voltaire in The Story of Civilization, Simon and Schuster, NY, 1965, pages 497, 780 and Part 22; Our Oriental Heritage, Simon & Schuster, 1954, pages 257, 829-830; The Life of Greece, 1939, page 47, 254. 565-6, The Age of Voltaire, pp 497, 780 and Chapt. 22.

Durkheim, Emile, The Elementary Forms of Religious Life, Allen & Unwin., London, 1968, pages 418-9

Eliade, Mircea, Cosmos and History, Harper, NY, 1954, page 3-5, 27-33.

Einstein, Albert, Out of My Later Years, Lyle Stuart Inc., 1956.

Eisler, Riane, The Chalice and the Blade, Harper and Row, S.F., 1987, page 10, Part 11.

Eno, Robert, Deities and Ancestors in "Early Oracle Inscriptions," Religions of China in Practice, editor Donald Lopez Jr., Princeton University Press, N.J. 1996, pages 43-44.

Fagan, Brian M., The Journey From Eden, Thames and Hudson, London, 1990, page 12-14, 23, 46, 157, 179.

Farb, Peter, Humankind, Houghton Mifflin Co. Boston, 1978, page, 17, 31, 435-438.

Fast, Julius, Body Language, Simon Schuster, NY, 1970, pages 120-121.

Fisher, Sidney N., The Middle East, Alfred A. Knopf, 1959, page 18, 23.

Fishman, Joshua. "Hard Evidence," Discover, January 1992, pp. 50-51

Flood, Gavin, An Introduction to Hinduism, Cambridge University Press, 1996, pages 116, 148-1668, 174-9, 197, 218-222, and 320-321.

Frazer, Sir J. G., The Golden Bough, London, 1949, i ff. and Totemism and Exogamy, 1910, chapter 34.

Freedman, Jonathan L., Crowding and Behavior, W. H. Freeman and Co., 1975, pagers 87, 90 and 96-98

Friedman, George, America's Secret War, Broadway Books, N.Y., 2004, pages 52-59, 69, 93, 108, 256-8.

Friedman, Milton & Rose, Free to Choose, Avon, 1979, pg 2, 45.

Frish, John E., Research on Primate Behavior in Japan, American Anthropologist, LXI, 1959, page 589

Frey, Arthur, The Cross and Swastika, translated by J. Strathearn, McNabb, London, 1938, pages 5, 78 and 79.

Furneaux, Rupert, Ancient Mysteries, McGraw-Hill, 1977, pages 120-5.

Galbraith, John Kenneth, Economics in Perspective, Houghton Mufflin Co., Boston, 1987, page 134

Gardiner, Sir Alan Henderson, Egypt of the Pharaohs, 1961, pages 109-111, 183, 269-270.

Galbraith, John Kenneth, Economics in Perspective, Houghton Mufflin Co., Boston, 1987, page 134

Gardner, Martin, Did Adam & Eve Have Navels?, w.w.Norton & Co. NY, 2000, pgs 144-152.

Gernet, Jacques, A History of Chinese Civilization, Cambridge University Press, NY, 1982, page 1, 390, 398-422.

Gibbon, Edward, Decline and Fall of the Roman Empire, Vol. I, Part XV, Section III

Gilbert, Susan, A Field Guide to Boys and Girls, Harper/Collins, N.Y., 2000, pages 40-76.

Gimbutas, Marija, First Wave of Eurasian Steppe Pastoralists into Copper Age Europe, Journal of Indo-European Studies 5, Winter 1977, pages 15, 20, 32, 168, 277, 177, 203, 277, 285, 293, 297, 304-5; The Language of the Goddess, Harper and Row, NY, 1989, pages 141, 159 318-20; The Goddesses and Gods of Old Europe, University of California Press, LA, 1982, pages 12, 16, 18, 27, 74, 93, 159-161, 178, 196, 201, 237 etc.

Glucksman, A., Sexual Dimorphism in Human and Mammalian Biology and Pathology, Academic Press, 1981.

Goldman, Wendy Z., Women, the State and Revolution: Soviet Family Policy and Social Life, 1917-1936, Cambridge University Press, 1993.

Goldsmith, Edward, The Fall of the Roman Empire, A Social and Ecological Interpretation, The Ecologist, 1975, Chapter 1.

Goodall, Jane, In the Shadow of Man, 1971, and in American Scientist, March-April, 1990, pages 121-124.

Graves, Robert, The Greek Myths, 1955, Introduction

Gray, John, The Canaanites, Frederick A. Praeger Inc., 1964, page 34-5.

Greenwood, David J., The Taming of Evolution, Cornell University Press, Ithaca and London, 1984, pages 199-204.

Glob, Peter Vilhelm, The Bog People, Cornell University Press, NY, 1969, pages 101, 132, 143, 159, and 168

Guirand, Felix, editor, Larousse Encyclopedia of Mythology, Paul Hamlyn Ltd., London, 1964, page 89-118, 213-4, 239.

Gulik, Robert H. van, "Erotic Color Prints," as referenced in Skeptic, 1951, vol 5, #4, page 13 and 74-76.

Hall, Norman and Lucia, "Is the War between Science and Religion Over?", The Humanist, May/June 1986

Halley, Henry H., Halley's Bible Handbook, Zondervan Publishing, 1962, page 40.

Hallowell, Irving, Self, Society and Culture in Phylogenetic Perspective, in The Evolution of Man, Vol II, The University of Chicago Press, 1960, page 332-4.

Hamblin, Dora Jane, "Has the Garden of Eden been located at last?, "Smithsonian, May 1987, pages 127-155.

Harding, R. S. O. and S. C. Strum, Predatory Baboons of Kekopey, Natural History, #85, pages 51-3.

Hargrove, Robert A., EST: Making Life Work, Dell Publishing, NY, 1976, pages 42 and 45

Harrison, Brian, Southeast Asia, A Short History, St. Martins Press, NY, 1966, pages 58-60.

Harris, Marvin, Our Kind, Harper & Row, NY, 1989, pages 83-94, 319-325. 393-395, 414-416, 429.

Hartman, Thomas, "Unequal Protection," Rodale, 2002. Parts 1-3.

Hathout, Dr. Maher M., The Sighting of the Hilal and the Role of Technology, Islamic Center of Southern California, LA, 1984, page 8.

Hawking, Stephen W., A Brief History of Time, Bantam Books, NY, 1988, pages, 13, 54-56, 140-141. A Brief History of Time, Stephen W. Hawking, Bantam Books, 1988, pages 140-141.

Hazlett, Andrew, "See Spot Run Multiculturally," Wall Street Journal, Feb. 22, 1999.

Heiden, Konrad, Der Fueher, translated by Ralph Mannheim, Houghton Mifflin Co. Boston, 1944, page 5-12, 738.

Hua, Cai, "A Society without Fathers or Husbands: The Na of China," Zone books, 2001.

Impoco, James, "What the Emperor Knew," U. S. News and World Report, November 26, 1990, page 67.

Isbell, Lynne A., "The Fruit, The Tree and the Serpent, why we see so well, Atlantic, April 2010, pg. 94.

Johnson, P., The History of Christianity; Atheneum, 1976. p. 28, 350-376.

Khan, Mahvish R., My Guantanamo diary, Public Affairs Group Pub. , 2008, pages 149-186.

Klein, Naomi, "The Shock Doctrine, H. Holt & Co., 2007.

Kroeber, Alfred. L. and Clyde Kluckholn, "A Critical Review of Concepts and Definitions," Papers of the Peabody Museum of American Archeology and Ethnology, Vol 47, 1952, Parts II and III, pages 3-223; Evolution, History, and Culture, in The Evolution Of Man, Vol II, Sol Tax, editor, University of Chicago Press, 1960, page 12.

Kung, Hans, Christianity and the World Religions, Doubleday & Co, NY, 1986, Part II, section 2, page 58.

Kurtz, Paul, "The New Age—an Examination, the Skeptical Inquirer, Summer, 1989

Laffin, John, The Arab Mind Considered, Taplinger Publishing Co., 1975, page 17, 19, 42.

Laird, Thomas & Michael Victor, A Woman's World -- Meghalaya; matrilineal culture, 1995, Whole Earth Review

Lamb, David, The Arabs, Random House, 1987, pages 12-4. Lawrence, Bruce B., Defenders of God, Harper and Row, 1983, page 10.

Lawrence, Bruce B., Defenders of God, Harper & Row, 1989, pp 11 , 63, 76 and 81.

Larson, Edward J. and Larry Witham, "Scientists and Religion in America," Scientific American, September 1999, page 90.

Larue, Gerald A., Marriage and Divorce, in What the Bible Really Says, edited by Morton Smith and R. Joseph Hoffman, Prometheus Books, Buffalo, 1989, page 78, 82, 90-91.

Lawler, Andrew, "Out of Eden," Discovery, December, 2009, pp. 64-68.

Lawrence, Bruce B., Defenders of God, Harper & Row, 1989, page 7-8, 11, 46, 51, 52, 62-63, 75-76, 81-82, Part 3, 172

Le Bon, Gustave, The Crowd, 1896.

Lee, Richard, Cultural Anthropology Today, editor, Communication Research Machines Inc., Del Mar, Calif., page 13.

Lehmann, Johannes, Hittites, People of a Thousand Gods, the Viking Press, NY, 1975 , page 269.

Leonard, Jonathan, Early Japan, Time-Life Books, NY, 1968, pages 77-79.

Lewis, Bernard, Istanbul and the Civilization of the Ottoman Empire, 1963, page 5.

Lewis, Henry T., "Indian Fires of Spring, Natural History, January 1980, page 76-83.

Lindbergh, David, The Beginnings of Western Science, University of Chicago Press, 1992, p 180.

Lissner, Ivar, The Silent Past, G. P. Putnam's Sons, 1962, page 33, 194-202.

Lloyd, Seton, Early Highland Peoples of Anatolia, McGraw Hill, 1967, page 8.

Loewe, M., Chinese Ideas of Life and Death: Faith and Reason in the Han Period, 202 BCE to AD 200, 1982, Taipei SMC.

Lorenz, Konrad, On Aggression, Harcourt, Brace & World, NY, 1963, page 31, 45, 51, 221-2, 241, 258, 269, 273; "Ritualized Fighting", pages 49-50 in The Natural History of Aggression, J. D. Carthy and F. J. Ebling, editors, Institute of Biology, Academic Press, London and NY 1964, page 49-50.

Ludwig, Emil, The Nile, Viking Press, 1937, pages 257-259

Lumsden Charles J., and Edward O. Wilson Genes, Mind and Morris, Ivan, "Oh, Lone Pine Tree," Horizon, Winter 1975, pages 33-37.

Luxing, Wu, 101 Chinese Deities, Asiapac Books, 1994.

Lyon, Quinter M., The Great Religions, 1957, pages 80-4.

MacKenzie, Norman, editor., Secret Societies, Collier Books, NY, 1967, pages 16, 21-22, 26,

Mack, Raymond W. and Kimball Young, Sociology and Social Life, The American Book Co., NY, 1968, page 127 and 4th edition, page 38, 371-372.

MacKay, Charles, Extraordinary Popular Delusions and the Madness of Crowds, London, 1984.

Maclay, George and Humphry Knipe, The Dominant Man, Delacorte Press, NY, 1972.

Malinowski, Bronislaw, Sex, Culture, and Myth, Rupert Hart-Davis, London, 1963, page 134-8, 215, 244, 257-8, 334; Magic, Science and Religion, Doubleday, NY, 1954, pages 59, 71, 125-126, 245-246, 261-265.

Mannheim, Karl, Ideology and Utopia, Harcourt, Brace and World, NY, 1936, pages 5-40.

Martin, Paul, "Pleistocene Overkill," Natural History, December 1967.

Marshack, Alexander, "Implications of Palaeolithic Symbolic Evidence for the Origin of Language," American Scientist, March-April, 1972.

Mathers, MacGregor, S. L., The Kabbaluh Unveiled, Routledge & Paul Kegan Ltd., London, 1957.

Mayer, Thomas, Truth Vs. Precision in Economics, Cambridge University Press, 1993, pages 15-20, 27-29, 44-47.

Mazar, Amihai, Archeology of the Land of the Bible, 10,000-586 BCE, Doubleday, page 56.

McAdams, Robert, Contexts of Civilizational Collapse, page 33.

McCrone, John, The Ape That Spoke, William Morrow, NY, 1991, pages 26, 30-7, 214-218.

McCutcheon, Mark, The Final Theory, 2002

McDowell, Josh and Don Stewart, Answers to Tough Questions, Tyndale House, Wheaton, Ill, copyright 1980 by Campus Crusade for Christ inc., pages 33, 38-39, 46-48.

McNeill, William H., The Rise of the West, McNeill, 1963, page 406.

Mee Jr., Charles L., "How a Mysterious Disease laid low Europe's Masses," Smithsonian, Feb. 1990, page 67.

Meeks, Wayne A., The First Urban Christians, Yale University Press, New-haven, 1983, pps 2-40, and The Venture of Islam: Conscience and History, University of Chicago Press, 1979, Vol. 3, p. 189.

Mekown, Delos B., "Science Vs. Religion in Future Constitutional Conflict," Free Inquiry, Summer 1984.

Mellaart, James, The Neolithic of the Near East, Scribner, NY, 1975, page 280.

Meyer, Marvin W., transl., The Secret Teachings of Jesus, Random House, NY, 1986, introduction XV-XVI.

Miles, Rosalind, The Woman's History of the World, Salem House, 1989, page 64.

Miller, Lisa, "Harvard's Crisis of Faith," Newsweek, 1/22/10, pp. 43-45.

Miller, Peter, Swarm Theory, National Geographic, July 2007, pages 136-147.

Mindell, David P., "Evolution in the Everyday world," Scientific American, Jan. 2009, p 83

Mirsky, Steven, "What's Good for the Group," Scientific American, Jan. 2009, pg 51.

Mitchell, H. L., One Hundred and Seventy-seven Alleged Bible Contradictions, NY, 1934.

Mitchell, Richard, Less than Words Can Say, Little Brown & Co., Boston, 1979.

Mohen, Jean-Pierre, The World of Megaliths, Facts on File, NY, 1990, 45-67, 87, 204, 213-216, 225-226, 262-266, 272-275.

Monard, Jacques, Change and Necessity, 1971.

Moore, Michael, "Dude, Where's My Country", Warner Books, 2001, chapters 1-10

Morgan, Elaine, Descent of Woman, Stein & Day, NY, 1972, pages 100-120; Demon Lover, W. W. Norton, 1989, page 26.

Morris, Desmond, The Naked Ape, Crown Publishing, NY, pages 10-88.

Morris, Henry M., A History of Modern Creationism, Master Book Publishers, San Diego, CA, 1984, page 333.

Morton, H. V., The Colosseum, Fodor's Rome, 1990, page 61.

Moscovici, Serge, transl. by J. C. Whitehouse, The Age of the Crowd, Cam-bridge University Press, 1985, page 68-69.

Muller, Herbert, The Uses of the Past, Oxford University Press, 1957, Part 4, Part 5, Part 5, part 4 and 6, page 79.

Mumola, Christopher, Suicide and Homicide in State Prisons and Local Jails, August 2005, Bureau of Justice Statistics, Special Report.

Needham, Joseph, Science in Traditional China, Harvard University Press, Cambridge, 1982, page 8, 26.

Nishida, T. and K. Kawanaka, Inter-unit Group Relations among Wild Chimpanzees, African Studies, Kyoto University, 1972.

Nixon, Bobbie, "Termite Battles May Explain Evolution of Social Insects," National Science Foundation, posted: 29 January 2010 http://www.livescience.com/animals/termite-social-insect-evolution-bts-100129.html

Ono, Dr. Sokyo, Shinto the Kami Way, Bridgeway Press, Japan, 1962, pages 2-12, 55, 79, 92-3, 98, 105-7, 111.

Packard, Norman interview, Omni magazine, January 1992, page 85, 97.

Packard, Vance, The Hidden Persuaders, 1957.

Palmer, Leonard R., Mycenaean and Minoans, 1962, pages 97, 100, 106, and 132-143.

Pan, Lynn, Sons of the Yellow Emperor, Little Brown & Co, 1990, page 44.

Paper, Jordan, The Spirits are Drunk, State University of New York Press, 1995, pages 15-17, 47-49, 77-79, 120.

Park, Andy, "Giants Once Ruled Australia, fossil discoveries reveal," Smithsonian, January 1990, page 142.

Partner, Peter, Two Thousand Years, The First Millennium, Granada Media, 1999.

Patai, Raphael, The Hebrew Goddess, Avon, NY, 1978, page 12-13, 48-50.

Patterson, James and Peter Kim, The Day America Told the Truth, Prentice Hall, 1991, page 268.

Pease, Allan, Body Language, Sheldon Press, London, pages 9-10.

Perlin, John, A Forest Journey, W. W. Norton & Co., NY & London, 1989, pages 70, 98-101, 138-140, 163-245.

Perry, John and Erna, The Social Web, Harper & Row, NY, 1976, page 93, 334.

Pfeiffer, John E., The Emergency of Society, McGraw Hill, 1977, page 35, 73-74, 165, 226, 289; Cro-Magnon hunters were really us, working out strategies for survival, Smithsonian, October 1986, page 77, 80, 82; "Was Europe's Fabulous Cave Art the Start of the Information Age?" Smithsonian, April, 1983, pages 38-39; "Man the Hunter," Horizon, Spring, 1971, page 31.

Phillips, John A., EVE: The History of an Idea, Harper & Row, 1984, page 7, 11-12, 64, 144-6.

Pinson, Koppel S., Modern Germany, Its History and Civilization, 1954, page 462-465, 491-492.

Pope Pius XI ordered *Index of Prohibited Books,* Vatican Polygot Press, 1930, p. xi.

Pouzzner, Daniel, The Evolutionary Psychology of Human Sex & Gender, 2000,

Powell, Corry S., "Twenty Ways the World could End," Discover, October 2000, pages 50- 57.

Pricknett, Lynn and Clive Prince, The Templar Revelation, Simon and Schuster, 1997, pages 265-329.

Pruyser, Paul W. , A Dynamic Psychology of Religion, Harper & Roe, 1968, page 331-333.

Putman, John J., "The Peopling of the Earth, National Geographic, October 1988, page 448.

Pym, Christopher, The Ancient Civilization of Angkor, Mentor Books, 1968.

Queen, Stuart A. and Robert Havenstien, The Family in Various Cultures, Lippencott, 1961, pages 73-4.

Ratnagar, Shereen, Enquiries into the Political Organization of Harappan Society, Ravish Publishers, India, 1991, pages 1-11, 160-169, 189-190.

Rawls, John, "A Theory of Justice," 1971.

Reed, Evelyn, Sexism and Science, Pathfinder, 1978, pages 125-126.

Renfrew, Colin, Archaeology & Language, Cambridge University Press, NY, 1988, page , 83-4, 137-139, 148, 153, 164-5, 173, 183-197, 216, 243-8, 253-5; Before Civilization, 1974, pages 147-9, 222.

Reynold, G. S., A Primer of Operant Conditioning, Scott Foresman & Co., 1975, 8, 131-142.

Ridley, Matt, The Red Queen, Penguin Books, NY, 1993, page 7, 18, 191, 204-5.

Ritzer, George, Sociological Theory, Alfred A. Knopf, NY, 1983, pages 11-12 and 15.

Roach, M., Almost Human, National Geographic Magazine, April, 2008, pages 124-144.

Roe, Richard L., Cultural Anthropology Today, Communication Research Machines Inc. Del Mar CA, 1971, pg 15.

Robertson, J. M., Pagan Christs, Dorset Press, N.Y.1966, pages 68, 70, 110, 128.

Rothkopf, David, "Averting Disaster," Newsweek, January 25, 2010, p 28.

Rubvinsky, Yuri, and Ian Wiseman, The History of the End of the World, William Morrow & Co., 1982, page 56.

Rybczynski, Witold, Taming the Tiger, the Viking Press, N.Y., 1983, page 122-125.

Russell, Bertrand, Religion and Science, Oxford University Press, 1935.

Sagan, Carl & Ann Druyan, Shadows of Forgotten Ancestors, Random House, NY, 1992, pages 184-8, 196-7, 214-7, 230, 234-7, 248-9, 254-6, 272-291, 301-2, 312-313, 325-7.

Saggs, H.W.F., Civilization before Greece and Rome, Yale University Press, 1989, page 73-77, 277, 737; The Greatness that was Babylon, 1962, pages 9-33, 52, 61, 84-139, 164, 186-200, 233, 369, 478.

Sahlins, Marshall D., Social Life of Monkeys, Apes and Primitive Man, "The Evolution of Man's Capacity for Culture," edited by J. N. Spuhler, Wayne State University Press, Detroit, 1959, page 58-64.

Sakellarakis, Yannis and Efi Sapouna-Sakellaraki, "Drama of Death in a Minoan Temple, National Geographic, February 1991, page 205-7.

Samuelson, Robert J "why school 'reform' fails: student motivation is the problem." September 13th, 2010, Newsweek, pg 21.

Sargent, Stansfeld, The Basic Teachings of the Great Psychologists, New Home Library, NY, 1944, pages 65-68.

Schoenberger, Karl, "A Royal Uproar in Japan," Los Angeles Times, November, 1990, page A20.

Schonfield, Dr. Hugh The Passover Plot, Bantam Books, 1966.Scott, John Paul, Aggression, University of Chicago Press, page 97.

Scott, John Paul, Aggression, University of Chicago Press, page 87.

Sears, P. S., Doll Playing Aggression in Normal Young Children, Psychological Monographs, 1951, pages 1-42, 65-66.

Seife, Charles, Sun in a Bottle, Viking Pres., 2008, pages 200-209.

Service, Elman R., of the University of Michigan, Primitive Social Organization, Random House, NY, Studies in Anthropology series, 1962, page 47.

Shapiro, Judith, Mao's War Against Nature, Cambridge University Press, 2001.

Shell, Ellen Ruppel, The Hungry Gene, Atlantic Monthly Press, 2002, pgs. 80, 172-219.

Shenkman, Richard, Legends, Lies & Cherished Myths of World History, History, Harper Collins, 1993, pp 204-209.

Shermer, Michael B., The Chaos of History, In Press, 1991, pages 52-57.

Shevoroshkin, Vitaly, work of by Harvey Hagman, Tracking Mother of 5,000 Tongues, Insight, Feb. 5, 1990, page 50-60.

Shills, Edward, Tradition, University of Chicago Press, 1981, page 94.

Shipman, Pat, "Old Masters," Discover, July 1990, pp 62-5.

Shotwell, James T., The Story of Ancient History, Columbia University Press, NY, 1961 edition, pages 341, 347-8, etc.

Silverman, David P. editor, Ancient Egypt, Oxford University Press, 1997.

Skousen, Mark, Playing the Price Controls Game, Alington House, New Rouchelle, N.Y., 1977, pages 26-27.

Smith, Robertson, The Prophets of Israel, D. Appleton Co. 1882, page 70-83.

Soffer, Olga, "The Caveman's New Clothes," Science American, November 2000, pages 42-4.

Sokal, alan, The Sokal Affair (by editors of Lingua Franca) and Fashionable Nonsense, with Jean Bricmont, 1999, MacMillan

Sommers, Christina Hoff, The War Against Boys, Simon & Schuster, 2000, pages 127, 172, 187, 200, 208.

Sone, Merlin, When God was a Woman, JB Publishers, 1976, pages 132-142.

Speer, Albert, Inside the Third Reich, The MacMillan Co, NY, 1970, page 115.

Speizer, E.A., Akkadian Myths & Epics in American Near East Texts Relating to the Old Testament, Princeton University Press, 1950, pp 99-100

Spender, Dale, Man Made Language, Routledge of Regan Paul, 1980, page 101.

Spiro, Melford E., Gender and Culture: Kibbuts Women Revisited, Duke University Press, 1979, pages 4-13.

Sprague de Camp, "Anghor, Jungle City of the Dead," in Lost Cities and Forgotten Tribes, Richard F. Dempewolff, Hearst Books, N.Y., 1974, pages 181-2.

Staniforth, Maxwell, translator, Early Christian Writings, Dorest Press, NY, 1968.

Starr, Chester, The History of the Ancient World, Oxford University Press, 1983, pages 38-47. 82, 86, 104-5, 135, 239, 359-373, 374-384, 418, 430, 445, 617.

Steinberg, Leo, "A Corner of the Last Judgment," Daedelus, 109, no. 2, Spring, 1980, pages 207-273.

Stein, George J., "Biological Science and the Roots of Nazism," American Scientist, Vol 76, January-February 1988, pages 50-58.

Steven F., Diet for a Small Primate, Natural History Mag., Jan. 1991, page 42.

Steward, J. H., Theory of Culture Change, University of Ill. Press, 1955, page 68, 71.

Stiendorff, George and Keith C. Seele, When Egypt Ruled the East, 1957, page 23, 104, 142.

Stone, I. F., The Trial of Socrates, Doubleday, 1988, Part I, page 252, and 1976 edition, pgs. xxii and xxiii

Stone, Merlin, When God was a Woman, HJB publishers, 1976, pages 132-142.

Streiker, Lowell D., The Gospel Time Bomb, Prometheus Books, buffalo, NY.

Swaan, Wim, Lost Cities of Asia, G.P. Putnam's Sons, 1966, page 124.

Swanson, Carl P., Ever Expanding Horizons, University of Massachusetts Press, 1983, pages 90-93.

Swartz, Jeffrey H., The Red Ape, Houghton, Mufflin Co., Boston, 1987, page 157.

Tax, Sol & Charles Collender, editors, Issues in Evolution, 1960

Tattersall, Jan and Jay H. Matternes, "Once We Were Not Alone," Scientific American, January 2000, page 62.

Taylor, Theodore and Charles Humpstone, The Reston of the Earth, harper & Row, 1973, pages 7-15.

Taylor, Timothy, The Pre-history of Sex, Bantam Books, 1996, page 184.

Temple, Robert, The Genius of China, Simon and Schuster, 1986, page 16, 248.

Thompson, James Westfall, Economic and Social History of the Middle Ages, 1928, pages 671-673, 743-755, 778-790.

Thorpe, W. H., Animal Nature and Human nature, Doubleday, NY, 1974, page 245, 257.

Tiger, Lionel and Robin Fox, The Imperial Animal, Henry Holt and Company, NY, 1971, pages 16-17, 29-34, 52, 156-157.

Toynbee, Arnold J., editor, Half the World, 1973, Holt, Rinehart & Winston, page 16.

Trattner, Ernest R., The Story of the World's Great Thinkers, New Home Library, NY, 1942, page 252.

Trigger, B. G. etc., Ancient Egypt, A social History, Cambridge University Press, 1983, pages 15, 37-38, 57, 173-174, 208-211.

Turnbull, Stephen, Samuri Warlords, Blandford, London, 1989, pages 110-114, 129-131.

Trotter, William, Instincts of the Herd in Peace and War, MacMillan Co., NY, 1915.

Tuck, Edward F. and Timothy Earle, Why C.E.O.'s Succeed (and Why They Fail): Hunters and Gatherers in the Corporate Life, 1996.

Turnbull, Stephen, Samurai Warriors, Blandford Press, London, 1987, pages 9, 30-5, 100, 107, and 128-9.

Turner, Frederick, "Life on Mars," Harper's Magazine, August 1989, pages 38-40.

Tuttle, Russell, H., "Apes of the World", American Scientist, March-April 1990, page 121.

Tylor, Sir Edward Burnett, Primitive Culture, 1871 Washburn, S. L. and B. Avis, Evolution of Human Behavior, "Behavior and Evolution," edited by Anne Rowe and G. G. Simpson, Yale Univ. Press, 1958, page 194.

Varley, H. Paul, Japanese Culture, University of Hawaii Press, 1981, page 14-17.

Vries, Jan de, Perspectives in the History of Religions, University of California Press, Los Angeles, 1967, page 204.

Walker, Benjamin, Sex and the Supernatural, Ottenheimer Publishers, 1970, pages 51-55.

Wallbank, T. Walter, A. M. Taylor, and N. M Bailkey, Civilization, Past and Present, Scott, Foresman and Co., 1967, page 77, 94-95, 171-174, 335.

Wanderlick, Hans, The Secret of Crete, 1974.

Ward, Peter, "What Will Become of *Homo Sapiens?*" Scientific American, January 2009, p 70

Washburn, S. L. and V. Avis, Evolution of Human Behavior, in Behavior and Evolution, edited by Anne Rowe and G. G. Simpson, Yale University Press, 1958, page 194.

Waters, Tom, "Traveling Man," Discover Magazine, June 1990, page 22.

Watson, William, China Before the Han Dynasty, 1961, pages 39-57, 109-116, 172-175.

Watters, Ethan, The Globalization of the American Psyche, Crazy Like Us, Free Press, 2009

Watts, Arthur P., A History of Western Civilization, 1939, Volume I, page 171.

Weaver, Richard, "Concealed Rhetoric in Scientist Sociology" in Scientism and Values" edited by Helmut Schoeck and James W. Wiggins, D. Van Norstrand Co. Inc., 1960, pages 83-93.

Webber, Philip, Ph., Chairman of Scientists for Global Responsibility, West Yorkshire, UK in the Bulletin of the Atomic Scientists, Vol.63, #5, Sept/Oct 2007

Wellard, James, Lost Worlds of Africa, E. P. Dutton, 1967, pages 164-8.

Wells, H. G., The Outline of History, Garden City Publishing, 1920-40, page 543, 986-8.

Wernick, Robert, "What were Druids like, and was Lindow Man one?" Smithsonian, March 1988, page 148, 154-6.

West, John Anthony, "Civilization Rethought," Conde Nest Traveler, February 1993, pages 100-177.

Westphal, Sylvia P., "High Hopes for New Kind of Gene," Smithsonian, July 2009, p 76.

Whipps, Heather, How the Hyoid Bone Changed History, Live Science, February 2008.

White, Kenneth D., The Efficiency of Farming under the (Roman) Empire, Agricultural History Society, 1956, p 85.

White, Morton, The Age of Analysis, Mentor Books, 1955, page 15.

Whitehead, A. W., Science and the Modern World, Mentor Books, 1955, pages 2-7, 188-9.

Whitehouse, Ruth, Megaliths of the Central Mediterranean, in the Megalithic Monuments of Western Europe, edited by Colin Renfrew, Thames and Hudson, 1982, pages 54-58.; with John Wilkins, The Making of Civilization, Alfred A Knopf, NY, 1986, page 54, 120., 130-134.

Wiet, Guston, Baghdad, University of Oklahoma Press, 1971, pages 120-58.

Winkless, Nels, and Iben Browning, Climate and the Affairs of men, Harper, NY, 1975, pages 170-190.

Willis, Delta, The Hominid Gang, Viking Penguin, 1989 page 19, 256.

Wilson, John F., Religion, A Preface, Prentice Hall, 1982, pages 21, 30-31, 36-48.

Wilson, Peter J., Man, The Promising Primate, Yale University Press, 1980, page 2, 66-67.

Witmer, Jeff, and Michael Zimmerman, "Intercessory Prayer As Medical Treatment?", Skeptical Inquirer, Winter 1991, pages 177-180.

Wolpert, Stanley, A., India, University of California Press, 1991, pages 32, 37, 44, 76, and 80-84.

Woodward, Kenneth L., "Society: The Changing Face of the Church," Newsweek, April 26, 2001, pages 46-52.

Wolferen, Karel van, The Enigma of Japanese Power, Alfred A Knopf, NY, 1989, Parts 10 and 11, page 259-260, 324, 426.

Wright, Karen, The First Americans, Discovery, February 1999, page 60.

Wright, Robert, Three Scientists and their Gods, Harper and Roe, 1988, Part III, pp 48-49.

Yoffee, Norman, The Collapse of Ancient States and Civilizations, University of Arizona Press, 1988, page 57, 65; The Dissolution of the Roman Empire, in The Collapse of Ancient States and Civilizations, edited by Norman Yoffee and George L. Cowgill, The University of Arizona Press, Tuscon, 1988, pages 168-9.

Youngblood, Ronald, editor, The Genesis Debate, Thomas Nelson Publishers, NY, 1986, pages viii and 12-249.

Yusuf al-Qaradawl, Non-Muslims in the Islamic Society, American Trust Publications, Indianapolis, 1985.

Zanger, W., The Mind of Adolph Hitler, London, 1973, pages 55-56.

Zepp, Ira G. Jr., A Muslim Primer, Univ. of Arkansas Press, 2000, pages 16-27, 130 and 183.

Zimbardo, Philip G. and Floyd L. Ruch, Psychology and Life, Scott, Foresman and Co., 1977, page 114, 144, 216, 230, 393-5.

Some of the assorted reference books used:

Introduction to Early Greek Philosophy, Houghton Mufflin Co., 1968, pages 13 and 14

The Quran, translated by N. J. Dawood, Penguin Books, NY, 1956, page 409.

The New World Dictionary-Concordance to the New American Bible, World Bible Publishers, 1970, page 31.

The Lost Books of the Bible and The Forgotten Books of Eden, World Publishing Co., 1926.

The Apocrypha of the Old Testament, edited by Bruce M. Metzger, Oxford University Press, NY, 1975, pages X and XI.

The New World Dictionary-Concordance, World Bible Publishers, 1970, page 280 under ISHMAEL

The New World Dictionary-Concordance to the New American Bible, World Bible Publishers, 1970, page 39 (Artemis).

The Living Bible, Tyndale House Publishing, 1971, page 944, Galactans 4:24

The Bible, The Quran and Science, American Trust Publications, 1976, page 1-106.